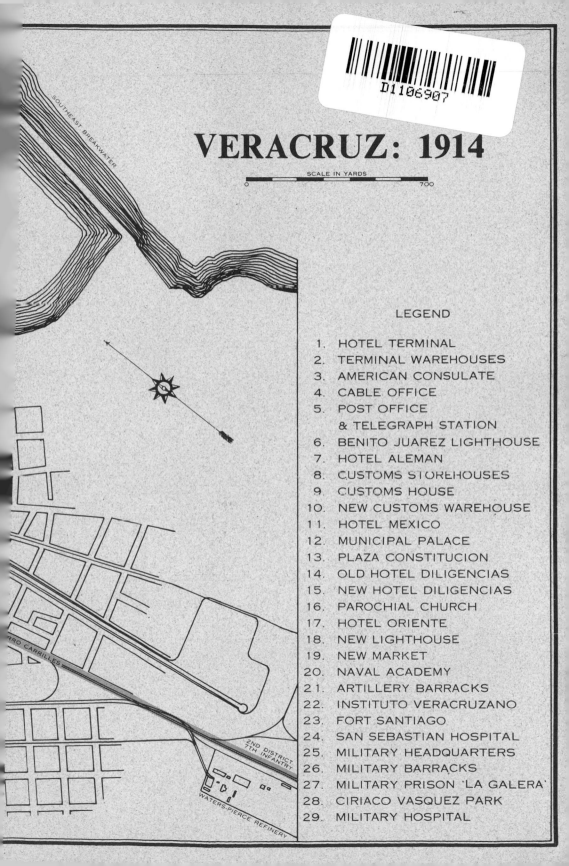

VERACRUZ: 1914

SCALE IN YARDS

0   700

SOUTHEAST BREAKWATER

RRO CARRILLES

2ND DISTRICT
7TH INFANTRY

WATERS-PIERCE REFINERY

LEGEND

1. HOTEL TERMINAL
2. TERMINAL WAREHOUSES
3. AMERICAN CONSULATE
4. CABLE OFFICE
5. POST OFFICE
   & TELEGRAPH STATION
6. BENITO JUAREZ LIGHTHOUSE
7. HOTEL ALEMAN
8. CUSTOMS STOREHOUSES
9. CUSTOMS HOUSE
10. NEW CUSTOMS WAREHOUSE
11. HOTEL MEXICO
12. MUNICIPAL PALACE
13. PLAZA CONSTITUCION
14. OLD HOTEL DILIGENCIAS
15. NEW HOTEL DILIGENCIAS
16. PAROCHIAL CHURCH
17. HOTEL ORIENTE
18. NEW LIGHTHOUSE
19. NEW MARKET
20. NAVAL ACADEMY
21. ARTILLERY BARRACKS
22. INSTITUTO VERACRUZANO
23. FORT SANTIAGO
24. SAN SEBASTIAN HOSPITAL
25. MILITARY HEADQUARTERS
26. MILITARY BARRACKS
27. MILITARY PRISON 'LA GALERA'
28. CIRIACO VASQUEZ PARK
29. MILITARY HOSPITAL

THE LANDING AT VERACRUZ: 1914

The Landing at Veracruz:1914

The First Complete Chronicle of a Strange Encounter in April, 1914, When the

United States Navy Captured and Occupied the City of Veracruz, Mexico

by
Jack Sweetman

United States Naval Institute
Annapolis, Maryland

To Mur

In 1914, Veracruz was written Vera Cruz; de Ulúa was, variously, d'Ulloa, de Ulloa, and de Ullua, and certain other Mexican place names were rendered according to an orthography no longer in vogue. As a rule, such spellings have been changed to conform to current usage.

PREFACE

It was 1914, and an Age was approaching an unsuspected and violent end. The comforting vision that had illuminated the Edwardian world was about to be lost in a darkness from which none other has emerged. One August dawn, Sir Edward Grey would watch the lights going out across Europe, and afterwards it would be impossible for anything to be quite the same again. But nothing is more specious than the wisdom with which we perceive the problems that awaited our fathers. At the time, there seemed no reason to fear that the most colossal accident in mankind's experience was soon to occur. To the contrary, there appeared every basis for belief that "The Good Years," as Walter Lord has named them, would meet that golden future into which civilization was so complacently advancing.

The events this book recalls took place in April of that last good year. Eclipsed by the outbreak of the First World War, they have been forgotten by all but the men who might have died in them. Yet it is doubtful if our history contains the record of a stranger, more confused, or exciting encounter. Its story deserves to be told.

The relations between the United States and Mexico had begun to deteriorate during the revolutionary turmoil which followed the overthrow of the moribund Díaz régime in May, 1911. The tension increased when General Victoriano Huerta emerged as provisional president of Mexico in a manner which aroused the righteous wrath of President Woodrow Wilson. While Wilson did not want war, he longed for an incident which could be used to the discredit of Huerta. Eventually, such an incident occurred; on April 9, 1914, a small party of American sailors was detained in the port of Tampico. The admiral commanding the American naval forces at Tampico promptly presented an ultimatum demanding that the Mexican government perform certain specified acts of contrition, the simplest being to fire a twenty-one-gun salute to the American flag. Mexico conceded everything except the salute, which it refused to fire without written assurance that it would be returned. That reservation was not acceptable to Wilson, who proceeded to ask Congress for authority to intervene in Mexico. Congress was still deliberating when Wilson learned that a tramp steamer carrying a huge cargo of arms to Huerta was about to dock at Veracruz.

Electing to intercept the arms, he ordered the Atlantic Fleet to seize the Customs House at Veracruz, an action unexpectedly resulting in a lively little battle and the loss of many lives.

That any of this could really have happened seems scarcely credible today. In point of time, Veracruz belongs to that deceptive past, so recent that we try to approach it in terms of our dwindling, nuclear world and so long ago that those terms do not apply. It is difficult for our generation, accustomed to round-the-clock radio and television coverage of world events, to appreciate the significance of the fact that the American ships at Tampico were not in direct communication with the United States. It is even more difficult for us to understand how Wilson could make such fateful decisions on the basis of the delayed and meager dispatches he received from Mexico. A representative opinion was expressed by the American historian who recently wrote: "In retrospect, . . . [it] was ludicrous. But considering the vested interests, chauvinism, and gross misunderstandings of both powers, it was a miracle that the comic episode did not become a tragedy." [1] One senses that author blushing at the thought that his country could have behaved so badly less than a lifetime ago. Yet the episode did not seem ludicrous to the bluejackets of the Second Seaman Regiment, who came under fire while marching in parade formation with the safeties on their rifles, or to the cadets defending the Mexican Naval Academy when the *Prairie's* shells began to fall; and its comic aspects were not apparent to the boy on the *New Hampshire,* who knew he would be killed.

To understand what transpired at Veracruz, we must adopt the perspective of the era. Momentarily, we must erase from memory the headlines of fifty intervening years. In the newspapers of 1914, accounts of Veracruz shared space with reports that Colonel Theodore Roosevelt had emerged from the Brazilian highlands after a harrowing journey down the River of Doubt; at the Winter Velodrome, in Paris, Jack Johnson had defeated Frank Moran for the heavyweight championship of the world; Representative Underwood, the Democratic house leader, had proclaimed his faith in the new income-tax law; Admiral Dewey had left Washington for a coastal cruise "to seek surcease from the heat"; and a harness shop was asserting: "The Horse is Still King." This is the context in which the landing at Veracruz must be viewed.

ACKNOWLEDGMENTS

M y interest in the landing at Veracruz grew from conversations with my father, who went ashore in the battalion from the battleship *New Hampshire*. His reminiscences added so much life and color to the dessicated framework of official reports that, when I decided to write this book, my first object was to seek the assistance of other veterans of the landing. Their response made it their book, in a literal as well as a figurative sense; and whatever vitality it may possess is the product of the counsel and cooperation of men who participated in the events it describes. Initially, most were inclined to doubt that they could contribute anything of value. One replied with the suggestion that I consult contemporary periodicals, commenting that the information they contained would be more useful "than the recollections of the survivors of Veracruz, most of whom are now septuagenarians, whose memories are, to express it charitably, less than perfect." No one claimed that, after fifty-two years, he could pinpoint every time and place; but what those years had edited was the sort of detail with which documentary sources were replete. In contrast, incidents of personal significance were often remembered with startling clarity. Time and again, recollections which appeared impossible to substantiate were subsequently verified by the discovery of "new" material. One veteran prepared an unusually detailed memoir. Several months later, a relative found and forwarded a copy of a letter he had written to his family four days after the landing. The letter not only described the same events as the memoir, but did so in much the same words. As my father succinctly remarked: "You get shot at once, you remember it a long time."

Vice Admiral Paul F. Foster, USNR (Retired), who won the Medal of Honor as an ensign at Veracruz, wrote a fascinating narrative. He is one of the three persons for whose encouragement and aid I owe the greatest debt. The others are Rear Admiral George M. Lowry, USNR (Retired), another Medal of Honor recipient, and my father, Mr. Arthur J. Sweetman, a teen-aged petty officer at the time of the landing. Admiral Lowry furnished a copy of an account he had written in June, 1914, and, like Admiral Foster, permitted me to copy a number of rare photographs in his possession. My father supplied much of the information regarding the *New Hampshire* battalion and the advance against the Mexican Naval Academy. All three read drafts of the manuscript, offering many useful comments and suggestions, and answered what must have seemed an interminable number of questions concerning the ways of the Old Navy.

Other veterans to whom I must express my gratitude are Captain Roy Dudley, USN (Retired), who jotted down his recollections of Veracruz and lent me his scrapbook, containing many unique snapshots; Chief Radio Engineer John Robert Johnson, USN (Retired), for his notes on Admiral Fletcher and Captain Rush; Commander George Cregan, USN (Retired), who furnished a copy of his Medal of Honor correspondence; Mr. Henry N. Nickerson, who lost a leg and won a Medal of Honor at Veracruz; Mr. Ralph Mitchell Crosby, for his account of the operations of the *Arkansas* battalion and the use of his unparalleled collection of Veracruz photographs; Rear Admiral Frank J. Fletcher, USN (Retired); Rear Admiral J. W. W. Cumming, USN (Retired); Commander William Masek, USN (Retired); Mr. George Junkin; Commodore Mark L. Hersey, USN (Retired); Lieutenant Commander J. F. Peck, USN (Retired), with whom a delightful evening was spent; and to Vice Admiral Carleton H. Wright, USN (Retired); Captain William L. Sayre, USNR (Retired); Commander John A. Brownell, USN (Retired); Captain E. B. Lapham, USN (Retired); Rear Admiral L. L. Hunter, USN (Retired); Captain H. B. Grow, USN (Retired); Lieutenant Colonel Roscoe Arnett, USMC (Retired); Captain R. B. Hammes, USN (Retired); Captain L. W. Comstock, USN (Retired); Captain J. A. Saunders, USN (Retired); Captain Schuyler Mills, USN (Retired); Lieutenant Commander G. S. Dale, USN (Retired); Captain George U. Gillespie, USN (Retired); and Commander J. P. Norfleet, USN (Retired): all of whom furnished accounts of their experiences at Veracruz. My only regret is that limitations of space required the omission of so much that was of interest.

Thanks are also due to Mr. Sherrod East, Acting Chief, Naval and Military Service Branch of the General Services Administration, for gathering the more than seven hundred pages of official reports on Veracruz from the Naval Records Collection of The National Archives, Washington, D.C.; Captain W. A. Morgan, late The Kensingtons, for his work in locating Admiral Cradock's logs and dispatches in the Admiralty Files of the Public Records Office, London; Vice Admiral W. S. DeLany, USN (Retired), Executive Vice President of the Naval Historical Foundation, Washington, D.C., and to the Foundation for authorizing the use of

Acknowledgments

Lieutenant Ellyson's Veracruz letter; Messrs. Robert Lane and Charles G. LaHood, Jr., of the Reference Department, Library of Congress, for their patience in replying to my many queries; Captain F. Kent Loomis, USN (Retired), Acting Director of Naval History, and Lieutenant Colonel T. P. O'Callaghan, USMC, Assistant Head, Media Branch, Division of Information, both of the Department of the Navy, and Lieutenant Colonel G. V. Glines, USAF, Chief, Magazine and Book Branch, Directorate of Information Service, Office of the Assistant Secretary of Defense, for their cooperation in providing official photographs from Veracruz; Mr. E. V. Niemeyer, Jr., Assistant Cultural Affairs Officer, U.S. Information Service, Mexico City, for information concerning the various Mexican archives; Dr. Robert E. Quirk, of Indiana University, author of *An Affair of Honor,* the only previous American work on the subject, for further notes as to Mexican references; Mr. Robert Feldmann, of the American Embassy, Mexico City, for procuring a copy of Palomares' book; Mr. José Socas, of Orlando, Florida, for translating Spanish-language material; Don Ignacio Rubio Mañé, Director, Archivo General de la Nación, Mexico, D.F.; Mr. Robert Scudder, of the Free Library of Philadelphia, Philadelphia, Pennsylvania; Rear Admiral Bruce A. McCandless, USN (Retired), for his interest; Mrs. Harriet Castle, for providing a photograph of her late husband, Commander Guy W. S. Castle; Mrs. Isabelle Badger and Mrs. Helen F. McDonnell, widows of Admirals Oscar C. Badger and Edward O. McDonnell; and to the Controller, H. M. Stationery Office, London, for permission to quote Crown-copyright material. And to Gisela, my wife, who understood.

JACK SWEETMAN

Orlando, Florida
July, 1966

CONTENTS

ILLUSTRATIONS

THE LANDING AT VERACRUZ: 1914

ONE: THAT TROUBLED COUNTRY

*The people of Mexico are striving for the rights that are funda-
mental to life and happiness—fifteen millions of oppressed men,
overburdened women, and pitiful children in virtual bondage in
their own home of fertile fields and inexhaustible treasure! Some of
the leaders of the revolution may often have been mistaken and
violent and selfish, but the revolution itself was inevitable and is
right.*

Woodrow Wilson [1]

O n the morning of January 31, 1914, the USS *Minnesota* swung
to her anchor off Veracruz, Mexico. It was Sunday and
her crew could hear the muted peal of church bells from the city.
Otherwise, Veracruz seemed to be slumbering in the warm sunlight,
a jumble of bright, pastel buildings between the sand hills and the
sea. To the men on the *Minnesota,* it was a depressingly familiar
scene. They had seen it every day for too many dull weeks. Months
earlier, the *Minnesota* had been stationed at Veracruz to protect
American residents against any danger from the revolution raging
in the interior of Mexico. But the fighting had not spread near
Veracruz and, as yet, there had been no need of the *Minnesota.*
Nothing had disturbed the tropic languor of Veracruz, and the
seamen and Marines of the *Minnesota* had grown heartily sick of
the monotonous, in-port routine. The date of arrival of a relief ship
was the favorite subject of speculation among all hands. The only
exceptions were two Marine sergeants who had a more pressing
mystery on their minds. First Sergeant Roscoe Arnett and his
friend Gunnery Sergeant Stout were trying to imagine what kind of
"secret and special duty" a Marine could pull in Veracruz.

Early that morning, Arnett and Stout had been summoned below
decks to see their battalion commander, Major Smedley Darlington
Butler. Speaking in the accents of his Quaker youth, Butler informed them that they had been selected for a "secret and special
duty." They were not to discuss the matter with anyone, not even
their company commander. To begin with, they were to report to
the paymaster. That was simple enough. The two Marines waited to

3

hear the rest, but Butler dismissed them with the comment that he could tell them nothing more.

Arnett and Stout were not aware of anything that might account for Major Butler's instructions. There had been no change in the routine aboard the *Minnesota* and Veracruz still looked the same. It was all very strange.

What followed was equally mystifying. The paymaster took them to a storeroom and told them to fit themselves in navy uniforms. Then he directed them to report back after dark, bringing their toilet articles and personal effects. These instructions gave Arnett and Stout a curious clue. Obviously, they were going to be sent off ship, and in disguise. That was an intriguing prospect, but it did not solve the puzzle of this "secret and special duty." Being Marines, Arnett and Stout wasted little more time in guessing what and where it might be. The afternoon would pass.

Arnett and Stout returned to the storeroom at the appointed hour. The paymaster was waiting; handing them the uniforms, he announced that they were to leave the ship at once. They would go over the starboard gangway. This was the officers' gangway, but the Officer of the Deck had orders not to interfere.

A launch was tied to the foot of the gangway. Arnett saw that it already held several passengers: Major Butler, two enlisted Marines, and a solid-looking, older officer whom he was startled to recognize as Rear Admiral Frank F. Fletcher, the commander of American naval forces on the Mexican Gulf Coast. To the two Marine sergeants, it would not have been much more of a surprise to find President Wilson holding the tiller. Admirals are rarely encountered in launches collecting details of Marines. Secret or not, this duty was certainly special.

The Marines sat in subdued silence as the launch moved away from the *Minnesota*. It stopped at another ship to take on two more Marines and proceeded to a third vessel. Here the six Marines were ordered to change into the navy uniforms, leaving their own clothing bundled and tagged. Pushing off from the third vessel, the launch bore across the harbor towards the point where the scout cruiser *Chester* lay beside the seawall. The launch made fast to the *Chester* and the Marines followed as the admiral and Butler crossed her deck to the shore. Trudging along in the darkness, the Marines perceived that they were being led towards the American Consulate. Consul W. W. Canada was on hand to receive them. Butler introduced the Marines; moments later, he and the admiral withdrew.

When the consul turned to them, the Marines realized that their secret and special duty was finally to be explained. Canada had never faced a more attentive audience. He began with the reminder that the Consulate was the temporary residence of Governor John Lind, President Wilson's unofficial ambassador to the Mexican government. Since most Mexicans were violently opposed to Wilson's policies, Mr. Lind was not exactly popular with the citizens of Veracruz. That morning, consular personnel had overpowered an armed Mexican lurking in the corridor outside Lind's rooms. The incident had convinced Canada of a need for more stringent security and to him, as to so many other officials in similar circumstances, stringent security meant the U.S. Marines. The agreement with Mexico, however, stipulated that consular orderlies consist of naval personnel. For this reason, it was necessary for the Marines to masquerade as sailors. Their duty was simply to protect Mr. Lind. Two of them would accompany him wherever he went, while two others stood guard at the Consulate. The two off-duty men would be free to go and come at will. This last bit of information dispelled any misgivings the Marines may have felt; it was not hard to see that the Consulate offered many more of the amenities than were available aboard ship. Continuing in a more intimate tone, Canada observed that Mr. Lind was apt to tell newsmen a little more than was proper, especially in informal interviews outside his office. The Marines would have the additional responsibility of curtailing these conversations.

Arnett and his men embarked upon their new duties with zest. The tone of their tour was set the first morning, when Lind went out for his regular walk. Arnett and Stout were sitting in an anteroom. Lind threw them a cheery "Good morning!" and strode into the street. The Marines trailed along behind.

Lind ran into reporters in a café around the corner from the Consulate. They greeted him warmly and asked what he heard from President Wilson. The opening words of Lind's reply satisfied Arnett that he was going to tell them. Giving a quick signal to Stout, Arnett edged in between Lind and the reporters. In a loud voice, he announced that the envoy was out for his exercise and was not to be disturbed. Both Lind and the newsmen objected to the interruption, but Arnett repeated that, though the newsmen could see the envoy in his office, they were not to interfere with his exercise. Then, one on each side, the Marines gently but firmly propelled Mr. Lind down the street. Thereafter the newsmen found the President's agent much less accessible. No other armed Mexicans were discovered on his threshold, either.

5

It was too good to last. A month later, Consul Canada learned that the Mexican authorities had become suspicious of his new orderlies. Sending for Arnett, Canada told him that the Marines must return aboard ship at once. He appreciated all they had done and hoped they wouldn't have to make a run for it. The Marines sauntered out of the Consulate expecting to be surrounded by Mexican secret police, but no one tried to stop them from reaching the *Chester*. Subsequently, the State Department obtained permission to use uniformed Marines at the Consulate.[2]

The chain of events in which this episode was far from the least likely link had begun on March 13, 1913, when Woodrow Wilson was inaugurated as the twenty-eighth President of the United States. In contrast to the caretaker Presidents of the late nineteenth century, Wilson was a man of whom great things were expected. A vigorous fifty-seven, he came to Washington from a highly successful term as governor of New Jersey and a distinguished academic career culminating in the presidency of Princeton University. Ostensibly, Wilson should hold a place among the most sympathetic figures in American history. A scholar, an idealist, a man of great courage and exemplary personal virtue, he felt a profound desire "to work for humanity and the happiness of men everywhere." Yet statesmen like Henry Cabot Lodge and veteran newsmen like C. W. Thompson considered him a pompous prig, lecturing Congressmen with an air of genteel condescension more appropriate to obtuse undergraduates. The impression embodies an element of truth. Wilson's altruism bore a deep strain of moral conceit, and he was acutely aware of his intellectual attainments. As a contemporary observed, he had "not only, as he himself has said, 'a single-track mind,' but a mind which is fully convinced of the everlasting righteousness of its own performance."[3] On the whole, however, the image is unwarranted. It has arisen from the fact that Wilson was one of those unfortunate men at whose expense it is easy to appear witty. Just as the features of that awesomely earnest, equine face seemed to invite caricature, certain aspects of Wilson's character—implacably fastidious, relentlessly benevolent, remorselessly sincere—lent themselves to levity. Wilson was aware of it. Contrasting the impact he and Theodore Roosevelt would have upon the voters of 1912, he wrote: "He appeals to their imagination; I do not. He is a real, vivid person, whom they have shouted themselves hoarse for . . . ; I am a vague, conjectural personality, more made up of opinions and academic prepossessions than of human traits and red corpuscles."[4]

Wilson entered the Presidency with very definite ideas about the nature of the office. "From 1865 until 1896," he said, "no President except Mr. Cleveland played a leading and decisive part . . . in our national life. Even Mr. Cleveland owed his great role in affairs rather to his own native force and the confused policies of the time, than to any opportunity for leadership afforded by a system which had subordinated so many Presidents before him to Congress." [5] In the course of his studies of American government, which he had taught for twenty years, Wilson had become convinced that the supremacy of the legislative branch was highly undesirable. This opinion had found repeated expression in his books and articles. "Nobody stands sponsor for the policy of the government," he lamented. "A dozen men originate it; a dozen compromises twist and alter it." [6] Policy-making should be the prerogative of the President; no compromises, no alterations. "Read what Mr. Wilson has written," an Englishman remarked. "It is as if . . . he is saying 'This is the perfect President; this is the President I shall be.'" [7] Wilson was determined to be a strong chief executive. He knew the job would be demanding; he had even prepared a list of the attributes imperative to that perfect President—"the eight horses that draw . . . the chariot of every leader . . . of free men." They were force of character; readiness of resources; clearness of vision; grasp of intellect; courage of conviction; earnestness of purpose; and instinct and capacity for leadership. [8]

Wilson had hoped that this team would draw him along the high road of domestic reform, for which he had great plans. Instead, he found himself assuming an office confronted with the worst foreign crisis in years. It involved, of all places, Mexico, a country with whom relations had been so good for so long they had come to be taken for granted.

American diplomacy had not experienced a Mexican problem since 1864. In that year, the Emperor Napoleon III, encouraged by Confederate agents, had established the Austrian Archduke Maximilian upon the throne of a satellite Empire of Mexico. With its own existence threatened by the Civil War, the United States was in no position to assert the Monroe Doctrine, and at first the imperial project had prospered. The Mexicans put up a gratifying resistance. There was an abundance of *la gloire,* and at a hacienda called Camerone, the 2ème compagnie, 1èr régiment was fortunate enough to be annihilated in what would become the most sacred chapter in the annals of the French Foreign Legion. Napoleon gave his troops a silver medal and dreamed of a French-oriented "Catholic Union" of Latin-American states.

Unhappily, the Mexicans never warmed to the idea of having an emperor, not even well-meaning Maximilian, and in 1865 the American Civil War came to an end. Shortly thereafter, General U. S. Grant and a large number of less-distinguished soldiers appeared on the Texas frontier. Napoleon divined that their purpose was not solely to chastise the Comanches; European waters were muddying, too, and in March, 1867, the last French forces sailed for home.

Abandoned by his sponsor, Maximilian elected to go it alone. Rebellion raced across the land. Maximilian placed himself at the head of his army; it evaporated midway through the campaign. The "lucky bullet" he had sought eluded him, and after the travesty of a trial, Maximilian was stood before a stone wall. He died with considerable aplomb, face to the firing squad and no blindfold over his blue eyes, and his wife went insane at the news. She was still alive in 1914.

With Maximilian out of the way, Mexican politics resumed their customary course. Benito Juárez, the dour, Indian patriot who had led the crusade against the French, became president. He soon discovered the Empire to have been a handy foe. As the mutual enemy, it had united the many, hostile native factions in a common cause. The moment that cause triumphed, they renewed their former rivalries. Juárez held power for ten frustrating years. He died in 1872, worn out in office, and was succeeded four years later by Porfirio Díaz.

In many respects, the paths which led Juárez and Díaz to the presidency were parallel. Both were of humble origin (Juárez had not learned Spanish until he was twelve and Díaz never spoke it correctly), had achieved prominence through their own abilities, and were heroes of the war with Maximilian. But their philosophies were as different as their lives had been alike. Juárez cherished the Mexican people; Díaz revered the kind of progress that is sometimes spelled with a capital *P*. Their conflict was inevitable. In 1871, Díaz proclaimed a revolution. He was driven into hiding, but Juárez succumbed of the strain.

On the surface, Díaz seemed a stereotype South American dictator. Yet he ruled Mexico for thirty years: longer than any other man, an accomplishment which exempts him from categorization. "Like a power of nature," was one writer's verdict, "he can scarcely be judged by ethical standards." [9] Gifted with an intuitive understanding of the usages of power, Díaz evinced a legitimate concern for what he conceived to be the interests of Mexico. That the scope of these interests was thought severely circumscribed by some did not disturb Díaz. He liked to say: A dog with a bone in its jaws neither kills nor steals, and in that metaphor expressed the rationale of his régime. Díaz never murdered a man he could buy. There was always the choice: *pan ó palo*—bread or the club. The landowners, the bureaucracy, and the clergy found this principle congenial, and from their favor Díaz developed a durable base of support. To Díaz the art of government consisted chiefly of providing an assured supply of bones. Accordingly, he set about the promotion of Mexico's primitive economy.

Trading on the country's untapped natural wealth, Díaz was able to attract vast amounts of foreign capital. During the three decades of his reign, American and European investors were granted immensely valuable concessions on Mexican soil. By 1912, the American investment exceeded one billion dollars,* a sum almost equalling the total capital of native Mexicans. Standard Oil, United States Steel, the Anaconda Corporation, Mexican Petroleum, and the Hearst and Guggenheim interests accounted for some of the more extensive holdings. In the aggregate, American firms owned 75 per cent of all the mines in Mexico and over 50 per cent of the oil fields. More than 40,000 Americans were living in Mexico in 1914, and few were not involved in some economic activity. The Europeans were not far behind. The English, with 300 million invested, vied with the Americans in oil, mining and public utilities; the French concentrated on textiles, the Spanish dominated retail sales, and the Germans, too late to stake out a private preserve, had made a sizeable, diversified penetration. Between 1880 and 1900, the value of the annual production of Mexican mines rose from 30 to 90 million pesos, foreign trade quadrupled, and over 9,000 miles of railway were laid.

So far as Díaz and the aristocracy were concerned, economic development was an eminently acceptable end in itself. But of the riches it generated, none reached the mass of the Mexican people. Many actually became more miserable than they had been before. During the years in which her economy made such phenomenal progress, the Mexican workers' wage remained at from twenty-five to forty centavos a day, while the price of food doubled. Three thousand families held title to over half of Mexico in 1910; one man

---

* Distributed approximately as follows: oil, 478 million; mining, 300 million; agriculture, 200 million; railways, 160 million; manufacturing, 60 million; mercantile, 50 million; federal bonds, 22 million; utilities, 10 million.[10]

owned seventeen million acres, and the seventeen largest haciendas covered almost twenty per cent of the country. Countless peasant proprietors had seen their farms swallowed in these giant tracts.

Though bread became scarce, the club remained omnipresent. In later years, Francisco Bulnes, the principal intellectual ornament of the Díaz régime, related that the duties of a provincial governor had been to "falsify . . . elections; to distribute nocturnal clubbings . . . ; to jail, and, if necessary, to kill troublesome journalists; to sentence to the army those inclined to rebellion; [and] to apply the *ley fuga*." [11] This *ley fuga* was among the least attractive native customs. A euphemism for political murder, it waived investigation of the death of prisoners killed trying to escape custody. Approximately 10,000 instances of the *ley fuga* were recorded during the presidencies of Díaz. The peculiar thing was that, in almost every case, the deceased was found to be an accused awaiting trial.

By the turn of the century, the classic ingredients of revolution were present: a repressive government, compromised by its association with foreign interests; the superconcentration of wealth in the hands of a politically incompetent elite; the agitation of an estranged intelligentsia; and a spirit of resentment in the factories and fields. The explosion occurred in November, 1910, two months after Díaz's eightieth birthday. By then, the sinewy *guerrillero* who had escaped Maximilian's prison yard by lassoing a water spout and pulling himself up the rope had become a dignified, if still semiliterate, old gentleman with a snowy white mustache and elegant manners. His régime, enfeebled and corrupt, lacked the stamina to withstand a widespread popular rising. Díaz resigned in May, 1911, and after the first reasonably honest election since 1867, Francisco I. Madero became President of Mexico.

A moderate intellectual with visions of economic reform, Madero soon succeeded in antagonizing both ultraconservative and extreme liberal factions. He was a gentle man, five feet, two inches tall and of frail physique, and he never understood the utter amorality of those who envied his office. Having surmounted the predictable flurry of counterrevolutions, Madero was toppled by treachery: a *coup d'état* engineered by General Victoriano Huerta, whose loyalty he had not questioned. General Felix Díaz, the dictator's nephew, was Huerta's principal confederate, and American Ambassador Henry Lane Wilson was privy to the plot.

The *coup* commenced on February 9, 1913, the first of what Mexicans refer to as *la decena tragica*—the Tragic Ten Days. Put under arrest on February 18, Madero was led to resign upon the assurance that he would be granted safe-conduct into exile. No one except Madero really relied on Huerta's word, however, and on February 21, the minister of foreign affairs appealed for an "effective guarantee" of the deposed president's safety. With a dramatic gesture, Huerta tore open his collar, revealing a golden chain from which was suspended a scapulary, a Virgin of Guadeloupe and a Sacred Heart of Jesus. "This was hung around my neck by my mother," he exclaimed. "By her memory, before these sacred images, I swear to you that I shall permit no one to make an attempt against the life of Señor Madero." [12] Two days later, it was announced that Madero had been shot to death while "attempting to escape."

Proclaiming himself provisional president, Huerta initiated a bloody purge of Madero supporters. Informing Deputy Serapio Rendón's family of his death, a member of the firing squad related, perhaps in consolation, "He was the one-hundred-and-fourth we had shot." [13] To President William Howard Taft, Huerta wired: "I have the honor to inform you that I have overthrown this government. . . . From now on, peace and prosperity will reign." [14]

The turbulent course of Mexican affairs was watched with acute concern abroad. Revolutions are notoriously bad for business. Foreign investments had already suffered substantial damage, and greater destruction appeared imminent. Madero had been dead less than a week when a group calling themselves Constitutionalists rebelled against Huerta. As the fighting became general, oil tanks were set ablaze, trains commandeered, herds of cattle stolen, and rich haciendas ruined; on isolated occasions, foreign nationals were killed. Longingly, the investors remembered the days of Díaz, when, as the saying went, Mexico was the safest country in the world—for everyone except the Mexicans.

Liberal sentiment outside Mexico had approved Madero's revolution. "Until the end of the Díaz regime," Woodrow Wilson once said, "eighty per cent of the people in Mexico never had a 'look in' in determining who their governors should be. Now, I am for the eighty per cent." [15] But to the business interests, Madero had been anathema. Henry Lane Wilson, whose opinions reflected those of the American colony, considered the Madero government "a wicked despotism," was "disposed to accept" the official version of Madero's death, and urged that the United States recognize Huerta.[16]

Throughout the disturbances, the United States had refrained from overt interference in Mexican affairs. In March, 1912, President Taft had imposed an embargo on arms shipments to everyone except Madero, but otherwise he had done nothing that could be construed as intervention. With only a month left in the White House when Huerta seized power, Taft deemed it advisable to defer action until his successor could take office. His last official statement on the Mexican situation, issued late in February, merely reiterated existing policy. "We must avoid in every way that which is called intervention," he declared, "and use all possible patience, with prayer that some power may arise within Mexico to bring peace throughout that troubled country." [17]

TWO: OUR FRIEND HUERTA

I hope they have got a man of the Díaz type who will do sufficient throat-cutting to restore peace. That seems an unpleasant thing to say, but it is apparently impossible to maintain order . . . in Mexico upon any other terms.

Senator Henry Cabot Lodge, on the Huerta *coup* [1]

T he universal practice of American diplomacy had been to extend *de facto* recognition to any government showing reasonable signs of stability. As the State Department's J. B. Moore endeavored to explain to the President in May, 1913, "The Government of the United States having originally set itself up by revolution, has always acted upon the *de facto* principle. We regard governments as existing or not existing. We do not require them to be chosen by popular vote. . . . Our depreciation of the political methods which may prevail in certain countries cannot relieve us of the necessity of dealing with the governments of those countries." [2] Wilson was not impressed. He had been in office less than three months when he vowed: "I will not recognize a government of butchers!" [3] and he was true to his word. Whatever Wilson undertook in regard to Mexico, the desire to see Huerta supplanted would remain foremost in his mind.

Wilson's Mexican policy may be compared to a play in three acts. In the First Act, Wilson believes that the Mexican problem can be solved through American mediation. The curtain falls when the offer of American assistance is rudely rebuffed. Act Two is a "flat," during which Wilson, hoping that events within Mexico will work themselves out, assumes an attitude called "watchful waiting." But in the closing scenes, Huerta seems stronger than ever; and as the Third Act opens, Wilson decides that he must intervene.

Wilson's attempts at mediation were the outgrowth of a plan prepared by a Kansas City businessman, Delbert J. Haff, approved by a group of American investors, and submitted to the President in the first week of May, 1913. According to its provisions, the United States would agree to recognize Huerta in return for his promise to hold "a free and fair election" at "an early date." An election already scheduled for October 26 was dismissed as "being, in our

U.S. Army Signal Corps

Woodrow Wilson, President of the United
States, 1913–1921

National Archives

Victoriano Huerta, Provisional President of
Mexico, 1913–1914

judgment, too remote." [4] Attracted as he was to this idea, Wilson was unable to reconcile himself to recognizing Huerta, even temporarily. He was still considering the Haff plan when its sponsor, Julius Kruttschnitt, Chairman of the Board of the Southern Pacific Railroad, proposed a more palatable alternative. Realizing the distaste with which Wilson regarded Huerta, Kruttschnitt deleted the reference to recognition: the United States would simply arrange an armistice between Huerta and the Constitutionalists pending an election whose result both parties would pledge to accept. Delighted, Wilson began to develop the details of an offer.

At this point, it is interesting to contrast the character of the two presidents. On the one hand, we have Woodrow Wilson, a minister's son, the personification of Presbyterian conscience; on the other, General Victoriano Huerta, late-protégé of Porfirio Díaz, "an ape-like old man of almost pure Indian blood." These are the words of William Bayard Hale, perhaps the most perceptive American observer in Mexico at the time. "He may almost be said to subsist on alcohol," the report continued. "Drunk or only half drunk (he is never sober), he never loses a certain shrewdness. He has been lifelong a soldier, and one of the best in Mexico. . . . A hard fighter, [he] glorifies in the exercise of power." [5] Huerta had achieved renown through his merciless suppression of the Yaqui Indian insurrection of 1901. Several years later, he had added to his fame by failing to account for five million pesos of government funds.

In spite of his somewhat unsavory past, Huerta enjoyed the support of the great majority of Americans with interests in Mexico. To be sure, their solicitude did not derive from any affection for Huerta; its motivations were purely economic. As Secretary of State William Jennings Bryan related, "Much of my time during the first few months of office was occupied in hearing delegations which came to urge Huerta's recognition. The pleas were all the same and ran in substance as follows: 'We do not care to say anything about Huerta individually, nor about the way in which he obtained power, but a strong man is necessary to preserve order in Mexico, and he is the only strong man in sight.' " [6] To preserve order: that was the sole object of the lobbyists' concern. Huerta was simply the best bet.

As Wilson pressed harder, however, many Americans began to respect the resolution with which Huerta resisted his demands. Wilson himself was among them. In August, 1913, he would write, "Our friend Huerta is a diverting brute! He is always so perfectly in character; so false, so sly, so full of bravado (the bravado of ignorance, chiefly), and yet so courageous, too, and determined—such a mixture of weak and strong, of ridiculous and respectable! One moment you long for his blood . . . and the next you find yourself entertaining a sneaking admiration for his nerve. He will not let go till he pulls the whole house down with him. . . . What an indomitable fighter he is for his own hand!" [7] After Veracruz, Richard Harding Davis carried it even further. "If Wilson and Huerta ran for President," he declared, speaking for the army of occupation, "Huerta would get all our votes. He may be an uneducated Indian, but he is a man." [8]

Under normal circumstances, the President's proposal to the Mexican government would have been presented by Ambassador Henry Lane Wilson. In the curious circumstances then prevailing, Wilson wondered whether the ambassador would be the man for the job. A few weeks earlier, in March, 1913, the *New York World* had run a sensational exposé of Henry Lane Wilson's complicity in the Huerta *coup*. The *World* disclosed the long conference Wilson had held with Huerta and Felix Díaz immediately prior to Madero's arrest; told how Wilson had led the applause at Huerta's introduction to the *corps diplomatique;* and contended that when Huerta had sounded the ambassador out on the disposition to be made of Madero, Wilson's nonchalant reply—"that which was best for the peace of the country" [9]—had sealed Madero's fate. The aggressively *Huertista* tone of Wilson's dispatches lent credence to the *World's* allegations, and the President's suspicions were aroused. Finally, he asked William Bayard Hale, his campaign biographer, to go to Mexico "ostensibly on your own hook" to discover "just what is going on down there." [10] A former Hearst correspondent, Hale had no special background in Mexican affairs, but he was a skilled observer, and Wilson trusted his judgment.

Hale's reports were not reassuring. In a telegram from Mexico City on June 3, he described Ambassador Wilson as a "vain busybody" with a "highly nervous temperament." [11] Subsequent dispatches confirmed the ambassador's peculiar part in the Tragic Ten Days. By the end of the month, the President had read enough. Ambassador Wilson was summoned to Washington "for consultation" on July 16. A barrage of laudatory letters and a special deputation from the American colony could not save him. "I have to pause and remind myself," said Woodrow Wilson, "that I am President of the United States and not of a small group of Americans with vested interests in Mexico." [12] After a mutually unsatisfactory interview, Henry Lane Wilson returned to private life.

In Mexico City, Nelson O'Shaughnessy, the elegant young Chargé d'affairs, assumed the duties of senior embassy official; a new ambassador could hardly be appointed to a government whose existence the United States denied. As Hale had nothing but praise for O'Shaughnessy ("a perfectly honest man"), one supposes that Wilson would have considered him capable of transmitting the offer to Huerta. O'Shaughnessy was known to be on excellent personal terms with Huerta, however, so Wilson chose to operate outside the established channels of diplomatic intercourse. The task of presenting his proposal was entrusted to John Lind, a prominent Midwestern politician, formerly governor of Minnesota.

The motives leading to the selection of Lind are difficult to discern. He was of good character and, a fact of paramount importance, a friend of Secretary of State Bryan; but he was also anti-Catholic, unable to speak Spanish, devoid of diplomatic experience, and wonderfully ignorant of Mexican affairs. His appointment was one more instance of that propensity for the amateur which the President exhibited throughout the Mexican imbroglio. Wilson seemed to suspect the professional. Veteran capital newsman Charles W. Thompson related that it was "a stock joke among the people who came to Washington, eager to lay their knowledge of the Mexican conditions before him, that the only way to get to him was to tell Tumulty [Wilson's secretary] that you had never been in Mexico." [13] Probably Lind did as well as anyone could have in his place, which is to say that he failed to accomplish the impossible, but Wilson's choices were not always as innocuous. Late in June, for example, he sent another of Bryan's acquaintances, an improbable individual named Reginald F. Del Valle, on a confidential mission to interview the Constitutionalist leaders in northern Mexico. Del Valle travelled south from Texas; on reaching Mexico City, he held a press conference to announce that he was a secret agent of the American government. His immediate recall did not redeem the highly negative effect of this revelation upon the already-strained relations between the provisional Mexican government and the United States.

Lind set out for Mexico on the afternoon of August 4. His instructions were contained in a remarkable letter which Wilson himself had composed. "Press very earnestly upon . . . those . . . exercising authority in Mexico," he had written, "the following considerations. . . . The present situation in Mexico is incompatible with the fulfillment of international obligations on the part of Mexico, with the civilized development of Mexico herself, and with the maintenance of tolerable political and economic conditions in Central America. It is upon no common occasion, therefore, that the United States offers her counsel and assistance. . . . We wish to act in the spirit of the most earnest and disinterested friendship. It is our purpose . . . not only to pay the most scrupulous regard to the sovereignty and independence of Mexico, . . . but also to give every possible evidence that we act in the interest of Mexico alone, and not in the interests of any person or body of persons with personal or property claims in Mexico. . . . The Government of the United States would deem itself discredited if it had any selfish or ulterior purpose in transactions where the peace, happiness, and prosperity of a whole people are involved." [14]

Presuming these protestations would win Huerta's heart, Wilson proceeded to delineate the terms upon which "a satisfactory settlement seems to us to be conditional." There were four such terms, only one of which departed from the provisions of the Kruttschnitt plan:

> The immediate cessation of hostilities throughout Mexico.
> An early election open to all parties.
> The consent of General Huerta not to be a candidate.
> The agreement of all parties to abide by the results of the election and cooperate in organizing and supporting the new administration. [15]

Point 3, of course, was the President's own innovation. In Wilson's opinion, once Huerta had been forced from the scene, the election of a government devoted to democratic processes would naturally follow. It was in vain that persons experienced in Mexican affairs pointed out that though free elections might remedy the political ills of an informed electorate, they would lose their efficacy in a land where ninety per cent of the voters could not read the ballot. Wilson remained convinced that free elections were the answer.

With a naïveté that seems touching today, Wilson was certain that the Mexicans would welcome his offer. He could "conceive of no reasons sufficient to justify those who are now attempting to shape the policy . . . of Mexico in declining the offices of friendship thus offered." [16] To the contrary, he expected them to be accepted with alacrity. Disillusionment came quickly. The State Department leaked the details of Lind's mission the day after he left Washington. Wilson tried to smother the story, but the damage had been done. Neither Huerta nor O'Shaughnessy had heard anything of the plan, and it bothered them to learn about it in the newspapers. A certain coolness would be evident in O'Shaughnessy's attitude towards Lind, while Huerta, declaring that his "limit of patience" had been reached, threatened to "absolutely ignore Lind's presence unless he bears official credentials as Ambassador." [17]

It did not get as bad as that. Huerta's foreign minister, Federico Gamboa, heard Lind out, but little more. The provisional government refused to accede to the President's program. In an infinitely pained letter of August 26, Gamboa informed Lind that it was "solely because of the sincere esteem in which the people and government of the United States are held by the people . . . of Mexico, [that] my government consented to take into consideration the representations of which you are the bearer. Otherwise, it would have rejected them immediately because of their humiliating and unusual character," which, he thought, would be "hardly admissible even in a treaty of peace" imposed upon a prostrate foe. "If even once we were to permit the counsels and advice (let us call them thus) of the United States to dictate the course of Mexico's internal affairs," he bristled, "we would . . . compromise for an indefinite future our destinies as a sovereign entity, and all the future elections for president would be submitted to the veto of any President of the United States. And such an enormity, Mr. Confidential Agent, no government will ever attempt to perpetrate." Lind's offer of an American loan, contingent upon the acceptance of mediation, was scorned with the lofty declaration that, "When the dignity of a nation is at stake . . . there are not loans enough to permit it to be lessened." [18]

THREE: THE IRONY OF FATE

It would be the irony of fate if my administration had to deal chiefly with foreign affairs.

Woodrow Wilson, on the eve of his inauguration [1]

W ilson had been intending to take the Mexican situation before Congress for several weeks past. The rejection of mediation presented a natural opportunity, and on August 27, he
appeared before a Joint Session. In an address of commendable
candor, Wilson reviewed the course of his Mexican policy. Ascrib-
ing the failure of the Lind mission to Mexican distrust of American
motives, he asserted: "It was our duty at least to volunteer our good
offices—to offer to assist." Though deploring the Mexican decision,
he cautioned that "impatience on our part would be childish.
. . . So long as the misunderstanding continues, we can only await
the time of their awakening to the actual facts. We cannot thrust our
good offices upon them. We can afford to exercise the self-restraint
of a great nation." Americans living in Mexico were urged to leave
the country, "not because we . . . mean to slacken . . . our efforts to
safeguard their lives and interests, but because . . . they should take
no unnecessary risks." As for those who chose to remain, Wilson
promised to "vigilantly watch their fortunes, . . . and . . . hold
those responsible for their sufferings and losses to a definite reckon-
ing." A complete embargo was declared on arms shipments from the
United States. In closing, Wilson predicted: "The steady pressure of
moral force will before many days break the barrier of pride and
prejudice down, and we shall triumph as Mexico's friends sooner
than we should triumph as her enemies—and how much more
handsomely, and with how much higher honor and satisfaction of
conscience." [2]

The response to the President's speech was encouraging. Demo-
crats applauded the nobility of his purpose and Republicans were
relieved to learn that he intended to stop meddling in Mexican
affairs. Several cabinet members sent congratulatory notes, and
across the nation editorial comment almost unanimously endorsed
non-intervention. "Watchful waiting," one of those pert phrases for
which Wilson had a flair, became a memorable if misleading head-
line. Even Huerta was happy. The embargo would be no great

21

inconvenience to him; he could bring arms in through his ports, but it would put the land-locked Constitutionalists at some disadvantage. "That is substantially what I expected," he said. "We never had any reason to doubt the United States." [3]

In view of Wilson's temperament, it is doubtful that "watchful waiting" would have endured, had not events begun to indicate the success of an earlier, more active policy. But within a few days of the President's address, it appeared that the Mexicans had consented to his offer, after all. The Gamboa letter must have been merely a matter of face. Huerta continued to plan for an election on October 26, 1913. The names of several relatively independent candidates were placed in nomination, and in Mexico City, the American Embassy was tactfully reminded that the Mexican constitution prohibited the permanent election of a provisional president. From Veracruz, where he had been reduced to the role of another special observer, John Lind wired: "Every point . . . is accepted in fact, though not in form. . . . The mission is a success." [4] Secretary Bryan was equally optimistic, declaring: "The crisis is past," [5] while Chargé O'Shaughnessy recorded his "opinion that . . . the Provisional President is desirous of coming to an understanding with our government." [6] At the end of September, Huerta was still promising to "spare no effort and no sacrifice . . . to . . . guarantee the free casting of the ballot." [7]

Such altogether good news might have been suspect, as it seems, to some extent, it was. In August, Wilson had written, "Every day the news from Mexico City unsettles the news of the day before," [8] and there is no reason to believe that he had abandoned all his reservations. But his slight skepticism was scant preparation for the enormity of what occurred. On October 10, liberal members of the Mexican Chamber of Deputies, encouraged by the Constitutionalist capture of Torreón, the last strong position north of Mexico City, proposed to transfer the seat of government behind Constitutionalist lines. Huerta found their suggestion extremely offensive, and on October 12, he indicated the extent of his displeasure. Troops closed round the legislative chambers and 110 deputies were put under arrest. The next day Huerta dissolved the remnant of the Congress, announcing that he would assume dictatorial powers pending the promised election. It was held on schedule, but after the balloting, Huerta declared that the vote had been too small to reflect the will of the Mexican people. He would continue in office until the "pacification" of the country had been completed. A Congress of hand-picked *Huertistas* was arbitrarily convened as soon as possible.

"Shocked" and "deeply distressed" were the words Wilson used to describe his reaction to this turn of events, but they fail to convey the intensity of his emotion. A more accurate index to Wilson's attitude lies in the diary of his closest adviser, Colonel Edward M. House. On October 30, House wrote: "The President has in mind to declare war on Mexico," speculated on his intention to throw two entrenched lines across Mexico from coast to coast, and concluded, rather gratuitously, "A real crisis has arisen." [9] Wilson did not pursue these plans. But from this time forward, his determination to eliminate Huerta would not stem solely from his dedication to an abstract moral concept. It would be supported by a passionate, personal commitment to an objective rather like revenge.

Acting with customary vigor, Wilson wired Mexico City. On November 1, O'Shaughnessy was instructed to advise Huerta that "the President of the United States feels that the recent *coup d'état* was in direct contravention of the assurances that had been conveyed to this government. . . . Unless General Huerta now voluntarily . . . withdraws from authority . . . , it will be necessary for the President of the United States to insist upon the terms of an ultimatum, the rejection of which would render it necessary for him to propose very serious practical measures to the Congress. . . . Huerta will only for a few days longer be free to act with apparent freedom of choice in the matter. . . . This Government cannot too earnestly urge him to make the inevitable choice wisely and in full view of the terrible consequences of hesitation or refusal." [10]

O'Shaughnessy had no better luck than Lind. After a day or two of doubt, Huerta decided to take whatever terrible consequence Wilson had in mind. It turned out to be an overture to the Constitutionalists. Hale was sent north to interview Venustiano Carranza, their "First Chief." If Carranza was cooperative, Wilson would lift the arms embargo. In the event, Carranza proved as obdurate as Huerta, informing Hale that he was not about to participate in any farcical election; he was going to enter Mexico City at the head of his army, and he saw no point in discussing other arrangements. But the news that negotiations were in progress so unnerved Huerta that momentarily he seemed willing to step down. Before the details of succession could be settled, however, he learned that the Constitutionalists had declined to make a deal. Never again did he weaken. By the end of November, 1913, Wilson's diplomatic offensive had ground to a halt.

The President was undismayed; overthrowing Huerta had become an obsession. Whatever obstacles it encountered would only harden his resolve. On November 24, he issued a State Department circular which must have removed any vestigal doubts of his goal. Forwarded to almost every government with which the United States maintained relations, this document was entitled "Our Purposes in Mexico." It opened with the declaration that "The purpose of the United States is solely and singly to secure peace and order in Central America. . . . Usurpations like that of General Huerta menace the peace . . . as nothing else could. . . . It is the purpose of the United States therefore to discredit and defeat such usurpations whenever they occur. The present policy of the . . . United States is to isolate General Huerta entirely; to cut him off from foreign sympathy and aid and from domestic credit, whether moral or material, and so to force him out. . . . If General Huerta does not retire by force of circumstances, it will become the duty of the United States to use less peaceful means." [11] No one, least of all Wilson, imagined that it would ever become necessary for the United States to resort to those "less peaceful means." Historically, Central American governments had existed on the good will of the United States. Its displeasure was supposed to be fatal.

The European powers made their customary commitment to follow America's lead. There was one misunderstanding, but it was easily resolved. The difficulty had arisen when the new British ambassador to Mexico, Sir Lionel Carden, presented his credentials to Huerta the day after the arrest of the deputies. Wilson felt that his action countenanced the *coup,* and hastily concluded that Britain had undertaken to sponsor Huerta in return for commercial advantages. The British had no desire to antagonize Wilson and Foreign Secretary Sir Edward Grey rushed his private secretary, Sir William Tyrell, to Washington to pacify the President. A cordial interview set the matter at rest, and in March, 1914, Great Britain withdrew recognition of Huerta. Besides repairing the entente, Sir William gained a startling insight into the President's mind. At one point in their conversation, he asked Wilson exactly what he hoped to accomplish in Mexico. Without a moment's hesitation, the President replied: "I am going to teach the South American republics to elect good men!" [12]

Surprisingly, it turned out to be not that simple. In the closing days of 1913, Huerta staged a remarkable rally. In December, his forces launched a series of counterattacks which resulted in the recapture of Torreón. Huerta himself stopped drinking so heavily and, while the Constitutionalist leaders fell to quarrelling among themselves, revived the Díaz régime's alliance with the Catholic Church. At the beginning of 1914, well-advised Mexicans were predicting that the war would last for years.[13]

On January 2, 1914, Wilson held a conference with John Lind aboard the USS *Chester*, off Gulfport, Mississippi. Lind told the President that only direct action could restore the Constitutionalists' flagging fortunes. He must have been convincing, for a month later Wilson played his trump: on February 3, he revoked the arms embargo. The Constitutionalists were exultant. Arms had been smuggled across the Mexican border, of course, but now even the minimal risk involved in these transactions was removed. Soon, however, it developed that the advantage the rebels gained through the President's decision was balanced by the reaction of the Mexican propertied classes. They had supported Huerta all along, but when the United States aligned itself with the Constitutionalists, they redoubled their efforts. In March, a domestic loan was so successful that Huerta was finally able to stabilize the rate of exchange. Aside from Wilson's animosity, the lack of foreign purchasing power had been Huerta's greatest handicap. Once the peso was sound, he began to order large quantities of arms and munitions from abroad.

Six months had passed since Wilson had publicly proclaimed his intention of ousting Huerta. That steady pressure of moral force, upon which Wilson had placed such reliance, had signally failed to affect the course of Mexican affairs. Huerta was still lodged in the President's Palace and Wilson's Mexican policy was beginning to be regarded as nothing more than a colossal bluff. "Watchful waiting" was already an object of editorial derision. A popular cartoon showed Bryan shaking his finger at Mexico and exclaiming: "I may say, I am most annoyed; and if you do not immediately reform, I hesitate to say what I may not be inclined to decide, perhaps!" [14] No President can afford a position in which he may appear silly, but unless Wilson did something decisive, and soon, he would be caught in one. At this impasse, one of those trivial incidents by which the turning points of history are usually marked occurred to offer the President an escape from his dilemma.

FOUR: THE PSYCHOLOGICAL MOMENT

What an utterly foolish thing, said his critics, it is to attempt in this day to oust a Mexican dictator by mere rhetoric and high-sounding phrases.

Joseph P. Tumulty [1]

I n October, 1913, Wilson had sent a squadron of the Atlantic Fleet to show the flag along the Mexican Gulf Coast. The oil industry was centered there, seaward of the Sierra Orientale, and thousands of Americans resided in the region; should a crisis arise, Navy units would be in position to protect their lives and investments. Rear Admiral Frank F. Fletcher, in the flagship *Rhode Island*, was designated Commander of U.S. Naval Forces off the east coast of Mexico.

"One had to become acquainted with Admiral Fletcher to appreciate his sterling character and his charm," said Major Smedley Darlington Butler, USMC. "He was a grand old sea dog." [2] Considering its source, this is exceedingly high praise: Smedley Butler did not incline towards charity when he spoke of Navy brass. His comments are even more remarkable in light of his introduction to Admiral Fletcher. When Butler reported for duty off Veracruz, Fletcher had given him a frosty reception. "I don't know why you men are here," the Admiral fumed. "Why didn't the Department consult me? I've no use for Marines and less for you. I don't need you." Butler had prepared a request for transfer before he learned that he had been a victim of Fletcher's heavy humor. "After he enjoyed his little joke, we became good friends," Butler related. "He was an efficient officer but no martinet. The human side was always uppermost." [3]

Electrician Second Class John Robert Johnson, Fletcher's flag radioman, endorsed Butler's opinion of the admiral. "He was a gentleman of the old school," said Johnson, "well-liked by all hands, especially the members of his staff." [4] Johnson's affection for Fletcher dated from the morning when, new aboard the flagship, he ventured aft to deliver a coded radiogram to Flag Lieutenant Rowan. Inadvertently bypassing the admiral's orderly, Johnson opened a door and found himself face-to-face with a stocky, middle-aged man with salt-and-pepper mustaches and dark, piercing eyes: he had blundered

Rear Admiral Frank F. Fletcher, commander of the
U.S. Naval Forces at Veracruz

into the admiral's stateroom. After an awful moment, Fletcher demanded: "Who are you?" Johnson gave his name and stammered that he had been trying to find the flag lieutenant. Fletcher called Rowan into the cabin and Johnson handed him the message. While Rowan studied the signal, Fletcher asked the young petty officer how he liked life aboard ship and other questions intended to set him at ease. Johnson replied as briefly as possible and was immeasurably relieved to be dismissed. "A lesser man would have prescribed a spot of bread and water, to say the least," he wrote.[5]

Johnson was also impressed by the observation that Fletcher never raised his voice. He noted, though, that the admiral could deliver the "most amazing" reprimand in a conversational tone. A Marine orderly gave Johnson the highlights of one of Fletcher's better efforts, directed at a very senior officer. "According to the Marine," Johnson related, "it took the varnish off the charthouse door, but that is an obvious exaggeration. . . . That the charthouse door got a new coat of varnish about that time was pure coincidence."[6]

Born in Oskaloosa, Iowa, in 1855, Fletcher had been appointed to the Naval Academy in 1871. In the course of his long career, most of which was spent at sea, he had commanded everything from torpedo boats to battleships. An ordnance enthusiast, he was the inventor of a gun mount and breech mechanism which had become standard equipment in the United States Navy. From 1910 to 1913 he had served as Aide to the Secretary of the Navy for Materiel. In June of the latter year, he had been given command of the First Division of the Atlantic Fleet.

Off Tampico and Veracruz, Fletcher's squadron met warships from the European powers involved in Mexico. The sleek new German armored cruiser *Dresden,* the French cruisers *Jeanne d'Arc, Condé* and *Descartes,* the antique Spanish cruiser *Carlos V* and the British Fourth Cruiser Squadron lay in Mexican waters in the spring of 1914. All were present to safeguard their respective nationals, and the community of interests fostered an atmosphere of camaraderie. At Tampico, the American ships even returned the salutes of Huerta's gunboats, though protocol prohibited the extension of this courtesy to vessels of governments not recognized by the United States; and at Veracruz, recalled Smedley Butler, "The harbor was like a busy city street. . . . There was a gay exchange of international . . . hospitality. Launches and barges were continually plying back and forth."[7] While officers entertained at formal dinners, members of the ships' companies took parties of enlisted visitors on tour. The invitations most eagerly accepted by American bluejackets were those to a German ship. British propaganda had yet to teach the world to hate the Hun, and every large American city had its German-American friendship *bund*. Moreover, the Kaiser's crews received rations of the *vaterland*'s beer, which they would share with their guests. Aside from the officers' wine mess, American ships had been dry since the 1880's, and the bluejackets thirsted for the moment when their hosts would bring forth the refreshments.

Shore leaves were limited, for fear of incident. The ships' athletic programs and libraries offered wholesome recreation; otherwise, for diversion the bluejackets could look forward to illicit crap and blackjack games, and the visits of the "bumboats"—the rickety craft in which native peddlers put out to hawk their wares. "Alligator pears" sold well to the younger seamen, until they discovered that these "pears"—the avocados of today—were not the succulent fruit they had expected. On the open seas, understanding skippers allowed their hands to fish for the giant sharks that cruised in the wake of their vessels. Great hooks were baited with galley scraps, and winches were used for reels. Seamen were still craftsmen, and sharks taken on this apparatus furnished hours of amusement. Their teeth were prized for watchfobs, and from their vertebrae were fashioned canes that put a black malacca stick to shame.[8]

In December, 1913, the presence of Fletcher's vessels had been invoked to compel the Constitutionalists to abandon an offensive into the oil fields around Tampico; but all that had happened on paper. On the whole, the American squadron had spent a tedious seven months. "The predominating features of this place are water, mist, fog, and heavy ground swells," wrote a bluejacket off Veracruz. "We have had rumors of wars, of reliefs coming, of landing the battalion . . . on this date, and that, all to naught."[9] The crew of the battleship *New Hampshire* went six months without setting foot ashore. The boredom became so excruciating that, after he had exhausted his ship's library, a young Eastern Shoreman took up knitting and crochet. Now the make-work routine of shipboard life was to be shattered in the unlikely aftermath of an event which, at any other time or place, would have passed almost unnoticed.

On the morning of Thursday, April 9, 1914, Lieutenant Commander Ralph K. Earle, captain of the gunboat *Dolphin,* met a German merchant named Max Tryon in the American Consulate at Tampico. Because the battleships could not pass Tampico Bar, the little *Dolphin* was serving as the temporary flagship of Rear Admiral Henry T. Mayo, commander of the Fourth Division of the Atlantic Fleet. Earle was trying to purchase gasoline for Admiral Mayo's launch. The launch was seeing steady service and the ships' stores were nearly exhausted. The usual sources of supply had been disrupted by the civil war and Earle had come ashore to ask if Consul Clarence Miller knew of any reserves.

When Earle mentioned his errand, Tryon told him that he had some gasoline for sale. It was stored in his warehouse, which stood on the canal connecting the Laguna de Carpentero with the Pánuco River on the northeastern outskirts of Tampico. Miller had a map of the city and Tryon pointed out its location.

Returning to the *Dolphin,* Earle ordered Assistant Paymaster Charles W. Copp to pick up the gasoline. Twenty-three years old, Copp was doing his first tour of sea duty; his previous two years' service had been spent at office work ashore. Collecting a detail of eight bluejackets, he put off in a whaleboat shortly before noon. In the Pánuco, the whaleboat caught a tow from a passing launch. Copp cast off near the mouth of the canal, and the bluejackets broke out the oars.

Usually, the Tampico waterfront was a scene of great commotion. Located ten miles from the sea on a bend of the broad Pánuco, the city was the center of the pipelines that radiated into the interior. The extent of the oil works impressed even world-travelled Jack London. "As we continued up the river," he wrote, describing his first trip to Tampico, "More and more terminals and tank farms lined both banks. . . . This was the Corona terminal, and that was the Aguila on both sides, and adjoining were the huge solid buildings of Standard Oil. There was the National Petroleum, there the Waters-Pierce, the Gulf Coast, the Mexican Petroleum, the Texas, the International Oil, the East Coast Oil—and thereat I ceased taking account of the companies. . . . 'Ah,' I remarked, 'there's the city at last,' indicating great masses of buildings on the north bank. But I was informed that the city was yet miles away, and that what I had mistaken for it were the boiler stacks, still stacks, warehouses, paraffin plants, and agitators of the refineries." [10]

In the fifteen years since the discovery of oil, Tampico had grown from a backwater village to a bustling city with a population of over thirty thousand, including the largest American colony outside Mexico City. But its allure was purely commercial. Mrs. O'Shaughnessy called it "one of the dreariest spots on earth, . . . a horrid, flat, mosquito-infested place," [11] and Admiral Cradock requested that the crews of British vessels in the Pánuco receive the

Climate Pay allowed for duty in unhealthy stations.[12]

Little activity was evident to Paymaster Copp's party, however. The Constitutionalists had appeared in the suburbs on April 6, and the life of the city had come to a standstill. "Enormous clouds of smoke from burning oil tanks and buildings"[13] downstream at Arbol Grande and Doña Cecilia hung over Tampico. Two banks had sent their specie to the *Dresden*'s Captain Koehler for safe-keeping, and over six hundred European and North American residents had taken refuge aboard the foreign warships. In the Pánuco, the Federal gunboats *Zaragoza* and *Veracruz* were lobbing shells over the city into the Constitutionalist lines. The gunboats had been ordered to blockade Tampico, but Fletcher had informed their captains that the port would remain open.

Despite these conditions, Copp was not expected to encounter any difficulties. General Ignacio Morelos Zaragoza, military governor of the state of Tamaulipas, whom Mayo found "most courteous and reasonable,"[14] had not proclaimed martial law, and no restricted areas had been declared. In any event, the American flags which fluttered fore and aft on the whaleboat were assumed to provide ample protection for its crew. No member of the party was armed.

Tryon's warehouse stood a few hundred yards below the Iturbidé Bridge, the grandiose title of a trestle of the Tampico-Victoria railway. A brisk fire fight had taken place at the bridge two days before, when a Constitutionalist patrol had taken the Federals by surprise. Copp found the warehouse without incident and brought his boat alongside Tryon's battered lighter. Tryon was waiting; he lived on Calle Altamira, a short walk away, and the transaction was quickly completed. Copp and Tryon stood by while the bluejackets loaded the gasoline drums. It was a pleasant day, refreshingly cool for that torrid season. A Mexican patrol boat chugged back and forth across the dark waters near the Iturbidé Bridge. Tryon noticed its officer peering towards the dock, but that scarcely seemed remarkable and he did not mention it to Copp.

Copp's men were stowing away the last of the gasoline when a squad of ten Federal soldiers appeared on the landing. Their leader, apparently an officer, spoke sharply to Copp. None of the Americans understood Spanish, but the Mexican's meaning was obvious—they were to come with him. Two of Copp's men, Coxswain G. H. Siefert and Seaman J. P. Harrington, were standing in the boat. Ignoring the Mexican officer's gestures, they made no move to leave the craft. The officer barked an order, and suddenly Siefert and Harrington found themselves staring into the muzzles of the Mexicans' rifles. They turned to Copp. He nodded, and they climbed ashore.

Tryon attempted to intercede in the Americans' behalf. Fluent in Spanish, he explained the reason for their presence and protested their arrest. He knew the officers at the Iturbidé Bridge; they were local men, members of the Tamaulipas State Guard. Unfortunately, they were not in a neighborly mood. Tryon was informed that their orders were to detain any persons found in the area without a military pass. The best the guardsmen could do was authorize Tryon to see General Zaragoza. Copp and his men were led away.

Tryon left the area at the same time. Instead of seeking General Zaragoza, however, he hurried to the *Dolphin,* moored at the Fiscal Wharf. There he told Lieutenant Commander Earle that Copp's party had been seized. Earle notified Admiral Mayo, who ordered him ashore to demand the bluejackets' immediate release.

Meanwhile, Copp's detail had been marched a few blocks up Calle Altamira and across the railway track to a Mexican regimental headquarters. Officers there spoke English, and the misunderstanding was explained. The forces defending the Iturbidé Bridge had been alerted to expect a Constitutionalist attack. Regular troops might well have been uneasy, and the Tamaulipas guardsmen, spooked by the previous assault, were in a state of acute hypertension. Furthermore, as General Zaragoza later declared, they were "ignorant of the first rules of war." [15] The sight of a boatload of men in uniform had inflamed their martial instincts, which seems natural; but the discovery that those men were Americans, and unarmed, had failed to allay their alarm, which is less easily understood. The guard commander, Colonel Ramón H. Hinojosa, told Copp that the area around the bridge was under military control. American sailors had no business being there. Nevertheless, he instructed his men to escort the bluejackets back to their boat. At the landing, Copp's party was detained a further few minutes to give Hinojosa time to clear his action with General Zaragoza.

By then, Earle and Consul Miller, whom he had asked along to interpret, had reached Zaragoza. The general was completely conciliatory. After sanctioning the Americans' release, he asked Earle to convey his "regrets" to Admiral Mayo. The entire episode had occurred in something like an hour and a half.[16]

It was an Incident, of course: guns had been pointed. But as Incidents go, it was a most innocuous affair. A similar occurrence had taken place the preceding afternoon, when a Marine noncom

Captain William L. Sayre, USNR (Ret.)

General Ignacio Morelos Zaragoza, Military Governor of Tamaulipas,
with members of his staff

U.S. Navy

Rear Admiral Henry T. Mayo, U.S. Navy,
whose demand for a 21-gun salute to the
American flag precipitated the Mexican crisis

carrying messages from the Consulate to the Fiscal Wharf had lost his way and wandered near the Iturbidé Bridge. He had been held for a few minutes, and nothing untoward had developed. There was one important difference, though: the Marine had not been compelled to leave a vessel flying the American flag. According to international law, seizing a man in this manner was tantamount to abducting him from the territory of the nation itself. Still, far more flagrant actions had been forgotten many times before. An over-zealous subordinate had exceeded instructions, but his commander's apology had been prompt and sincere.

The possibility that such thin stuff could be parleyed into a *casus belli* proceeded from the pugnacity of Rear Admiral Henry T. Mayo. Having spent forty-two of his fifty-seven years in the uniform of the United States Navy, Mayo was not at all disposed to overlook any token of disrespect to that service. Nor, in all probability, was he especially adverse to the prospect of what Teddy Roosevelt liked to call "a splendid little war." By nature an aggressive man, Mayo had been dogged by routine duties throughout his career. An un-lucky assignment had prevented him from seeing action in the Spanish-American War, and prior to June, 1913, when he had been given a division of the Fleet, his most distinguished post had been Commandant of the Mare Island Navy Yard, in California, near San Francisco. Mayo's star had begun to rise in 1912, when he made a highly favorable impression upon newly appointed Secretary of the Navy Josephus Daniels during Daniels' first tour of naval installa-tions. Not long afterwards, Mayo had been called to Washington to act as Daniels' aide and promoted to rear admiral over several more senior officers. In naval circles, Mayo had a reputation for forceful-ness and cool judgment. His features were the hallmark of his nature: stern and inflexible, they seemed to have been carved from the granite of his native New Hampshire. "He does what he thinks is right," a friend said, "and as a rule he does not lose a lot of time doing it." [17]

On April 9, 1914, Mayo acted entirely in character. He repri-manded Assistant Paymaster Copp for allowing Siefert and Har-rington to leave the boat, and sent Commander W. A. Moffett ashore, starched and straight, with dress sword and gloves, to per-sent the following ultimatum to General Zaragoza. Neither Admiral Fletcher at Veracruz nor the Navy Department was consulted prior to its dispatch.

I need not tell you that taking men from a boat flying the American flag is a hostile act, not to be excused. Responsibility for hostile acts cannot be avoided by a plea of ignorance. In view of the publicity of this occurrence, I must require that you send me, by suitable members of your staff, formal disavowal of and apology for the act, together with your assurance that the officer responsible for it will receive severe punishment. Also that you publicly hoist the American flag in a prominent position and salute it with twenty-one guns, which salute will be duly returned by this ship. Your answer to this communication should reach me and the called-for salute be fired within twenty-four hours from 6 P.M. of this date.[18]

The furor produced by this document lasted for eleven days. At the end of that period, diplomatic resources being exhausted, Wilson asked Congress for authority to "use the armed forces of the United States in such ways and to such an extent as may be necessary to obtain from General Huerta and his adherents the fullest recognition of the rights and dignity of the United States." [19] Before that request was made, almost every leader in both nations endeavored to achieve a less drastic solution—every leader, that is, except Wilson himself. For the record makes it clear that, pacifism notwithstanding, Wilson exploited the Tampico Incident to promote a situation which would appear to justify intervention. "Really," he said afterwards, "it was the psychological moment." [20]

Wilson's resolve was reinforced by the curious conviction that intervention could be accomplished without recourse to arms. The abhorrence with which he professed to view war was sincere. "It is not a difficult thing for a President to declare war," he told Tumulty, "especially against a weak and defenseless nation like Mexico. . . . The thing that . . . holds me back is the aftermath of war, with all its tears and tragedies. I came from the South and I know what war is, for I have seen its wreckage and terrible ruin. It is easy for me . . . to declare war. I do not have to fight and neither do the gentlemen on the Hill who now clamor for it. It is some poor farmer's boy, or the son of some poor widow . . . or perhaps the scion of some great family who will have to do the fighting and the dying." [21]

In advocating intervention, Wilson did not sacrifice his principles. By a magnificent rationalization, he managed to persuade himself that they would be preserved. As late as April 20, he could warn reporters, in all good faith, "not to get the impression that there is about to be war between the United States and Mexico. That isn't the outlook . . . at all. . . . This need not eventuate into war if we handle it with firmness and purpose." [22]

Wilson was spending a long weekend with his ailing wife in White Sulphur Springs, West Virginia, when the State Department advised him of the incident. Endorsing the admiral's action with the comment, "Mayo could not have done otherwise," [23] the President returned to his golf; he had a standing Saturday game. Secretary of the Treasury McAdoo, the only cabinet member at White Sulphur Springs, was not even informed.

Meanwhile, Zaragoza had requested an extension of the twenty-four-hour time limit, explaining that it would be necessary for him to forward the ultimatum to Mexico City. He lacked the authority to consider its demands. On April 10, Mayo asked the commander of the British cruiser squadron, Rear Admiral Sir Christopher Cradock, what he thought of the request. "I told him," wrote Cradock, "that Mexicans are not quite like other people; that it was their natural habit to move slowly, and I suggested granting . . . a week if necessary." [24] Mayo agreed, and that afternoon, in Mexico City, O'Shaughnessy prodded the Mexican foreign office into assembling a preliminary note. It was not altogether satisfactory. "It is perfectly understood," insisted the Mexicans, "that a military commander who sees the arrival of men in uniform at the port he is guarding should proceed to arrest them pending an investigation as to whether the presence of those men is . . . justifiable." [25] But the over-all tone was more accommodating, and the next day the Mexican government all but capitulated. Huerta issued a formal apology, promising that Colonel Hinojosa would receive his just deserts—he had already been relieved of command.

The only requirement Huerta resisted was the twenty-one gun salute. Perhaps, as a soldier, he found that condition particularly offensive. And perhaps, as a schemer, he entertained the idea of risking war with the United States on the chance that the revolution might be forgotten in the feelings of national unity produced by the threat of a foreign invasion. Unlikely as it sounds, this was the opinion of the German ambassador, Admiral von Hintze. "Huerta's personal position is desperate," he said. "Whether he fights the rebels . . . or the United States, it is disaster for him. Only, I fancy, he has less to lose in the way of prestige if he chooses the United States. His nation will make some show of rallying around him in this latter case." [26] Huerta himself lent support to this view when he answered a newsman's question about the effects of America's belligerence with the exclamation, "It is the best thing that could happen to us!" [27]

At any rate, in a long letter of April 12, Huerta contended that for his government to salute the flag of a power which had refused to recognize the legitimacy of his régime (and, he might have added, was devoted to its downfall) in penance for an act for which it had already apologized, would be a gesture of abject submission. "The old Indian was more eloquent than I have ever seen him," O'Shaughnessy reported. "I was impressed that he is imbued with a certain amount of patriotism in his statements, and I believe that he will probably not yield." [28]

To many Americans, Huerta's apology seemed good enough. They were willing to forego the salute. None of Wilson's cabinet members except Secretary of War Garrison attached much importance to it, and on April 12, Bryan had said, "I am inclined to believe that Admiral Mayo, who after all has the whole matter in his hands, will regard the apology as sufficient. . . . If the Federal commander at Tampico should not actually salute the flag, Admiral Mayo will pass by the matter, satisfied with what Huerta has said." [29]

The operative phrase here is "who has the whole matter in his hands." It seems a curious statement for a Secretary of State, but it was entirely true. In the accounts of those April days, one seeks vainly to discover the role of the Secretary of State. He had none. Bryan's appointment had been a political necessity; he was an institution of the Democratic Party, and at the deadlocked 1912 convention it had been his delegates, thrown to Wilson, who had assured the President's nomination. But as a cabinet member, Bryan was hopelessly out of his depth. The extent of his thought on the Mexican problem appears to have been the hope that it could be handled without anyone getting shot. History had slipped past the "Boy Orator of the Platte." Once the Populist decade had ended, William Jennings Bryan was a man out of his time.

Wilson returned from White Sulphur Springs on Monday, April 13. To the newsmen waiting at the Washington station, he promised: "The salute will be fired." [30] A radiogram from Admiral Fletcher, volunteering to go to Mexico City in the belief that "in conference with the Embassy as to the technical details and naval customs . . . I could personally reach an agreement with the Mexican authorities that will be satisfactory to both parties," was ignored.[31] Wilson's position became even clearer after the cabinet meeting of April 14, in which he declared his determination of "backing up . . . Admiral Mayo." John Lind, who had just arrived from Mexico, encouraged him to force the issue. That afternoon, Wilson ordered the Atlantic Fleet to concentrate on the east coast of Mexico. Rear Admiral Charles J. Badger, the commander in chief of the Atlantic Fleet, led the battleships out of Hampton Roads that evening.

At this eleventh hour, the President's program was almost upset. O'Shaughnessy finally convinced Huerta of the importance of the salute. The fleet was still off Virginia when Huerta stated that he would direct his forces at Tampico to raise and salute the American flag. He made one reservation: there must be a written agreement that it would be returned round for round. This was exactly what Mayo had demanded in the first place, but it was no longer sufficient. Wilson replied that compliance must be unconditional. The United States had abandoned the "generous attitude" which had characterized its previous dealings with Mexico; the psychological moment must not be let slip. On Saturday, April 18, Wilson established a final deadline of 6:00 P.M. Sunday. Unless Huerta agreed to the salute by that hour, Wilson would go before Congress. The expiration of this ultimatum was accepted as a matter of course.

Wilson addressed the Congress in Joint Session at three o'clock on the afternoon of Monday, April 20. He had conferred with Congressional leaders earlier in the day. To his recital of the events at Tampico, Wilson added accounts of two subsequent "incidents." The first had occurred on April 10, when Seaman F. C. Larue, a mail orderly from the battleship *Minnesota,* had become engaged in an altercation with a Mexican soldier in the post office at Veracruz. A policeman had taken them both to the station, from which Laruc had been immediately released. The other incident had taken place in Mexico City on the evening of April 11. A blundering Mexican censor had caused a two-hour delay in the transmission of a coded telegram from O'Shaughnessy to the State Department. It made no difference that Admiral Fletcher had concluded his report of Seaman Larue's misadventure with the statement that "the attitude of the Mexican authorities is correct; there is no cause for complaint," [32] or that O'Shaughnessy had declared that the non-delivery of his telegram "was really due to the ignorance of the censor." [33] Wilson did not see fit to repeat their remarks. Instead, he maintained that this series of incidents made it clear that the Mexican government had adopted a policy of "studied contempt" for the United States.

"The [Tampico] Incident cannot be regarded as a trivial one," he asserted, "especially as the . . . men . . . were taken from the boat itself—that is, from the territory of the United States. . . . If it had stood by itself, it might have been attributed to the ignorance or arrogance of a single officer. . . . Unfortunately, it was not an isolated case." The only logical conclusion was that "the Government of the United States was being singled out . . . for slights and affronts in retaliation for its refusal to recognize the pretensions of General Huerta." The danger was that "such offenses might grow from bad to worse until something happened of so gross and intolerable a sort as to lead directly and inevitably to armed conflict." [34]

In closing, Wilson expressed his opinion that the measures he proposed could be peacefully enacted. But "if armed conflict should unhappily occur, we should be fighting only General Huerta and those who adhere to him . . . and our object would be only to restore to the people of the distracted Republic the opportunity to set up again their own laws and their own government." [35] Wilson's final words were received with a standing ovation.

Later, Wilson wondered if the applause had been too prolonged. Before leaving the White House, he had mused, "I had an uneasy feeling as I read the papers this morning, as if the country were getting on fire with war enthusiasm." [36] There were critics, of course; Republican Senator Henry Cabot Lodge thought the President's grievances were too flimsy to support intervention. Commenting on Wilson's address, Lodge said, "It seemed to me weak and insufficient, although of course well expressed." [37] Others argued that what Wilson really wanted was war against an individual named Huerta—a thesis not far from the truth. Asserting that Wilson's request proceeded primarily from "personal resentment," Representative Mann, the Republican floor leader, exclaimed, "I am not willing to declare war because the President of the United States doesn't like Victoriano Huerta." [38]

But the rebel yells that had punctuated the President's remarks revealed the spirit of the majority. A resolution authorizing the use of force against Huerta carried the House by the comfortable margin of 337 to 37.

Things did not go so smoothly in the Senate. Lodge and Elihu Root had drafted an amended version of Wilson's resolution, expanding it to authorize the employment of United States troops against any Mexican party, Federal or Constitutionalist, which threatened American interests. The Republicans lacked the strength to pass the bill, but they were numerous enough to force a debate. It lasted until the early morning of April 21, when the Senate adjourned without taking action on either proposal. The resolutions were set at the top of the agenda for Wednesday, April 22.

✠✠

FIVE: THERE IS NO ALTERNATIVE

On Saturday 11th April I lunched with the Admiral and as I left the gangway he told me in these words, "I have given them 24 hours extension before taking any action." As I steamed down the river that night I passed the USS Des Moines, *prepared for action, guns cast loose, with ensigns at the masthead and jack on the stay.*

Admiral Sir Christopher Cradock [1]

Radiograms from the Navy Department, though often long delayed in transmission, provided Fletcher with a running account of events on Capitol Hill. On April 20, he was advised that "General Huerta has refused to salute the American flag. . . . President Wilson will lay the matter before Congress today with a view of taking such action as may be necessary to enforce respect for nations' rights." [2] Everyone assumed that the Navy would be ordered to occupy a Mexican port; and though the administration seemed confident that a landing could be carried through without opposition, the Atlantic Fleet did not share that certainty. Junior officers reviewed the infantry tactics they had been taught at Annapolis, while bluejackets were issued field packs, rifles, bayonets, and other equipment for service ashore. [3]

Standing Fleet Orders prescribed the exact organization of the "battalion" each vessel was required to maintain. Rifle companies followed the lines of the gun divisions, the First Company being composed of the personnel assigned to the First Division (Number One Turret), and were divided into two sections, corresponding to infantry platoons. A battleship battalion consisted of three rifle companies plus an artillery company with a few heavy machineguns and a 3-inch "landing gun"; altogether, it amounted to over three hundred men. So no one found it strange that an army brigade encamped at Galveston had not been embarked for Mexico.

There seems to be a flavor of Kipling and Henty in the terms "Seaman Regiment" and "Naval Brigade," but in 1914 there was nothing unusual in the idea of sending sailors to fight on land. Throughout naval history, seamen had been expected to double as soldiers; Marines were regarded essentially as seagoing police. Sir William Peel's naval gunners had manned most of the British

41

batteries before Sebastopol in 1854 and 1855 and detachments of the Royal Navy had served ashore in colonial campaigns from New Zealand to the Soudan. The decisive land battle in the French conquest of Indochina had been won by sailors led by an admiral, and in the decades since the Civil War, American bluejackets had fought in Hawaii, Korea, Samoa, China, the Philippines, and on almost every seacoast in Latin America.

To understand this state of mind, it is necessary to know something of the Navy as it was in the days before the First World War. It was, in many ways, a world apart: a small—in 1912, the entire establishment numbered 3,094 officers and 47,515 men—supremely self-assured society existing outside the mainstream of American life. The stern, sometimes callous, traditions of wooden ships and iron men still ran strong. The Civil War was only two generations distant; the petty officers who trained the recruits of 1912 had been trained by men who remembered the ironclads on the Mississippi and chases after blockade runners off the Carolina capes. At the Newport News Training Station, one drill master corrected men marching out of step by hurling a dull dress sword into their shins. Before-breakfast calisthenics included a race hand-over-hand through the rigging of the old *Constitution*. The recruit lived in anticipation of the day he would join the fleet; but his life was little less rugged there. Advancement was agonizingly slow; not many bluejackets would receive a rating during their first enlistment, and the odds of obtaining a commission were infinitesimal. Discipline was rigid and punishment swift. Yet the Navy had much to offer: the security of three meals a day; the allure of travel; the opportunity to share in the fraternity that exists among every good crew; the prospect of romance (largely illusory) and danger (real enough) ; and, to some wayward youths, the alternative to a term in the house of correction.[4]

Professionally, the Navy was in a period of transition. In the midst of the dreadnought era, with the potential of aircraft and submarines already evident, many senior officers thought in terms of experiences antedating the Spanish-American War. Since 1906–1907, when Teddy Roosevelt had sent the Great White Fleet around the world, a group of younger officers, led by Captain W. S. Sims, had begun to evolve a new school of gunnery and tactics; but as yet their theories had attracted scant support among the upper echelons. Long-range fire control and radio procedure were in their infancy. Recently "modernized" drill in the gun sheds along the seawall of the Naval Academy at Annapolis included such archaic commands as "Stand by to ram!" which called for a belly flop, and "Stand by for raking fire from aft!" at which everyone ran around and crouched down in front of the gun platform. The midshipmen's summer cruise was still made on a square-rigger, and plebe-year fencing lessons featured instruction on the use of sword and cutlass and the etiquette of handling a cane. At the Atlantic Fleet's winter gunnery and torpedo exercises at Guantánamo, junior officers were expected to demonstrate their ability in handling small boats "under sail and oars," and an ensign's efficiency rating might depend largely upon how well he could bring his cutter alongside a ship's gangway.[5]

Throughout the second week of April, 1914, international attention centered on Tampico. The bulk of American naval forces were located there, in the mouth of the Pánuco and off Tampico Bar: the battleships *Connecticut* and *Minnesota,* the cruiser *Des Moines,* the scout cruiser *Chester,* the mine depot ship *San Francisco,* the collier *Cyclops,* and the hospital ship *Solace,* which had been with Sampson at the battle of Santiago in 1898. Admiral Mayo had laid plans for taking Tampico. While the *Chester* and *Des Moines* engaged the Mexican gunboats, the *Dolphin* would land parties to seize the Fiscal Wharf and Customs House, and the battleships would send their battalions upriver to augment the *Dolphin* contingent.

It sounded quite simple, but around April 13, Mayo began to have second thoughts. During a storm, not unlikely at that time of year, his ships could not cross Tampico Bar. The battleship battalions would be unable to disembark, and forces already in the Pánuco would be cut off from support. Even without a storm, there were grounds for concern. If the landing were opposed, the battleships' whaleboats would be easy targets while they were being towed up the Pánuco. A landing from the open sea could be made on the beach at La Barra, but there was a sand bar one hundred yards offshore. The landing parties would have to wade the rest of the way, and machine gunners in the dunes could make that a bloody business. On the 14th, Mayo discussed the situation with Sir Christopher Cradock, whose courteous demeanour concealed the conviction that he was confronted with a bungling provincial. "He promised to let me and others know if violent action was likely to take place," Cradock noted. "I fear the Admiral is in a high state of nervous tension." [6]

Informed of Mayo's misgivings, Secretary Daniels lost no time in sending reinforcements. On April 19, the transport *Hancock,* bearing the First Marine Regiment, eight hundred men of the famed

Camp Mitchell "Panama Brigade," under Colonel John A. Le-jeune, appeared off Tampico. Reassured by their presence, Mayo declared his numbers sufficient to cope with any situation which might arise before the arrival of Admiral Badger's battleships, expected late Wednesday, April 22.[7]

At Veracruz, Admiral Fletcher had only three vessels: the battleship *Florida,* which flew his flag; the battleship *Utah;* and the old gunboat *Prairie,* which carried the First Provisional Battalion, Second Advanced Base Regiment, USMC, commanded by Lieutenant Colonel Wendell C. Neville. Though Tampico held the headlines, Veracruz was of greater military significance. Its harbor, while not ideal, was the best on the east coast of Mexico, which made it the natural port of supply for an advance on Mexico City. The American army had used it as such in 1847. Fletcher appreciated the city's strategic value. "In the event of hostilities beyond retaliatory measures," he radioed Daniels, "Veracruz will become center of operations."[8] It was also the most convenient refuge for Americans fleeing the interior.

Orders to "afford every possible protection" to Americans were, in fact, the only operational orders Fletcher had received. He believed that his forces would be ample to accomplish this "in case of trouble, following any action taken at Tampico."[9] During the fighting around Tampico, Fletcher had been authorized to charter the Ward Line steamer *Esperanza* for use as a refugee ship. The Constitutionalists had broken off their attack the same day a navy crew boarded the *Esperanza,* but Fletcher had retained her for future contingencies. On the morning of April 20, he was empowered to impress a second Ward Liner, the *Mexico,* which had carried a cargo of arms into Veracruz a few days before. With these two ships at his disposal, Fletcher could accommodate hundreds of refugees without having to crowd them aboard the battleships.[10]

At this uncertain point, the Mexican situation was suddenly cast in a wholly new and dramatic perspective. On Saturday, April 18, William W. Canada, the American Consul at Veracruz, informed the State Department that the steamer *Ypiranga* was scheduled to dock on Tuesday, April 21, with what was believed to be the largest cargo of arms and munitions ever consigned to a Mexican port: 200 machine guns and 15,000,000 rounds of ammunition. To permit these supplies to reach Huerta was unthinkable; and Tampico was soon forgotten amid the quickening pace of events at Veracruz.[11]

The administration's first impulse was to temporize until the Senate had acted on Wilson's request to use force. In anticipation of its approval, Daniels decided to concentrate the entire Atlantic Fleet off Veracruz. At 2:00 P.M. (Washington time) Monday, April 20, he sent Admiral Mayo orders to proceed at once to Veracruz, leaving a single vessel, the *Des Moines,* at Tampico, and an hour later he instructed Admiral Badger, whose squadron had been doing twelve knots towards Tampico, to make full speed for Veracruz.[12]

What Daniels envisioned was a simple maneuver. Owing to faulty communications, however, it introduced a new element of confusion into a situation whose outlines had been fuzzy from the first. Radio was still a primitive instrument. At Tampico, Mayo was not in direct communication with Washington. At best, his signals could carry no more than three hundred miles. Messages to and from Tampico had to be relayed through Veracruz. Fletcher's battleships were newer, and, in the evening, when atmospheric conditions were most favorable, their radios could raise the naval station at Key West. Even then, there was heavy static, and coded messages of any length were usually garbled in transmission. Fletcher's only prompt and assured communication with the United States was through the cable office at Veracruz. But as the cable operators were Mexican, this facility left a great deal to be desired. It was probably on account of these circumstances that Mayo had not attempted to contact Washington before presenting his ultimatum to General Zaragoza.[13]

In an age when instantaneous communications are taken for granted, it is interesting to follow the sequence of events attending the transmission of Daniels' two orders. The message advising Fletcher that Badger's squadron had been diverted to Veracruz reached Fletcher around 4:15 P.M., three hours after it had left Washington, a good record considering the two-hour difference in time between Washington and Veracruz; but nine more hours were to pass before he received the order for Mayo to withdraw from Tampico. Fletcher questioned the message to Badger, citing the critical "situation at Tampico and ample forces at Veracruz." [14] It was duly confirmed, but with the order to Mayo still in the air, Fletcher remained unaware of the concentration Daniels intended to effect at Veracruz. Therefore, at 5:00 P.M., Fletcher asked Mayo to send him the *San Francisco.* With a draft too deep to cross Tampico Bar, the *San Francisco* would be of limited value to Mayo, but Fletcher could use her within the inner harbor at Veracruz.[15]

Four hours later, Fletcher received the first of a series of radiograms, diminishing in length as they increased in urgency, concerning the *Ypiranga*. Daniels had sent it at 6:00 P.M. Washington time. "*Ypiranga* should not land her war stores," he declared. "Dissuade captain if you can do so without offense. If he should depart from [word missing] send vessel to follow into any Mexico port she may enter and make request there." [16]

This placed Fletcher in a difficult situation. The *Ypiranga* was a German ship, a member of the Hamburg-American Line. Dissuading her captain from landing the arms would have been relatively simple had not Daniels stipulated that it must be done "without offense." Were the United States and Mexico at war, Fletcher could have seized the *Ypiranga*'s cargo as contraband; but the two countries remained, however precariously, at peace. Under the circumstances, Fletcher had no right to overt action. An essay at diplomacy was his only recourse. At 10:00 P.M., he directed Commander H. I. Cone, the acting captain of the *Utah,* to take his vessel ten miles out and attempt to intercept the *Ypiranga* as she neared port. If successful, Cone was to advise the *Ypiranga*'s captain of the troubled conditions at Veracruz and urge him to wait in the outer harbor until the crisis should subside. [17]

Soon after the *Utah* weighed anchor, the *Florida* picked up a signal from the *Arkansas,* Admiral Badger's flagship. Badger requested information concerning the forces available for operations ashore, and asked Fletcher to meet him for consultation off Tampico. It was becoming a hectic night. "Total landing force 1225 bluejackets and 1800 Marines, including 325 on *Prairie,*" Fletcher replied. "Not advisable for me to leave. . . . Forces now at Tampico and Veracruz ample for present contingencies and I suggest you come first to Veracruz." [18] Badger answered at 10:35 P.M., agreeing to rendezvous at Veracruz. He mentioned the order for Mayo to leaveTampico, but as the original had not reached Veracruz, Badger's reference did not cause much concern.

It was not until 1:36 A.M. Tuesday, April 21, that Daniels' message was received at Veracruz. When Fletcher forwarded it to Tampico, Mayo was appalled. At 7:55 A.M., he advised Fletcher of his "fear that our ships leaving Tampico will result in loss American citizens' life and property due intense anti-American feeling prevailing. Position USS *Des Moines* and American citizens will be untenable therefore request repetition of order. . . ." [19] In addition to the anxiety he felt for the Americans at Tampico, Mayo was distraught by the eclipse of his plans for taking the city. Consul Miller related that Mayo was "almost in tears when he informed me of his orders." [20] Mayo's men were no less disappointed. During the period in which they had expected to land, their mood had struck Miller as "joyous"; now they seemed "downcast and despondent." [21]

Miller believed Mayo's apprehensions were eminently justified and, with the admiral's blessing, used his ship's wireless to send a strong protest to the State Department, via Veracruz. Later Miller wrote: "I would have done anything possible to have prevented their going out (that is, anything honorable) ." [22] Anything honorable evidently included passive resistance, for Miller professed himself unable to procure a Mexican pilot to take Mayo's vessels across Tampico Bar.

Miller's message to the State Department did not even receive a reply. In Washington, affairs at Tampico were no longer of interest. Concern was focused on the *Ypiranga,* and growing greater by the minute. There was always the possibility that the *Ypiranga* might elude Fletcher; and assuming he did intercept her, there was no guarantee that he could persuade her captain not to land his cargo. While the munitions remained aboard the *Ypiranga,* forcible action could not be taken without the risk of provoking an incident with Germany. The only alternative was to seize them as they entered the Mexican customs. That the administration found this option far more attractive was reflected by Daniels' next dispatch, which reached Veracruz at 3:04 A.M.: "Be prepared on short notice to seize Custom House Veracruz landing force sufficient for security of same and to preserve order in the city. If offer resistance use all force necessary to seize and hold city and vicinity. Interfere with municipal government as little as possible." [23] This was followed by a third transmission, logged in on the *Florida* at 4:00 A.M., exhorting Fletcher to "Use all possible precautions to prevent landing of arms and ammunition by the *Ypiranga.* If you cannot persuade ship not to land stores, endeavor to secure delay until Congress acts. Congress will act Tuesday morning." [24]

Matters rested there when, shortly past 2:00 A.M. Washington time, the State Department received an electrifying message from Consul Canada. Canada had continued to investigate the *Ypiranga* situation. Now he had learned that she was due to arrive around 10:30 that morning, and that three trains were waiting on the waterfront siding to rush her cargo into the interior.[25] There would be no time to wait for Congress. The State Department notified Bryan. He telephoned Daniels, and at 2:30 A.M., they rang the White House for Joseph Tumulty, the President's buoyant young secretary.

Tumulty was in bed, but the White House operator put through the call. Bryan told Tumulty when the *Ypiranga* was expected to reach port. "He thought the President should be notified," Tumulty remembered, "and, in his opinion, drastic measures should at once be taken to prevent the delivery of these munitions. . . ." While Tumulty was questioning Bryan, Daniels came on the line and confirmed all Bryan had said. In the end they decided that the situation was serious enough to warrant waking the President. The operator arranged a four-way connection, and soon Wilson was heard, in a voice indicating that he had been aroused from sleep.

"Mr. President," Bryan began, "I am sorry to inform you that I have just received a dispatch . . ." and proceeded to read Canada's cablegram. Bryan recommended that the Navy seize the arms as they were landed. "I want your judgment on how we shall handle the situation," he concluded.

"Of course, Mr. Bryan," Wilson replied, "you understand what drastic action in this matter might ultimately mean in our relations with Mexico?"

"I thoroughly appreciate this, Mr. President," Bryan assured him, "and fully considered it before telephoning you."

For a moment, Wilson was silent. Then he said, "What do you think, Daniels?"

"The munitions should not be permitted to fall into Huerta's hands," Daniels declared. "I can wire Admiral Fletcher to prevent it and take the Custom House. I think that should be done."

Bryan spoke up to emphasize the danger of allowing the munitions to reach Huerta. "The thing that determined the . . . recommendation of both Secretaries," wrote Daniels, "was the feeling that if the ammunition was landed it would strengthen the usurping president and increase the loss of life in Mexico, and that the guns might later be turned upon American youths."

When Bryan had finished, Wilson conceded, "There is no alternative but to land." Then, without a moment's hesitation, it seemed to Tumulty, the President said "Daniels, send this message. . . . 'Take Veracruz at once.' " [26]

Bryan and Daniels hung up. Tumulty sat holding the receiver, struck by the terrible irony of the decision. Here were three men, he reflected, pacifists at heart, men who had been criticized and lampooned throughout the whole country as being too proud to fight, now agreeing on a course of action that might result in bringing two nations to war. Suddenly the President said, "Tumulty, are you there? What do you think of my message?" Ever faithful, Wilson's

Secretary asserted that, under the circumstances, "there was nothing else you could do." [27]

"It's too bad, isn't it," Wilson sighed; "but we could not allow that cargo to land. The Mexicans intend using those guns on our own boys. It is hard to take action of this kind. I have tried to keep out of this Mexican mess, but we are now on the brink of war and there is no alternative." [28]

Daniels' radiogram reached Fletcher at 8:00 A.M., April 21:

Seize Custom House. Do not permit war supplies to reach Huerta or any other party.[29]

✶✶

SIX: GIVE 'EM HELL, YANKS

The orders for action came with unexpected suddenness and at a time when the Naval Forces off Veracruz had been reduced by the exigencies of the service much below its usual strength.

Rear Admiral Charles J. Badger [1]

F letcher was in conference aboard the *Florida* when the order from Daniels arrived. Fletcher's chief of staff, Captain Henry McL. Huse, the *Florida*'s Captain William R. Rush, Lieutenant Colonel Neville, and Commander Herman O. Stickney of the *Prairie* had been called to the admiral's cabin to review the plans for a landing.[2]

Captain Rush had been appointed to command the Naval Brigade. Rush was a thrusting, thick-set man of the "damn-the-torpedoes" school. A turret division commander aboard the battleship *Brooklyn* in 1898, he had been cited by Commodore Schley for distinguished conduct in the battle of Santiago. Rush's officers thought him "a good skipper . . . strict but . . . fair," if "erratic at times,"[3] but his men's view was less favorable. In his relations with them, Rush seemed guided by a determination to justify his nickname of Wild Bill. "The word 'martinet' . . . does not adequately describe [Captain Rush]," a bluejacket wrote, "but it will have to serve. *Florida*'s crew, officers and men alike, had one special uniform which they set aside solely for Saturday Captain's Inspection. It was never worn on any other occasion and was carefully laundered after each inspection. We could wear them only for inspections, as, otherwise, we might get a spot of paint on them and have to get another made up to specifications suitable to Captain Rush. The sleeves had to hit the wrists at exactly the right spot, and other measurements were exactly as Captain Rush said they should be."[4] Captain Rush was also very serious about good grooming. One of his customs was to lay his open hand on the top of a man's bare head; if the hair stuck up above his fingers, the man was given extra duty for an unmilitary haircut. And the outraged bluejacket who dared give Rush a hard look was likely to be put on report for "contumacious conduct." "Then," as a sympathetic officer said, "the poor bastard spent three days in the brig trying to figure out what 'contumacious conduct' was."

51

Superficially, the task before Rush appeared to be an easy one: seizing the Customs House ought not to prove difficult. Diplomatic sources indicated that the landing would be unopposed, and in the unlikely event that the Mexicans did offer resistance, the guns of Fletcher's squadron could obliterate any position they sought to defend. The sister ships *Florida* and *Utah* were among the most powerful vessels in the United States Navy. Commissioned in 1911, they had been America's mightiest entries in the dreadnought race then under way between the world's great navies. Each carried ten 12-inch guns, mounted in five center-line turrets so that all could be brought to bear for a single broadside, in which eight 5-inch deck guns could join.[5]

In reality, the situation was not that simple. Fletcher's mission was actually fourfold: to occupy the Customs House; to prevent the *Ypiranga* from delivering her cargo; to provide every possible assistance to distressed Americans; and, through it all, to treat the Mexican population with utmost consideration. No two of these purposes were wholly compatible. Attempting to combine all four was like trying to make an omelette without breaking any eggs.

Fletcher distrusted the administration's confidence that the Mexicans would accept the docile role in which they had been cast. On April 20, he had learned that convicts from the prison-fortress of San Juan de Ulúa were being freed and armed to augment the garrison of Veracruz.[6] That the Mexican authorities denied this fact made it appear even more ominous. Moreover, should the Mexicans choose to defend Veracruz, Fletcher felt that respect for humanity constrained him not to turn his big guns on the city. Throughout the landing he would concern himself as much with averting and, once they had commenced, arresting hostilities as with carrying them to a military conclusion. Fletcher's philosophy was reflected by one of his bluejackets, Boatswain's Mate Henry N. Nickerson. "I remember," wrote Nickerson, "an English naval officer made the remark that he admired the way we went into the city; that they would have shelled the city . . . before they landed. I could not agree to that, as there would have been women and children killed. I would rather risk my own neck than fight that way."[7]

The plans for the landing had been made on April 13, the date on which the Naval Brigade was organized. There were two regiments. The First Marine Regiment, under Lieutenant Colonel Neville, was composed of the battalion aboard the *Prairie* and the Fleet Marines from the two battleships, a total of 22 officers and 578 men. The First Seaman Regiment, commanded by the *Florida*'s Lieutenant Commander Allen Buchanan, consisted of the *Florida* and *Utah* bluejacket battalions, 30 officers and 570 men altogether. The landing parties would disembark in whaleboats to be towed ashore by motor launches. All craft would make for Pier Four.[8]

Immediately upon receipt of Daniels' order, Fletcher directed Mayo to send him the scout cruiser *Chester* from Tampico, which he intended to employ inside the breakwater; [9] he did not, however, give the order to land. For two excellent reasons, Fletcher wished to postpone that moment as long as possible. He did not want to commit his forces until the *Ypiranga* had arrived at Veracruz. Were the *Ypiranga* to learn of the landing while still at sea, she might change course and make a dash for Puerto Mexico,* 125 miles to the south, which also had a railhead. Furthermore, he would have preferred to wait until Badger's squadron was nearer Veracruz. From his own ships, Fletcher could put approximately 1,200 men ashore. The Military Commandant of Veracruz, General Gustavo Maass, could field around 600 regulars.[10] They would have the advantage of fighting in familiar surroundings, and should they be supported by the populace and police, the landing party might find itself hard pressed.

There was another factor, though, to which all other considerations must be made subordinate—the weather. April 21 had dawned windy and grey. There were whitecaps in the outer harbor, and the battleships rolled in heavy swells. From all indications, there was a storm brewing. No vessel could navigate the narrow passage through the breakwater into the inner harbor in a storm, and a good blow might last for days. The bluejacket battalions would be unable to leave the battleships, and the Marine battalion was too small to go ashore alone. If a storm was on the way, the landing would have to be made before it broke.

As minutes passed, the weather continued to deteriorate. Around 9:00 A.M., Fletcher noted the breeze suddenly shift to the north, "increasing in force," he wrote, "with all the appearance of an approaching 'norther.' . . . It was decided to land." [11]

Once he had concluded that the landing could not be delayed, Fletcher lost no time in setting it in motion. Neville was ordered to prepare the Marines to disembark, and a radiogram was sent directing the *Utah* to return to the outer harbor. Captain Huse went ashore to inform Consul Canada, and other officers were detailed to

---

* Present-day Coatzacoalcos.

notify the commandant of San Juan de Ulúa, Admiral Cradock, and the captain of the *Carlos V.*[12]

So far as the landing was concerned, there was nothing further for Fletcher to do; the stage was set. But one important matter remained unresolved: the withdrawal from Tampico. Fletcher had not yet replied to Mayo's anguished message of 7:55 A.M. His answer depended upon an analysis of a situation which had become extremely complex. In Fletcher's simplified summary:

> Tampico was in a state of excitement and resentment against Americans.
>
> Mayo was under orders to withdraw all ships except the *Des Moines* and proceed to Veracruz.
>
> The Atlantic Fleet was 250 miles at sea en route to Veracruz.
>
> The *Florida* was in the outer harbor and the *Prairie* alone in the inner harbor.
>
> There were approximately six hundred regulars plus several hundred prisoners released from San Juan de Ulúa available for the defense of Veracruz.[13]

Fletcher could have used Mayo's bluejackets to advantage to increase the strength of his landing party; the ships at Tampico could reach Veracruz sooner than the Atlantic Fleet. But Fletcher was convinced that Mayo's departure would result in an uprising against the Americans in Tampico, and, in the outcome, that consideration was decisive. He assumed the responsibility of modifying Daniels' directive; most of Mayo's ships should remain at Tampico. At 9:55 A.M., Fletcher advised Mayo: "Your orders to leave were verified. I approve of your recommendation and you can retain *Connecticut, Dolphin, Des Moines, Cyclops, Solace* to look out for Americans and other foreigners' lives until other provision is made. I have been ordered to seize Custom House Veracruz." [14]

In the meantime, the officers detailed to give notice of the landing had begun to reach their destinations. Captain Huse entered the American Consulate at 9:30 A.M. and told Canada that the first troops would come ashore around 11:00. Canada was requested to advise the other consuls of the action and urge all foreign nationals to report to Pier Four to be taken aboard the *Mexico*. Huse also asked Canada to play a supporting role in the landing itself. The Consulate, a boxlike, two-story building on the corner of Calles Montesinos and Morelos, commanded a clear view of the waterfront. When Canada saw the *Prairie*'s boats shove off, he was to inform General Maass that "overwhelming" American forces were about to "take charge" of the Customs House; that Fletcher hoped

Maass "would remain and lend all assistance in his power to keep order in the city, and that he trusted no resistance would be offered." Canada was authorized to promise Maass that the landing party would be restricted to the waterfront, to avert the danger of a collision with his troops. Similar messages were to be given the collector of customs and the chief of police.[15]

The commander of the Spanish cruiser *Carlos V* learned of the impending action from Ensign Edward O. McDonnell. Upon hearing McDonnell's report, he asked whether General Maass was aware of the program. McDonnell replied, quite truthfully, that he did not know. The Spanish captain then inquired if he might go ashore. McDonnell was hardly empowered to answer such questions, and merely repeated his original announcement. There was little to be said after that, and McDonnell took his leave. Casting off from the *Carlos V*, he proceeded to HMS *Essex*, the flagship of Admiral Cradock.[16]

Rear Admiral Sir Christopher G. F. M. Cradock, K.C.V.O., C.B., was a superb representative of the Royal Navy officers of his day. He had fought in shore battles in the Soudan and China, served aboard the Royal Yacht, and been Naval A.D.C. to King Edward VII. Paying official calls, he disdained to use a motor launch, sailing his own gig instead.[17] Bachelorhood had left him the leisure to pursue a literary bent, and he had written several pleasant, unassuming books on naval life and sport.[18] A singularly handsome, spade-bearded man, "shining with that special, well-groomed English look," [19] his appearance was as distinguished as his career. Off Mexico he had renewed acquaintances with American officers he had met in China during the Boxer Rebellion. They found him a charming host, "very much the English gentleman." [20] Edith O'Shaughnessy was taken by the appointments of "his delightful room." Herself a fancier of *objets d'art*, she was quick to note "old silver from Malta, a beautiful twelfth-century wood carving (suitable for a museum) from Greece, fine enamels from Peking, and many other lovely things. . . . He is really a connoisseur, but he said that the ladies, God bless them, had robbed him of most of his possessions." [21]

Entering Veracruz on April 19, Cradock had requested and received Fletcher's assurance that he would be granted advance information of any operations which might lead to the outbreak of hostilities.[22] The news that American troops would be going ashore in less than two hours came as a jolt, and the fact that his ships were anchored squarely in the line of fire between San Juan de Ulúa

La Invasion Yanqui, Palomares

General Gustavo Maass, Military Commandant of
Veracruz

and the American squadron did nothing to relieve his pique. He told McDonnell that "Admiral Fletcher had promised them plenty of notice, and he got none, but that he would stay where he was and take his chances." He supposed that Fletcher would want him to get out of the harbor, but it would take time for his ships to build up steam. As McDonnell departed, Cradock asked him to tell Admiral Fletcher that he desired to call.[23] At 9:30 A.M., Cradock boarded the *Florida* to inquire if Fletcher had any objection to the dispatch of HMS *Berwick* to Puerto Mexico. "I told him," wrote Fletcher, somewhat abashed, "that there was no objection whatever." [24]

Ensign E. P. Nickinson, of the *Prairie,* landed at San Juan de Ulúa. Its commandant, Commodore Alejandro Cerisola,* was cautioned that "any aggressive move on his part would be immediately followed by our opening fire with heavy guns on the fort." [25] The fortress itself was scarcely a threat—its garrison consisted of 160 men and its ordnance belonged in museums; but there was the disturbing possibility that it might fire torpedoes into the inner harbor. Visiting the fortress several days earlier, Commander Stickney had observed a torpedo tube and a shed containing five torpedoes. Nickinson called special attention to the inadvisability of any movement indicating the use of torpedo tubes. When Cerisola asked if he were really delivering a declaration of war, Nickinson answered that this was not the case at all; the Marines were to land for the purpose of maintaining law and order only. Cerisola replied that he understood the message, and would not fire unless fired upon.[26]

The *Utah,* returned from her search for the *Ypiranga,* dropped anchor in the outer harbor at 9:40 A.M. Minutes later, Commander Cone boarded the *Florida* to report his battalion ready and waiting for any service. Fletcher told him that the Marine company aboard the *Utah* was to go ashore with the landing force. Pending further orders, Cone should be prepared either to disembark his bluejackets or make full speed for Puerto Mexico. It was still possible that the *Ypiranga* would run for that port.[27]

Matters were now fast approaching a head. At 10:15 A.M., Mexican customs officials ordered the *Mexico* to pull away from Pier Four; she was occupying the berth in which the *Ypiranga* was scheduled to dock. Fifteen minutes later, as the *Esperanza* was tying up to the Sanitary Wharf to receive late-coming refugees, Neville signaled: "Am ready." [28] "Upon receipt of this message," wrote Fletcher, "I directed Captain Rush to land his brigade and carry out

---

* Actually, there was a dual command on de Ulúa. Cerisola was in charge of the naval facilities; the garrison was under a Colonel Vigil.

orders." [29] Rush in turn signaled the *Prairie*, "Land and take Pier Four. Be prepared to cover landing with necessary gunfire." [30] Beyond the breakwater, the launches towing the *Florida*'s bluejackets and the *Utah*'s Marines began to move towards shore. As they passed Cradock's cruisers, the British sailors lined the rails and cheered, "Give 'em hell, Yanks! Give 'em hell!" [31]

From the roof of the American Consulate, where he had trained his field glasses on the *Prairie*, Canada saw the first boatload of Marines leave the ship. Making a mental note of the time, he hurried downstairs to telephone General Maass. It was precisely 11:12 A.M.[32]

Maass was astounded, though it seems strange that the news should have taken him completely by surprise. "No!" he exclaimed. "It cannot be!" Canada assured him that, indeed, it was. Maass requested a conference with Admiral Fletcher; his orders, he protested, had not been designed to cover such exigencies. Canada replied that this was not practical; the landing was already under way. Maass hung up without declaring his intentions.[33]

Next Canada rang Señor Azcarraga, the collector of customs, and Antonio Villavenecio, the chief of police. Azcarraga was not much help. "He became greatly excited," Canada wrote, "and in spite of assurances that he could keep on with his regular duties and would not be molested, he begged for time to warn his subordinate and lock up his office in order that he might reach his family without delay." [34] Villavenecio took the news with more aplomb, promising that he would assist the American forces in keeping order in the city. "This, however," Canada commented, "he failed to do." [35]

From the information at his disposal, Canada concluded that Maass would withdraw without disputing the occupation. At 10:30, the terminal superintendent, an American, had advised Canada that he thought Maass intended to seize the morning passenger train from Mexico City, the implication being that Maass planned to use it to evacuate the garrison.[36] Shortly before the *Prairie*'s boats put off, Canada had sent one of his Marine orderlies to the roof of the Consulate to signal the *Florida:* "We think they are evacuating. The terminal superintendent states that there is an order out for a train of six hundred soldiers to stop at the roundhouse, probably to take on more. . . . The train is now waiting for the morning train to arrive. . . . The superintendent's idea is that they will take the passenger train out also. . . ." [37]

Canada's suppositions were all very reasonable, and all very wrong. After their conversation, Maass had sent an aide to the radio station in the suburb of los Cocos to request instructions from Mexico City. Then he hurried to the Military Barracks, a group of buildings occupying an area of almost two square blocks on the Plaza Zamora, where the two regular infantry battalions at Veracruz were billeted.[38]

In some respects, Maass was a comic figure. A suavely handsome, long-headed man with Imperial mustaches and a failing for plumed helmets, he bore a resemblance, probably cultivated, to Kaiser Wilhelm II. It was hardly what one expected of a *Huertista* general. Months earlier, one look had convinced Edith O'Shaughnessy that he would not prove efficient. "A blue-eyed Mexican who wears his sandy grey hair in a German brush effect *can't* be!" [39] she exclaimed. But like Consul Canada, she had misjudged her man. That opera-bouffe air was deceiving.

The assumptions from which Maass proceeded are evident from his actions. He doubted, but did not discard, the possibility that he might be ordered to make a determined stand in the city. Far more likely, his instructions would be to put up enough resistance to uphold the national honor while extricating the principal portion of his command.

In the quarters of the 19th Battalion, Maass encountered Lieutenant Colonel Albino Rodríguez Cerrillo. After a quick briefing, Cerrillo was directed to take a scratch force, around one hundred men, down Avenida Independencia to "repel the invasion." At the headquarters, Maass found General Francisco Figueroa, the battalion commander. He told Figueroa to deploy his remaining troops in position to defend the Barracks pending further orders.[40]

Entering the 18th Battalion area, Maass instructed its commanding officer, General Luis B. Becerril, to release the *rayados* * of la Galera, the military prison adjacent to the Barracks. At the same time, he was to distribute the contents of his armory to the people of Veracruz.[41]

Arming civilians was not as desperate a measure as it would appear. In August, 1913, a group of citizens had come to the Commandancia Militar and asked to be taught to handle arms and execute simple military movements. Their request had been approved by the Ministry of War, and a weekend training program was initiated. By January, 1914, over three hundred men had completed the course of instruction and five hundred more were en-

---

* Literally, "stripers," a slang term referring to the blue-and-white striped prison uniform.

rolled. Together they had formed the "Society of Defenders of the Port of Veracruz," a militia-type organization whose members pledged to take arms against any foreign power attempting to land at Veracruz.[42]

The officer who had conducted the training, Lieutenant Colonel Manuel Contreras, was now in charge at the armory. He had 450 rifles, Mausers and Winchesters of identical calibers, and 2,000 rounds of ammunition requisitioned for target practice to be held the following Sunday. Many of Contreras' civilians had already appeared to claim weapons, but there were still numbers of rifles left on the racks. Contreras had received orders to free the 50 men and 3 women who were political prisoners at la Galera. Under the circumstances, he decided to free all the inmates of la Galera and issue the remaining arms to them. Assembling the *rayados,* he made a brief address. Announcing that the *Yanquis* had invaded Vera-cruz, Contreras reminded the convicts of "the obligation of all good Mexicans to die for the land where they saw light for the first time." Those who were not in position to defend the homeland should leave the arms "to someone who had guts." The *rayados* proclaimed their determination to resist the enemy, and Contreras let them at the rifles. Outside, they joined the group of volunteers who had stood by in Calle Ocampo. When the arms room was empty, Con-treras led the crowd into Avenida Cinco de Mayo, paralleling Cerrillo's route towards Pier Four.[43]

A few minutes later, Maass received the reply to his message to Mexico City. The Minister of War, General Aureliano Blanquet, ordered him to withdraw to Tejería, a village on the National Railroad ten miles inland from Veracruz. That was generally what Maass had expected, but by then it was not altogether possible. Maass could evacuate the troops at the Military Barracks, but the hedge he had made on defending the city could not be reclaimed. Cerrillo's men had disappeared down Independencia, and the impa-tient mob Contreras had raised was moving towards the waterfront. Events had acquired a momentum of their own.[44]

SEVEN: A CALMNESS PREVAILED

The tropical somnolence here was scarcely disturbed by the situa-
tion between Mexico and the United States. . . . The tables in the
outdoor dining and drinking places about the central plaza of
the city were filled as usual with people who laughed and chat-
ted. . . . Mexicans in many cases fraternized with Americans, and
in a saloon down near the cable office a dozen American sailors who
had strayed . . . from the swimming beach sang popular American
songs for hours while a good-natured policeman on the corner
twirled his club and smiled.

Dispatch from Veracruz to the Washington Post, April 21, 1914

April 21 had begun like any other day in Veracruz. Despite the
international situation, there was no intimation of trouble in
the city. In the shaded *portales* along Avenida Independencia, men
gossiped over coffee cups and reread their morning papers. Whining
beggars patrolled the streets and servant girls passed on the way to
the market. The sight of long strings of whaleboats converging on
Pier Four aroused interest but not apprehension, and a curious
crowd gathered along the granite-coped seawall to watch. Workers
returning home for the midday meal paused to augment the number of idlers. Robert H. Murray of the *Washington Post* stood on
the Fiscal Wharf while the *Prairie's* Marines "tumbled smartly
down the gangway to their places in the boats," and counted
"launches, half a dozen of them, . . . wallowing shoreward from the
Florida." [1]

The landing party numbered 787 officers and men, of whom 502
were Marines.[2] "Except on the bronze of their monuments," Richard
Harding Davis wrote, "the Mexicans had never seen men so
imposing." [3] Khaki fatigues, broad-brimmed campaign hats, and
huge, Civil War-style knapsack rolls made the Marines unmistak-
able, but aside from their white uniforms the seamen could scarcely
be recognized as such. Their V-necked blouses were crisscrossed with
the straps of towering haversacks and their bell-bottom trousers
were gathered in canvas leggings. Around their waists they wore

61

cumbrous cartridge belts and, like the Marines, they shouldered long-barreled, bolt-action Springfield '03's. Their officers were similarly dressed, with choke-collar tunics and sidearms.

The landing was accomplished without incident. "In a moment," a witness recorded, "the Marines and bluejackets were clambering up the stone steps and concrete pavement along the immense stretch of asphalt opposite the Customs House." [4] The handful of American civilians present quickly realized what was happening, and cheered as each boatload came ashore.[5] They had hoped for intervention. One enthusiastic lady was waving a tiny American flag. For their part, the *Veracruzanos* perceived that so many men with guns could mean only one thing, and the crowd began to disperse. When one *peon* ran for cover, having had the temerity to shout "Viva Mexico!" the American onlookers laughed.[6] As word spread, iron grilles rang down over store fronts across the city and children were called off the streets.

Outside the American Consulate, the *New York Times* correspondent met Commodore Manuel Azueta, the Commandant of the Mexican Naval Academy, whom he mistook for a general. Azueta had been trying to see Consul Canada. Falling in step with the commodore, the reporter asked the key question: would the landing be opposed? Azueta replied, in so many words, that he did not know whether resistance would be offered to the Americans or not. He added that he could not find General Maass.[7]

At that moment, the troops Maass had held at the Military Barracks were in the act of withdrawing from the city. Upon receiving the order to evacuate, Maass had instructed his railway officer, Major Diego E. Zayas, to run all the locomotives at the Terminal Station out to the roundhouse, coupled with cars enough to accommodate the garrison and its 3-inch battery. The troops took train there. They left the barracks in such haste that afterwards ammunition cases containing over five thousand rounds were found placed along the firing-step behind the parapet.[8]

By 11:40 A.M., when the landing parties began to move towards their objectives, an ominous silence had fallen over Veracruz.

Veracruz retained the appearance of a Spanish colonial city. Most of the buildings were two or three stories high, of brick or adobe, with flat, parapet roofs. Above them at intervals rose the jagged, green fronds of the coconut palms that grew in the public plazas and the patios of the homes. Wooden balconies, with delicate, wrought-iron railings, connected the houses along each block.

Usually the buildings were painted blotchy pastels; they reminded one American of the scenery in "a tawdry theatre . . . , pale greens, greys, corals, cartwheel blues, and leprous whites . . . , turned gorgeous by the calcium blaze of tropic sun." [9] Seen from the sea, it was beautiful. The snowy summit of Orizaba, at 18,700 feet the highest in Mexico, provides a majestic backdrop; and at a distance, even as experienced a voyager as Smedley Butler was enchanted by a panorama of "indigo water, sand hills, white walls and coconut palms, [and] mountain peaks piercing the clouds." [10] To keep that impression, however, it was necessary to keep at a distance. At close quarters, Veracruz was filthy, foul-smelling, and incredibly ill-kept.

A city of forty thousand souls in 1914, Veracruz made no pretense towards a program of public sanitation. On one occasion, a Red Cross worker made a routine inspection of the city's eating places. In the kitchen of a restaurant favored by foreign residents, he discovered hens roosting over the stoves. With unsuspected candor, the menu featured: "Chicken cooked in its own moist." [11] Garbage was thrown into the streets, and in the poorer sections the carcasses of dead animals rotted where they fell. No one could recall the last time the municipal dump had been burned clean. In the summer, when the temperature often exceeded 100° F. and the humidity became almost absolute, dysentery, malaria, and other insect-borne diseases were rampant. Waste disposal was left entirely to the *zopilotes,* the great, black vultures by which Veracruz was overrun. Protected by a municipal ordinance imposing a fine of five pesos on anyone doing a *zopilote* harm, they flocked along the seawall, perched on the cupolas of the Municipal Palace, and vied with packs of mongrel dogs at the refuse heaps which littered the city. [12]

Like all Spanish cities, Veracruz had been built around a central square, then called the Plaza Constitución or, less frequently, the Plaza de Armas. It lay not far from the waterfront, in the heart of the commercial district. In its center, surrounded by stone benches and a scattering of scrubs, was a low bandstand where, in the cool of early evening, concerts would be given while the *Veracruzanos* made their nightly promenade. [13] Around the plaza stood the Municipal Palace, the Parochial Church, and the Old and New Hotel Diligencias, where the foreigners stayed. The Municipal Palace was an imposing stone structure in whose domed tower and graceful arcade the Moorish influence was marked. As Veracruz was the administrative center of the state of that name, it housed many offices of the state government as well. In its rear and a story lower was the city jail. Diagonally opposite the Municipal Palace was the Parochial

Church, dating from the 1700's. Decades of wind and rain had given its grey walls a rich patina of age. In contrast to the white pilasters, they created the effect of a giant piece of Wedgwood.[14]

Encircling the plaza were narrow, cobbled streets fronted by boarding houses, small shops, warehouses, and the ubiquitous *cantinas* which accounted for roughly half the city's retail establishments. North and south, generally parallel to the waterfront, ran a series of avenues—Morelos curving to become Zaragoza, Independencia, Cinco de Mayo, Cortés, Hidalgo, Bravo, and Guerrero—on which the leading stores were located and along which the traffic of the city flowed. To the northwest were the Terminal Station, Terminal Hotel, roundhouse and yard, from which the tracks of the National Railroad extended 263 miles inland to Mexico City; the solid protrusion of Pier Four, with its stone warehouses and railroad siding, also called the Terminal Wharf, where the Ward Line steamers docked; the Cable Office; the Post Office and Telegraph Station, a semi-classical stone building with flaring cupolas at either end; and the municipal power plant, beyond which the coastline fell sharply away to the west. To the south stood the rusting steel skeleton of the New Market, an unfinished project of the Díaz régime; the Naval Academy, a quadrangle of severe, two-storied barracks-type buildings; the new Customs House, a rambling stone and marble structure with pretensions towards the Romanesque; and the massive Military Barracks. Further inland, along the foot of the sand hills that ring the city, was the residential district.

Seaward, in the center of the principal breakwater around the inner harbor, the knuckle of Gallega Reef was crowned with the grim, grey outlines of the Castilo San Juan de Ulúa. Begun by the Spanish in 1518, de Ulúa had proved one of the most dismal failures in the history of military fortification. Impotent against the freebooters by whom Veracruz was repeatedly ravaged, the fortress's great moment had not come until 1823, during the revolt against Spain, when its loyal garrison had used de Ulúa's guns to pulverize the city it had been intended to protect. Díaz had converted the fortress into a federal penitentiary and navy signal station and dry dock, and its claim to military significance had long since been abandoned. Most of its prisoners had committed political offenses, usually an attempt to evade conscription. Hundreds of them were herded in dark, salt-encrusted dungeons into which fresh air and light could enter only through slitted apertures in the walls and patios, at places ten feet thick. At high tide, many of the cells filled waist-deep with water.[15] When Mrs. O'Shaughnessy visited de Ulúa in January, 1914, she was nauseated by a "horrible, indescribable stench" that even the sea breeze could not dispel. Throwing boxes of cigarettes into the blackness—*noblesse oblige*—she was rewarded by "vague, human groans and rumbling noises." Afterwards, she wondered: "If above we could scarcely stand the stench . . . what must it have been like in the depths below?" [16] But like the rest of Veracruz, the fortress was attractive as long as one did not get too near, and when the United States decided to issue a medal to the men who had served in Mexico, a silhouette of San Juan de Ulúa was chosen to appear on its face.

The plans for the landing had divided Veracruz into two sectors, northern and southern.[17] Neville's Marines had been assigned the northern sector. Their mission was to occupy the Terminal Station, the railway yard and roundhouse, the Cable Office and the power plant, advancing inland as far as Avenida Guerrero. The leathernecks were in good hands. Seizing a city was hardly a novelty to Lieutenant Colonel "Buck" Neville; he had been in combat, in the Philippines, China, and throughout the Caribbean, intermittently ever since the Spanish-American War. Hard fighting had not impaired his good humor, and he had the reputation for being the most cheerful man in the Corps. "Nobody could be down-hearted when Neville was one of the company," [18] a brother officer said. Neville led his men almost due inland from Pier Four, crossing the littered brown field before the buildings nearest the waterfront.

Just then, on his rooftop perch, Consul Canada saw a carriage careen past the Consulate and clatter into the railway yard. "It contained three Mexican officers and one machine gun," he reported. "The officers leaped to the ground, carrying the machine gun with them . . . towards the entrance to the station facing the American landing force." Concluding that it was the intention of these officers to open fire, Canada rushed a messenger to warn the Marines.[19]

Expecting to be greeted by a burst of fire, the advance guard entered Calle Montesinos. But no shots rang out; the Marines occupied the Terminal Station unopposed. There they made the disappointing discovery that the trains were gone. The rolling stock remaining in Veracruz consisted of a broken-down locomotive, a handful of decrepit passenger cars, and several hundred empty boxcars on the siding at Pier Four. A search of the station revealed no trace of the Mexican officers Canada had reported, but scattered beside the tracks the Marines found the parts of a machine gun.

Captain Roy Dudley, USN (Ret.)

A group of officers aboard the USS *Florida*. From left, unidentified; Lieutenant (jg) Francis Cogswell, aide to Captain Rush; unidentified; Ensign Mark L. Hersey, aide to Admiral Fletcher; Lieutenant Frank Jack Fletcher, in command of the refugee ship *Esperanza;* extreme right, Ensign George M. Lowry, the *Florida*'s First Company commander

The officers had dismantled it before commandeering an engine to carry them out of the city.[20]

While Neville's main body fanned out to block the western approaches to the Terminal Yard, Captain Harllee's *Florida* Marines turned north towards the power plant and Corporal Curtis' squad was sent to seize the Cable Office.[21] Corporal Curtis, a knowledgeable type, double-timed his men up to the American Consulate to ask directions. The building was just around the corner, and at 11:45 A.M. he forced his way through a throng of excited newsmen to announce, "I take possession of this office and cable in the name of the United States." The Mexican superintendent arose from his desk. "It is useless to resist, Señor," he observed, bowing and forcing a smile; "I obey." [22] Atop the Consulate, a Marine signalman wigwagged the *Florida:* "Cable station O.K." [23]

The *Florida*'s three rifle companies, commanded by Lieutenant Richard Wainwright, Jr., moved southeast from Pier Four. Their objectives had been set by Captain Rush at a conference in his cabin on the evening of April 19.[24] The responsibility for seizing the Customs House—the focal point of the landing—was assigned to the First Company, under Ensign George M. Lowry. Blue-eyed and boyishly slender, with aquiline good looks, Lowry had filled one post of honor already in his brief career. A year earlier, he had commanded Commodore Perry's War of 1812 flagship in the centennial celebration of the battle of the Great Lakes; but the nature of his duties on that occasion had nothing in common with those he was about to undertake.

The Second Company was led by Ensign Theodore S. Wilkinson, a trim young man whose ardor for ping-pong had caused his Annapolis classmates to nickname him Ping. His men were to occupy the Post Office and Telegraph. The Third Company, with Lieutenant (junior grade) Leland S. Jordan, Jr., in command, was to remain in reserve near Pier Four. Ensign James McD. Cresap, the Brigade Ordnance Officer, had orders to set up the *Florida* "battalion artillery"—an impressive title for a single, hand-drawn, 3-inch gun—in an open area, so-called the Terminal Plaza, in front of the American Consulate.[25]

Captain Rush had come ashore with the *Florida* battalion. He made his headquarters in the Hotel Terminal, a tortuously-ornamented, two-story, granite building facing Pier Four. The Signals Officer, Ensign Edward O. McDonnell, was ordered to take a semaphore section to the hotel roof and establish communication with Admiral Fletcher on the *Florida*. McDonnell's men sent their first message at 11:50 A.M. The Second Company reached its destination around the same time, and at 11:55, McDonnell signaled: "Telegraph and post office occupied and doing business as ever." [26]

Ensign Lowry's company was now approaching the intersection of Morelos and Emparán. The Customs House stood in the next block. Skeptical of the assurances that the Mexicans would not resist, Lowry was on the lookout for trouble. "As the streets of Veracruz are narrow," he wrote, "the Company marched slowly in two single columns under cover of the houses and shops on each side of Morelos. . . . Houses and shops were shuttered and tightly closed. The city was quiet—a calmness prevailed." [27]

EIGHT: A NUMBER OF MEXICANS SHOOTING

It's a funny feeling, being shot at by snipers. It isn't like lying in a trench and fighting an organized force, but anybody that can lay hold of a gun, takes up a convenient place in a sheltered window or on the roof, and takes a pot shot at you.

Seaman J. R. Copeland, of the *Utah* [1]

The advance of the American columns had been observed by countless unseen eyes. The forces sent by Maass to "repel the invasion" had dispersed throughout the district bounded by Calle Montesinos, Avenida Bravo, and Calle Esteban Morales. Their deployment was virtually spontaneous. Stray civilians and *rayados* took positions of their own selection. Many climbed to rooftops or found posts at upper-story windows; others congregated in the *portales* along Avenida Independencia.[2] The regulars showed scarcely more regard for tactics. "In the side streets opening into . . . Independencia," Consul Canada could see blue-coated "squads of Federal soldiers . . . lying flat on their breasts or moving excitedly to and fro as the orders were countermanded."[3] One unit occupied the Hotel Diligencias and the Municipal Palace, covering the Plaza Constitución, but neglected to barricade the approaches to the square. Another detachment displayed more energy but no better judgment by manhandling a one-pounder to the top of the old Benito Juárez Lighthouse. The only professional touch in the operation was provided by the machine gunners who placed their pieces to sweep some of the larger streets.[4] Lieutenant Colonels Cerrillo and Contreras met briefly in the Plaza Constitución. After a moment's discussion, they decided to station the main body of volunteers around the Parochial Church.[5] This conversation comprised the sum of the arrangements for concerted action made among the city's defenders. Otherwise, every little band of riflemen, each individual sniper, was left on his own initiative.

The mystery is that firing did not break out sooner; snipers were afterwards active in blocks American troops had passed before the shooting started. It seemed as though everyone were waiting for everyone else. Then, as the *Florida*'s First Company began to cross Calle Emparán, a single shot rang out. It was fired by Aurelio

Mexican firing line in the Plaza Constitución. The picture was taken moments before the fighting began.

Corner of Morelos and Miguel Lerdo, where the first shot was fired. The barricades at right were rolled forward by bluejackets advancing from the Customs Warehouse; Boatswain's Mate Nickerson was wounded here.

Monffort, a municipal gendarme on duty on the corner of Morelos and Miguel Lerdo.[6] The echo was lost in the crackling report of the fusillade that followed.

The firing in the Customs Zone was a stimulus to the Mexican forces throughout Veracruz. Bullets began to rain down on Pier Four and splatter against the sides of the *Esperanza*.[7] The Marines marching up Montesinos were "fired into from all directions"[8] as they came abreast of Avenida Bravo, and the signalmen atop the Hotel Terminal, splendid targets against the sky, began to hear a peculiar whine in the air. Coincidentally, the hotel guests who had been keeping them company remembered pressing reasons to return to their rooms.[9] Hurrying outside to investigate, Captain Rush was shot through the fleshy part of the calf. "He tied an oversized handkerchief around his leg," a bluejacket wrote, "and went on. . . . Several crew members of the *Florida*, upon hearing he had been hit, fervently hoped it would prove fatal." But Rush came back aboard a week later, dishearteningly healthy and "just as hard to get along with as before."[10]

Ensign Lowry's bluejackets had taken cover in doorways and against the sides of buildings on Calle Morelos. After the initial shock, they returned the Mexican fire. Gendarme Monffort fell, riddled with bullets, on the curb outside the Cantina y Miscelanea a La Flor de Lis, the first Mexican killed in the defense of Veracruz. Above his head, tattered, once-bright broadsides advertised the excellence of Superfinos cigarettes.[11]

Though snipers were everywhere, the heaviest firing came from four points: a pink stucco building at the foot of the Juárez Light; a machine gun on the east yard of the Naval Academy; the New Customs Warehouse, a huge iron shed opposite the Customs House; and a machine-gun nest in the Hotel Oriente, at the intersection of Zamora and Landero y Cos.[12] The machine gun outside the Naval Academy had been set up by Lieutenant of Naval Artillery José Azueta, the commodore's son. Though assigned to the Naval Academy staff, Azueta had started a machine-gun school for the garrison of Veracruz. From a corner of the Customs Warehouse wall, Boatswain's Mate Second Class Joseph G. Harner lowered his sights on Lieutenant Azueta's gun. Aiming with deadly precision, Harner began to squeeze off his shots. Two of the first struck Lieutenant Azueta. Ignoring his pain, Azueta ordered his men to stay by the gun. They were still firing when he was hit again. Mortally wounded, Azueta lost consciousness. That was enough for the gunners. Scooping him up in their arms, they retired into the Naval Academy.[13] The snipers in the pink house were silenced seconds later.[14]

Still, a murderous rifle and machine-gun fire from Avenida Landero y Cos raked the block between the bluejackets and their objective. "My job was to capture the Customs House," Ensign Lowry said, "but I did not wish to lose my entire company doing it." [15] Reluctant to order a general advance, he called for volunteers to approach the Customs House from the side. Five men were chosen: Harner, Coxswain J. F. Schumaker—one of "the really decent chaps," Boatswain's Mate Second Class George Cregan, and Seamen Lawrence C. Sinnett and Harry C. Beasley. All were crack shots.[16]

Instructing the other men to give them cover, Lowry led the volunteers into the narrow alley separating the Customs House and Warehouse. There they came under a cross fire from riflemen in the customs buildings and the machine gunners in the Hotel Oriente. Machine-gun slugs shattered the asphalt in front of them, and the sharp, spiteful sound of riccochets sang in their ears. "The firing from the windows and balconies of the Hotel Oriente was heavy," Lowry related, "but the Mexicans were poor shots. Otherwise, we would have been easily picked off." [17] Midway down the alley, Lowry decided they would have to knock out the machine-gun nest before going any further. Crouching beside the Customs House wall, he directed his men to concentrate their fire on the Oriente. At first, the duel went in the Mexicans' favor. A bullet clipped one of the buttons off Lowry's cap and another tore through his right legging, creasing the flesh.[18] Beasley was slightly wounded, and Schumaker was shot through the head. Cregan pressed his handkerchief against Schumaker's wound with his left hand, continuing to fire his rifle with his right. Then the bluejackets' marksmanship began to tell. The white-clad body of a Mexican policeman came hurtling out a second-story window, and the gun ceased to fire.[19]

Lowry stepped a few paces to the rear to call an aid man for Schumaker. A Mexican soldier had hidden behind a row of crates in the Customs Warehouse. While Lowry was looking the other way, the soldier stood up and took aim at him. Intent on his target, the soldier failed to observe that Boatswain's Mate First Class Percy A. Decker had followed the volunteers to the entrance of the alley. Of the three, Decker was the only one who saw both the others. Shouting a warning to Lowry, Decker raised his rifle. The Mexican swung around as Decker fired. The impact of the bo'sun's bullet sent him spinning out of sight.[20]

Hospital Apprentice First Class William Zuiderveld had heard Lowry call for corpsmen. Dashing down the alley, Zuiderveld reached Schumaker's side. He knelt to tie a bandage around Schumaker's head, hoping to staunch the flow of blood, but it was a futile effort. The coxswain's wound was mortal.[21]

The bluejackets continued firing at the Mexicans in the Hotel Oriente until Zuiderveld could carry Schumaker to the rear. When they were gone, Lowry and the other men worked their way up the alley to the south end of the Customs House. The machine gun did not resume fire, but they could hear the patter of rifle bullets striking around them. Several days later, Lowry returned to the scene and counted twelve holes at the point where his party had scaled the Customs House wall. Clambering over the balustrades, the bluejackets broke out a window and dropped into the Customs House. Inside they found the customs personnel throwing down their arms. After the Mexicans had been rounded up, Lowry sent a runner to inform Captain Rush that the First Company had secured its objective.[22]

Upon receiving the first ragged volley, the Marines had retired into the railroad warehouses lining the northern side of Calle Montesinos. While rifle squads answered the sniping from the south, Neville's company commanders set up Colt machine guns to enfilade Avenidas Independencia, Cinco de Mayo, Cortés, and Bravo. A brisk fire from the roof of the Waters-Pierce Oil Company office on Independencia was silenced by guns sited by Captains Dyer and Hughes. After a few minutes, Neville decided to take the offensive. Files of skirmishers darted into the streets intersecting Montesinos, covered by Marine sharpshooters posted on the tops of the Hotel Alimon and the American Consulate. The leathernecks' advance carried them into the area occupied by Lieutenant Colonel Cerrillo's detachment, the largest regular Mexican force. Cerrillo was hit in the arm as he stood in a doorway, directing his men, and made his way to the rear. With his departure, the last semblance of organization disappeared from the defense. Soon the Marines controlled the block from Montesinos to Calle Constitución. There Neville was ordered by Rush "to fall back to original positions."[23]

Cristóbal Martínez Perea was typical of the townsmen who took arms in the opening hours of the fight. Learning of the landing,

Martínez had bundled his wife of four months into a taxi, driven to the Sanitary Wharf, and seen her safely aboard the *Carlos V*. He returned to his home, which stood on the corner of Calle Emparán opposite the Post Office, in time to see the *Florida*'s bluejackets come marching up Calle Morelos. With mounting resentment, he watched one group halt at the Post Office, while the others continued towards the Customs Zone. The firing that followed gave Martínez all the encouragement he needed. He knew nothing of the *Ypiranga*'s arms, nor of the good intentions with which the twisted track of Wilson's Mexican policy was paved. He only knew that there were foreign forces in the streets of his city, but like hundreds of other *Veracruzanos,* he did not feel obliged to make inquiries. Traditionally, Veracruz has the highest homicide rate in Mexico; its inhabitants should not be expected to take the long view.

Using his two rifles, Martínez opened up at the invaders from a second-story window. The Americans were not long in locating his position and a heavy fire began to beat against the walls of his house. When it grew too hot at the window, Martínez withdrew to the roof. Those handy parapets had already attracted many of his neighbors. Martínez joined them in the sniping at the intersection of Morelos and Emparán, where Ensign John Brownell's section of the *Florida*'s Third Company lay behind the curbstone wondering where everyone was. Soon American marksmen appeared on the tops of nearby buildings. The volume of Martínez's fire made him a prominent target. Eventually, as he rose to peer over the parapet, one of the Marines on the roof of the Consulate put a bullet through his brain.[24]

By now, it was evident that the landing party had encountered a numerous nondescript force stiffened by detachments of regular troops. At 12:30 P.M., Rush signaled Fletcher: "One thousand men with machine guns reported in this vicinity; desultory firing; heavy at intervals; hurry *Utah*'s troops." [25] Upon receipt of this message, Admiral Fletcher ordered the *Utah* to land her battalion of 17 officers and 367 men. "Urgent," he added; "you may steam in closer; orders to Puerto Mexico canceled." [26]

The sound of firing in the city had been audible aboard the *Utah* since noon. "We realized that our attempt to seize the Customs House was being met with armed resistance," wrote Ensign Paul F. Foster, the Fourth Company's twenty-four-year-old commander. A sturdy young Midwesterner whose leadership abilities had been recognized by his appointment as Brigade Commander throughout his first-class year at Annapolis, Foster had anticipated the moment that his battalion commander, Lieutenant Guy W. Castle, ordered the company officers to assemble their men. "My company was the first to form on the quarter-deck and report . . . that we were fully equipped and ready to go ashore," he related. "By this time . . . , our sailing launches and whaleboats were at the gangway ladders and our steam launches were tied up at the ship's booms waiting to take their assigned boats in tow. According to schedule, my company was supposed to be the last to embark and thus would have been at the tail end of one of the two towlines, but because my company was ready and the others were not, Lieutenant Castle ordered me to embark my company immediately." [27] The battalion shoved off at 1:12 P.M.[28]

Captain Rush had made his first casualty report half an hour earlier. Fletcher instructed him to evacuate the wounded to the *Prairie* and radioed Admiral Mayo to send the *Solace* to Veracruz. Later in the afternoon, as casualties mounted, the medical officers of HMS *Essex* and the *Carlos V* boarded the *Prairie* to volunteer their services. "Their assistance," wrote Fletcher, "was gratefully accepted." [29] The *Essex* flew her flag at half-mast as small craft bearing the dead and wounded shuttled back and forth from Pier Four.[30]

At the corner of Morelos and Benito Juárez, the main body of Ensign Lowry's company was taking fire from three directions. It was especially hot around the company machine gun—one of the two in the battalion—which had been set up at the intersection without cover of any kind. In spite of their exposed position, the four crewmen stayed with the gun while Gunner's Mate Wertman directed a searching fire across the surrounding roofs. A heavy machine gun is not the ideal weapon for use against snipers, however, and the gunners' efforts did not materially reduce the volume of the enemy's fire. One of the gun crew was wounded; two other bluejackets were hit by soldiers in the Juárez Light, and a fourth by a sniper in the Hotel Mexico. At this point, a runner was dispatched to advise Captain Rush of the detachment's predicament. Rush promptly ordered Ensign Cresap to shell the Juárez Light. Cresap's 3-inch gun fired six rounds, every one of which struck on target. Several sizeable chunks were blown out of the tower, and the fire from the platform ceased. The *Florida* section went forward to join Lowry's volunteers around the Customs House, and Rush moved Cresap's gun to the intersection of Independencia and Montesinos, where it could support the Marines.[31]

Rear Admiral George M. Lowry, USN (Ret.)

Ensign G. M. Lowry led the volunteers who took the Customs House

Mrs. Harriet Castle

Lieutenant Guy W. S. Castle, USS *Utah* battalion commander

U.S. Navy

The *Utah* battalion being towed ashore under small arms fire early on the afternoon of April 21. San Juan de Ulúa appears at the left

Around 12:30 P.M., the *Utah's* lookouts reported a plume of smoke on the horizon: it was the *Ypiranga,* coming into port. She anchored five hundred yards west of the *Utah,* and Lieutenant Lamar R. Leahy was sent to board her. The *Ypiranga's* captain was a German named Bonath. Mincing no words, Leahy informed him that American forces had seized the Customs House to prevent a shipment of arms believed to be aboard the *Ypiranga* from reaching the Mexican government. Bonath volunteered his bills of lading, which proved that the information provided by Consul Canada was essentially correct.[32] The *Ypiranga* carried an immense cargo—1,333 crates, altogether—of arms and ammunition. But Consul Canada had believed that the shipment had originated in Germany, and in that he had been mistaken. The munitions had been purchased in the United States, from the Remington Arms Company, and routed through Hamburg to escape the embargo.[33]

Leahy told Bonath that the *Ypiranga* might enter the inner harbor, but that she would not be permitted to leave Veracruz without landing the arms. Bonath stated that, in view of the situation ashore, he would prefer to wait in the outer harbor. He promised to remain at anchor unless a storm broke, and to keep within gunshot range of the *Utah.* Leahy replied that these arrangements would be perfectly satisfactory, and cautioned him against any impromptu deviations.[34]

In Mexican history, there are no patriots more revered than the Chapultepec cadets of 1847, the *niños heroiques,* who hurled themselves off a cliff rather than surrender when the Americans broke through their lines. The cadets at the Naval Academy knew the story by heart; and upon learning of the "invasion," they had resolved to emulate that luminous example. Around noon, the Director of the School, Frigate Captain Rafael Carreón, assembled all his personnel in the central patio. "Gentlemen, leaders, pupils, and employees," he said, "I remind you of the obligation we all have to defend the homeland when it is in danger. At this moment, we hear the fire of the invaders. I remind you of the debt we have as Mexicans and as soldiers." [35] Commodore Azueta appeared a few moments later. Assuming that Maass intended to put up a fight, Azueta made a few remarks exalting patriotism and military honor and gave the boys their head. Buttressing the walls with mattresses and furniture, they prepared the Academy for defense. Soon they were joined by soldiers who brought several small cannon from the Artillery Barracks across the street. In the intervening hour, they maintained a continuous fire on Pier Four.[36]

Shortly before 1:00 P.M., Rush ordered the *Florida*'s Chief Boat-swain John McCloy, whom he had made beachmaster, to locate the source of this fire. A chief bo'sun since the age of twenty-four, McCloy was an almost legendary figure. "Efficient in every respect," wrote a *Florida* ensign, "he was like a bull; nothing could stop him." [37] McCloy had won the Medal of Honor at Tientsin, China, during the Boxer Rebellion; [38] now, fourteen years older but still "hard as nails," he was about to win another.

As beachmaster, McCloy was in charge of three steam launches —two from the *Florida* and one from the *Utah*—being used to tow men and supplies ashore. Each boat mounted a one-pound gun in its bow. Putting off from Pier Four, McCloy led the launches at full speed south along the waterfront. Passing the Fiscal Wharf he veered inshore, bearing towards the Naval Academy. At a prear-ranged signal, the little flotilla fired a volley into the Academy.

McCloy's salvo stirred up a hornet's nest. One-pounders barked at the boats out of the Academy windows, and snipers in the New Market and aboard the scow *Verano,* anchored off the Fiscal Wharf, peppered them with rifle fire. Three one-pound shot struck McCloy's own launch. One flew through the steering station and another penetrated the superstructure, neither doing much damage, but a third smashed a valve on the steam line. Clouds of vapor hissed out into the engine room, and within moments the launch lay powerless upon the waves. Hurrying below, the engineer managed to make a temporary repair. McCloy boarded the launch from the *Utah* and sent the crippled craft limping back towards Pier Four.

In the meantime, the Mexicans had found the flotilla's range. A solid shot crashed through the open engine-room skylight of McCloy's new boat and another entered her hull. Forward, the gun crew came under a withering fire. The pointer was mortally wounded, the loader was shot through the throat, and McCloy was hit in the thigh.[39]

Despite the casualties, McCloy's maneuver had accomplished its object. The Mexicans had revealed their positions. The *Prairie*'s 3-inch guns were firing over the launches as they returned to Pier Four. A couple of shells scattered the riflemen in the New Market; three others silenced the snipers aboard the *Verano,* and a like number put an end to the fire from the Naval Academy.[40] The projectiles were too light to pierce the Academy's thick, masonry walls, but razor-sharp fragments shot through the windows. Sixteen-year-old Cadet Virgilio Uribe was struck in the forehead and fell dying into the arms of Cadet Melendez. His body was carried to the Hall of Flags and four cadets were detailed to mount an honor guard over the remains. Upstairs, the other boys were ordered to keep away from the windows.[41] The one-pounders in the Naval Academy would not fire again that day, and it was hours before appreciable numbers of snipers ventured to re-enter the New Market.

Back at Pier Four, McCloy refused to be put out of action. After receiving first aid, he returned to duty. Not until the following evening and under direct orders from the brigade surgeon would he allow himself to be evacuated. During his convalescence, McCloy received a letter which, had it been made public, might have improved the *Florida* crew's opinion of their skipper. Captain Rush wrote:

> We have talked of you very often and thought of you very often and we never can forget the cool brave way you led your flotilla into action and successfully did the job you set out to do. The boats bear the scars of the bullets now—the men won't sew up the bullet holes in the cushion covers—though they have to mend their planking.
>
> I am writing now to ask about your planking. How are you getting on—if you keep it up there won't be enough of you left to hang all the medals of honor on that you deserve and win.* [42]

On the roof of the Hotel Terminal, Ensign McDonnell's detachment continued to wigwag messages to the *Florida* amid a hail of fire. After the shooting started, Rush sent a Marine rifle squad to protect the signalmen. The first Marine to reach the roof was Private Daniel Haggerty. He was shot through the stomach as soon as he stepped into the open. Electrician Third Class Edward A. Gisburne darted forward and began to pull him to cover. Gisburne had not been on orders to go ashore. Fletcher's flag radioman, Electrician Second Class John Robert Johnson, was to have had that honor; but he had developed an abcessed toe, and Gisburne had been sent in his stead. Furthermore, it is difficult to imagine what business, as an electrician, Gisburne had atop the Terminal. But there he was, dragging the dying Haggerty out of the line of fire, and a bullet shattered his knee. When Gisburne fell, Seaman Berrie

---

* McCloy's second Medal of Honor, together with most of the others for Veracruz, was awarded by authority of General Order No. 177, 4 December 1915. He thus became one of the six men who, in the 105 years since its institution, have been decorated with the Medal of Honor for deeds performed on two different occasions.

H. Jarrett, an orderly Rush had attached to McDonnell, ran out and succeeded in moving both Gisburne and Haggerty to safety.[43]

To reduce further casualties, Rush ordered the Marines off the roof. He could not withdraw the signalmen, as it was imperative for him to maintain contact with Fletcher; and for that purpose, their position, so clearly visible to the ships in the harbor, and, incidentally, to the snipers in the city, was ideal. This left Ensign McDonnell, Jarrett, Quartermaster Third Class Charles F. Bishop, Seaman James A. Walsh and Ordinary Seamen Charles L. Nordseik and Fred J. Schnepel alone on the roof. Nordseik was wounded around mid-afternoon, and the remaining signalmen carried on without replacements. The quality of self-discipline manifested by these men, in circumstances hardly calculated to generate that sort of adrenal exaltation in which so many acts of heroism are performed, makes praise seem presumptious. Again and again throughout the day, they exposed themselves to the fire of an unseen enemy to whom they could do no harm; so that in the end, Admiral Fletcher could assert, in simple testimonial to their valor, "Communications . . . were never interrupted." [44]

Nearing Pier Four, the *Utah* battalion's boats came under a sprinkling of small arms fire. In the bow of Lieutenant Castle's launch, a crisp young ensign stood with two sailors beside the one-pounder. Suddenly, one of the seamen groaned and crumpled to the deck. The ensign instinctively ducked behind the gun. An instant later, he heard a stinging reprimand and turned to see Castle standing upright in the cockpit. Cursing his reflexes, the ensign resumed his position at the gun.

The battalion, four companies with as many machine guns, landed at 1:40 P.M. There had not been time for more than a fragmentary briefing before it left ship, and neither Lieutenant Castle nor his company commanders had much idea of what was going on ashore. Ensign Foster, the first of the *Utah*'s officers to land, found Lieutenant Commander Buchanan waiting for him at the end of Pier Four. "He informed me that a company of bluejackets under Ensign Lowry of the *Florida* had been badly shot up in attempting to seize the Customs House," Foster related. "I was ordered to take my company 'on the double' towards the Customs House until I encountered Ensign Lowry. I was directed to relieve him and tell him that Commander Buchanan's orders were for him to fall back and take a breather." [45] Leading his men forward, Foster reflected that his promptness in preparing them to disembark had resulted in their being sent to the hottest part of the fight.

As the other companies came ashore, Buchanan routed them to various points in the city. Ensign Withers' section of Ensign Badger's company was rushed north to reinforce the Marines, plugging the gap between the companies at the power plant and the railroad roundhouse. Lieutenant Archibald Stirling's company and the balance of Badger's company were deployed to defend the space between Calle Morelos and the seawall. Lieutenant (junior grade) Philip Seymour was told to double time his company down Morelos after Foster.[46]

Approaching the Customs Zone, Seymour observed a group of soldiers in Calle Miguel Lerdo, below the Hotel Mexico. "If we can get to the top of that hotel," he shouted, "we can clean them out of there. Come along!" One of the men who came along, Seaman James R. Copeland, gave a graphic account of what followed.[47]

Seymour, Copeland, Boatswain's Mate Second Class J. J. McLaughlin, and several seamen sprinted up to the hotel. The door was locked, and there was no response to the bluejackets' pounding.

"Break it in!" ordered Seymour.

Someone found a post heavy enough to serve as a battering ram. McLaughlin guided the end of the ram against the door as Copeland drove it forward with all his strength. "The door fell in like matchsticks," he related. "We jumped inside and the first thing to confront us was the figure of a Mexican, wildly waving his arms and gibbering Spanish. He started to oppose us and he looked pretty dangerous.

"'Shoot him!' shouted the lieutenant.

"I was standing mighty close to him, so close, in fact, that I couldn't raise my gun to my shoulder. But I put it up as far as I could and fired. The bullet struck him right in the heart. There was a gurgle, and I remember that he stared at me in surprise and then he fell back—dead. It was the first man I had ever shot and I felt mighty queer.

"But we didn't have time to stop to analyze our sensations. . . . Right in back of this fellow were three others, alarmed, and they opened fire. We made a dash for them, and they fled up a winding stairs. The lieutenant chased them, and I followed. We stumbled up the stairs and all the time they kept firing down the stair well. But I guess our shots were better than theirs, for by the time we reached the roof there wasn't anyone to bar our way. . . .

"Once we got to the roof, we crawled on our stomachs to the parapet, and looked over. It was mighty ticklish there, too, for there were snipers on the other roofs. . . . I know that some of our boys who had rooftop positions got very reckless, and even tried sitting on the parapets, but after one or two of them had been hit, they were more careful."

Coxswain Frederick E. Norman, Seaman Robert E. England, and two or three others followed Seymour to the roof. This position proved much less attractive than it had appeared from the ground, for it was swept by fire from the tower of the Municipal Palace, the Parochial Church steeple, and the roofs of the Hotels Universal and Diligencias. Three of the party were wounded in a space of ten minutes. Copeland was one of them. "A soft-nosed bullet . . . tore through the back of my hand," he said. "It must have been fired by a sharpshooter, for his aim was good. It just missed going over the gun and catching me in the head. The bullet went clean through my hand [and] tore the strap of my gun. . . ." Prior to that time, Copeland believed that he had shot "about six [Mexicans] in all."

Noticing that Copeland had been wounded, Seymour crawled to his side. "I bled pretty freely," Copeland continued, "and the pain was almost unbearable, as the big bone in the middle of my hand was shattered."

"You'd better get out of here at once, and get that tended to," Seymour told him. "If you don't, you're going to bleed to death in a short time."

"That scared me pretty much," Copeland admitted. He was already feeling light-headed from loss of blood. "So I crawled to the stairway and down those winding stairs, stumbling over the bodies of the four men we had shot on our way up." After a hectic dash through sniper fire in the street outside, he reached the dressing station on Pier Four.

At the Post Office, Ensign Wilkinson's company was busily trading shots with snipers on the buildings on the Plaza Constitución. Scorning a passive defense, Wilkinson ordered Chief Gunner Robert Semple, his Second Section leader, to set up a counterfire from the top of the Post Office. Passing through the postmaster's handsomely-furnished, second-floor apartment, Semple's bluejackets emerged on the bullet-swept roof. It was not a healthy place. In the first few minutes there, Seaman Poinsett was killed and Seaman James Anderson wounded in the neck. Anderson refused to leave his post until Wilkinson gave him a direct order to report to the aid station. The young sailor obeyed with obvious reluctance and returned to the Post Office as soon as his wound had been dressed, insisting on resuming his place on the roof. By then, Chief Gunner

Semple, directing his men's fire "with great coolness and precision," had driven many of the snipers to cover. In the midst of this action, Ensign Foster's company appeared along Morelos.[48]

Foster deployed his company, fifty-four bluejackets, into two sections: one led by Ensign George Junkin, the other under Chief Turret Captain Niels Drustrup. Both sections were ordered to converge on the New Customs Warehouse, which was still occupied by Mexican soldiers. The warehouse was approximately a block long, with massive, open iron grillework at sides and ends. "There appeared to be quite a number of Mexicans shooting at us," Foster reported,[49] but his men's fire drove them away. Reaching the warehouse, the bluejackets found the stout iron doors locked and heavily barred. They were unable to enter the building until someone spied a length of railroad iron lying nearby. Foster and his men threw the rail on their shoulders to use as a battering ram. The doors gave way under the pounding, and the seamen surged inside. There they found huge cotton bales, barrels of rum and molasses, and sacks of sugar and rice. At the sight of these goods, Foster had an inspiration. Quickly, he and Junkin organized squads of men to load the assorted stores on the warehouse hand trucks. At a given signal, the trucks were pushed into Landero y Cos and Zaragoza to form a mobile breastwork. "I am convinced," wrote Foster, "that our good fortune at not suffering a great number of casualties was due in a great measure to the use of our movable . . . barricades, which gave our men quite effective protection against snipers on the ground and . . . firing out of first-story windows." [50]

But not all of the fire to which the men behind the barricades were subjected came from a low level. Two of the most dangerous positions were held by detachments under Boatswain's Mate Second Class Henry N. Nickerson at the corner of Calles Morelos and Lerdo, and Turret Captain Drustrup at Lerdo and Landero y Cos. Nickerson had been lightly wounded three times earlier in the afternoon, but he had returned to the company after receiving first-aid. Not long after his barricade had been put in position, Nickerson was hit by three shots, two of which splintered the bone in his left leg above and below the knee. Ensign Foster ran through a cross fire to pull him to cover and applied a tourniquet to his leg. Within minutes, Nickerson was on a stretcher headed for Pier Four.[51] "His grit after having been wounded three times," wrote Admiral Fletcher, "and the bravery he displayed when his many wounds made it necessary to carry him to the rear was an inspiration to all the men who saw him." [52] A week later, the surgeons on the *Solace* were forced to amputate Nickerson's leg at the hip.

After the arrival of the company led by Ensign Foster—his Annapolis classmate—Lowry moved his men back to the Terminal Plaza. When he reported, Captain Rush insisted on examining his shot-scorched cap, and joked with him about the similarity of their wounds—both had been hit by bullets which ripped through their leggings.[53] Rush had intended to hold Lowry's company in reserve, but by then the snipers had returned to the waterfront and the aid station on Pier Four was again under fire, the most persistent of which seemed to come from the Mexican Navigation Company steamer *Sonora,* moored to the seawall just north of the Fiscal Wharf. Brigade Surgeon Middleton S. Elliott continued to attend the wounded, heedless of the bullets falling a few feet away, but it was a dangerous situation. Soon after Ensign Lowry appeared, Rush gave him orders to clear the enemy out of the dock area south from Pier Four.[54]

Forming his men in skirmish order, Lowry led them along the waterfront, under fire from the *Sonora,* from wooden shacks, and from behind boxes and bales along the seawall. At the dock office, Lowry encountered the captain and two first officers of the *Sonora.* Holding his Colt .45 at the captain's back, Lowry and two bluejackets pushed him before them up the wharf. The *Sonora's* crew had hauled in the gangway and were sniping from the portholes and deck. "I remember so well the few minutes' tension in using the captain as a hostage and shield," Lowry recalled, "and knowing if his crew did not obey his command, I must shoot him." [55] When within hailing distance of the *Sonora,* Lowry told the captain to order his men to cease fire. Fortunately for all concerned, they obeyed. Nothing more menacing than sullen stares greeted the party Lowry led on board. The crewmen were lined up on the Fiscal Wharf while the bluejackets scoured the *Sonora,* confiscating all arms. Upon the completion of the search, the crew was permitted to return aboard ship. The waterfront was quiet when the First Company retraced its steps towards the Terminal Plaza.[56]

On Avenida Cinco de Mayo, Lieutenant of Infantry Benjamín Gutiérrez Ruiz, one of the heroes of the defense, had just been wounded by Marine fire from Montesinos. The bullet broke his right ankle, and one of his men assisted him to the Military Hospital. After his ankle had been bandaged, Gutiérrez determined to return to the fight. Persuading a slightly wounded soldier to help him, he made his way to the corner of Cortés and Benito Juárez. At the Ciriaco Vasquez Park, he found a sergeant's squad pinned under a cross fire from the Marines to the north and seamen to the east. Hobbling into the street, Gutiérrez began to fire at the Marines. The sergeant implored him to take cover, shouting, "Get off the curb, lieutenant! They're going to let daylight through you!" Gutiérrez ignored the warning. At length, the pain in his ankle became agonizing and, aided by the soldier from the hospital, he started to move back. Before he could reach cover, he was struck by a shot which fractured the femur in his wounded leg. A party of soldiers picked him up and began to carry him out of the line of fire. On the way, Gutiérrez was hit again, this time in the head. He died a few days later.[57]

Heeding Consul Canada's advice, several hundred American and other foreign nationals had availed themselves of the opportunity to board the *Mexico* and the *Esperanza* prior to the landing. But many had refused to take the warning seriously, with the result that they were caught in the city when fighting broke out. A number of families subsequently made their way to the American Consulate. Grave fears were felt for others, known to be trapped behind Mexican lines. Shortly past 2:00 P.M., Canada learned that around forty Americans, mostly women, had remained in their rooms at the Hotel Diligencias. "This news caused some consternation," he reported, in a classic understatement, "as the main body of Mexican forces were located in the hotel and on its roof." [58]

Moving closer to the scene of action, Admiral Fletcher transferred his headquarters to the *Prairie* at 1:55 P.M.[59] For all the control he could exercise over the course of the engagement, he might as well have stayed aboard the *Florida*. The first day at Veracruz was strictly a small-unit fight; the junior officers were on their own. Once a section had been sent to the front, the nature of the action and lack of communications made it impossible for brigade headquarters to exert more than a vague influence on its operations. A company advancing down one block had no idea what was happening to the company a block away. General orders to advance, withdraw, or defend were the most definite instructions which Fletcher on the *Prairie* or Rush at the Hotel Terminal—just then remarking: "It would be too bad, too bad, to have to shoot up this town" [60]—could issue to their subordinates.

The confusion was even more pronounced on the Mexican side. The tragedy of master carpenter Andrés Montes Cruz, killed on Avenida Zaragoza in the mid-afternoon, illustrates the conditions confronting the city's defenders. Montes Cruz was one of the civilians who had taken arms at the Military Barracks. Proceeding to the Plaza Constitución, he fell in with a group of volunteers. Being a man of some presence, Montes Cruz assumed command. Firing had not broken out and, in the absence of any instructions, Montes Cruz led his party to the corner of Avenida Hidalgo and Calle Miguel Lerdo. Here he left them for a few minutes while he hurried home to kiss his wife and children and make out his will. The sound of shots could be heard from the waterfront when he said good-bye. Rejoining his men, Montes Cruz moved east up Calle Arista to the corner of Avenida Zaragoza. Finding no other Mexican forces there, he decided to halt and prepare to defend the intersection. By sheer chance, Montes Cruz had chosen a position squarely in the path of the American advance.[61]

Meanwhile, the *Utah* battalion had begun to consolidate its positions. As the unit nearest the Plaza Constitución, Ensign Foster's company had become the spearhead of the drive into the heart of the city and was opposed by the most active and numerous Mexican forces. There had been a lull in the fighting after the *Utah* bluejackets reached the Customs Zone, but snipers in the small hotels and other buildings along Zaragoza soon increased the intensity of their fire. Seaman Walter B. Weeks, the youngest member of Foster's command, was the first man in the Customs Warehouse to return the enemy's fire, inspiring his comrades by his pluck.[62]

After Lowry had withdrawn, Foster posted a detachment under Boatswain's Mate Second Class James J. Dermody on the Customs House roof. Dermody's men engaged the snipers on Avenida Zaragoza, while, from a corner of Customs Storehouse Number Three, Chief Turret Captain Abraham de Somer's squad dispersed those along Landero y Cos. Master carpenter Montes Cruz was mortally wounded around 3:00 P.M., after which the Mexican fire from Zaragoza slackened. Around the same time, Boatswain's Mate Second Class George Berton and Seaman Hutchinson made a daring reconnaissance through the streets southeast of the Customs House, exposing themselves to the riflemen in the New Market and the Hotels Oriente and Buena Vista, in an attempt to locate the Mexican strongholds on Landero y Cos. To the north, Seymour's men pushed out from Morelos to establish barricades along Emparán and Benito Juárez. Bluejackets led by Gunner's Mate Third Class Arthur J. Fogarty occupied the public library in the base of the Juárez Light, battering the doors down under fire. Several soldiers were captured in the tower, where they had been trapped when Cresap's shells blew away the stairs.[63]

In the course of the afternoon, Ensign Foster's men were able to trundle their hand-truck barricades to the intersection of Landero and Zaragoza with Avenida Zamora, a block east of the enemy positions on the Plaza Constitución. When he made the rounds of the *Utah* battalion, Lieutenant Castle told Foster that his company was under a heavier fire than any other formation ashore.

In many instances, buildings had to be entered and cleared floor by floor. "These operations sometimes encountered resistance on the stairways leading to the roofs as well as on the rooftops," Foster related. During one such foray, Ensign George Junkin took a bullet through his cap. "This did not seem to bother him in the least," wrote Foster; "Junkin was not excitable by nature." [64] Ensign Harold Grow of the battalion staff had an equally disconcerting experience. Grow was walking across a rooftop with his friend Ensign Otto Forster when a sniper's bullet grazed his leg. The impact threw him off balance and he fell headlong through the skylight. Scrambling to his feet amid a medley of soprano shrieks, Grow discovered that he had plunged into a Catholic school for girls.[65]

One hundred and sixty miles off the coast of Mexico, on Admiral Badger's battleships, the men assigned to the bluejacket battalions learned that they would land at Veracruz. Reactions varied according to the individual: some men were delighted at the prospect of getting a crack at the "spigs"; others inclined to a less bellicose view. Aboard the *New Hampshire,* bluejackets were permitted to swap in and out of the ship's battalion providing they could find a man of equal rank willing to exchange. Arthur J. Sweetman, at eighteen the youngest quartermaster third class in the Atlantic Fleet, was able to trade his way into the landing party. "After seven months aboard ship," he said, "I was so anxious to set foot on land that I didn't particularly care whether someone was shooting at me or not." [66] But it was impossible for everyone to get his choice. Ordinary Seaman E. H. Frohlichstein, a young Jewish sailor from Mobile, Alabama, could not find anyone to take his place in the battalion. Convinced that he would be killed if he went ashore, Frohlichstein made a circuit of the ship, trying desperately to promote a trade. No one was interested. Friends laughed when Frohlichstein spoke of his premonition, and tormented him with gruesome speculations on the manners in which he might meet his death. That evening, young Frohlichstein wrote to his parents. He told them he felt that the letter would be his last one.[67]

NINE: ADVANCE AT YOUR DISCRETION

4:00 to 8:00 p.m.

At 4:00 disconnected boiler No. 12. At 4:15 HMS Berwick *got under way and stood out to the south-eastward. Three-masted schooner sighted standing back and forth to southward.*

At 5:00 the remains of Daniel Aloysius Haggerty, private USMC of the 8th Company, 1st Provisional Regiment, 2nd Advanced Base, was brought on board, killed in action on shore. Rickerd, E. G. (Elec.-1 cl.) was brought aboard with shot wound in left hand. At 5:29 shifted berth and anchored at 5:39 with 60 fathoms out on port anchor in 8¾ fathoms water. Bearings of anchorage: Benito Juárez, 255½° (true); Blanquilla Reef Light, 312° (true).

— Log of the *Utah*, April 21, 1914 [1]

A round 3:00 P.M., as the firing began to die down, Admiral Fletcher took stock of the situation. All things considered, Fletcher felt that he had fully complied with Secretary Daniels' essential instructions. "We were in possession of the Custom House, wharves, the Consulate, the cable and telegraph stations, railway terminal, rolling stock, tracks out to the roundhouse, the power and light plant, and the pumping station. . . . The landing of the ammunition had been prevented and the main object of our mission had been accomplished." [2] The question was what to do next. Fletcher's men were under fire from the Naval Academy, the New Market, some small craft on the waterfront, the Municipal Palace, the Parochial Church steeple, and the roofs of the Hotel Diligencias and other buildings bordering the Plaza Constitución. That something must be done was obvious; which of the available courses of action would bring the best results was not. "The condition of the enemy's forces in the City was not accurately known," Fletcher explained. "There were reports that the main part of the organized forces under General Maass had withdrawn, and it was known that nearly all the engines of the railway had been sent out while we were landing. I had . . . reason to believe that it was not General

Maass' intention to offer serious resistance within the city itself, as we both realized the unnecessary loss of property and noncombatants' lives that would ensue. . . . I did not desire to force the fighting through the city and use of the guns of the ships as long as there existed a reasonable chance to avoid this severe measure." [3]

Deciding to explore that reasonable chance, Fletcher sent Captain Huse to the Consulate to ask Canada to try to arrange an armistice. If a military officer could not be found, Huse told Canada, Fletcher felt that an endeavor should be made to have some civil authority stop the Mexican attack. Huse reported that the landing parties were losing men and that unless the fire could be stopped, he feared that it might become necessary to shell the city.[4] Canada was as anxious as anyone to avert shelling, and rushed a Mexican messenger out under a white flag to find Maass.[5]

At the Consulate, Huse recommended that the Americans who had gathered there after the fighting had started take advantage of the comparative calm to reach the *Esperanza*. Canada was not altogether receptive to this suggestion, as snipers were still active in the area. Finally he concurred, and the refugees made a dash for the Sanitary Wharf. They were in fact fired upon, both in the streets and on the wharf; happily, no one was hit.[6]

Though appearances were to the contrary, once aboard the *Esperanza* the refugees were as safe as they would have been on the Staten Island Ferry. Their guardian was Lieutenant Frank Jack Fletcher, Admiral Fletcher's imposing young nephew. Afterwards, they would remember the comfort they drew from his stalwart presence. The *Esperanza* was under fire all day; a bluejacket was wounded on her deck, and over thirty bullet holes were later counted in her hull. But not a single refugee, and eventually there were over 350 of them, was harmed.[7]

At 3:45 P.M., Admiral Fletcher cabled the first news of the landing to Washington. "In face of approaching norther landed Marines and sailors," he stated. "Mexican forces . . . opened fire with rifle and artillery after our seizure of the Custom House. . . . *Ypiranga* arrived Veracruz two P.M. anchored in outer harbor and [was] notified he would not be allowed to leave port with munitions of war aboard. Holding Custom House and section of city in vicinity of wharves and Consulate. Casualties two P.M. four dead twenty wounded." [8]

President Wilson was stunned. Everyone had assured him that there would be no bloodshed. "Preternaturally pale, almost parchmenty . . . [and] positively shaken," [9] Wilson paced back and forth across his office. Four dead, twenty wounded. The responsibility was almost too much to bear. To the faithful Tumulty, Wilson exclaimed: "I cannot get it off my heart. It had to be done. It was right. Nothing else was possible, but I cannot forget that it was I who had to order those young men to their deaths." [10]

The State Department was stunned, too, though for a different reason. Informing the *Ypiranga*'s captain that he could not leave Veracruz without unloading his cargo was in direct contravention of maritime law. It could very well provoke precisely the sort of incident the alternative of landing had been adopted to avoid. Upon receipt of the dispatch, Secretary of State Bryan hurried to call on the German ambassador, Count Johan von Bernstorff. Through a misunderstanding, Bryan told him, Fletcher had exceeded his instructions.[11] While the United States might hope that the *Ypiranga*'s captain would voluntarily discharge his arms at Veracruz, he was, of course, free to carry them wherever he might wish. Any resemblance to the Mexican apology for the Tampico Incident was purely coincidental.

In the meanwhile, at the American Consulate in Veracruz, Huse and Canada had vainly awaited their messenger's return. When he failed to appear after three-quarters of an hour, they decided to send a man to try to find the mayor, Roberto Díaz. In his report, Canada did not bother to name, much less commend, this second messenger, but he must have been a man of considerable courage. The disappearance of the first messenger was clearly an ill omen for those engaging in such errands. It must have seemed probable that he had been killed, as was later found to be true.[12]

The second man had better luck. Though frequently fired on en route, he managed to reach the mayor's residence. The doors were locked and no one answered his knocks and shouts. "He finally made his way to the roof," Canada related, "gaining entrance to the house by way of the court, and at last located the mayor barricaded in the bathroom. This individual received the message and replied that he had no jurisdiction in the matter and that the chief of police was the proper person to communicate with. . . ." [13] But the chief of police was not to be found, and after being shot at several more times, the messenger returned to the Consulate.

Two hours had been lost in the futile attempt to contact Mexican authorities. It was now around 5:00 P.M. "Any further advance at this time of day," wrote Fletcher, "would have brought the fighting into the most densely populated section of the city after nightfall." [14] The action had been expensive enough in broad daylight; there was no telling how costly it might become after dark, when tactical control would be almost impossible and the snipers, at home in the backstreets and alleys, would gain an immense advantage. Fletcher decided to remain on the defensive until dawn.

Special details, under the *Utah*'s Chief Gunner's Mate George Bradley, had already begun to bring food and ammunition ashore. Ignoring the fire to which the ration parties were subjected, Bradley personally supervised the landing and distribution of the supplies. He performed this duty with such efficiency, said Admiral Fletcher, as to relieve the staff of all care in attending to matters relative to supplies.[15]

There was still the problem of the foreign warships. Cradock's cruisers had steamed out of the inner harbor a few minutes after 4:00 P.M. A stray bullet had already wounded Paymaster A. W. Kimber, of HMS *Essex*.[16] The *Essex* dropped anchor beyond the breakwater, while HMS *Berwick* sailed for Puerto Mexico. Their departure left only the Spanish *Carlos V* in the inner harbor, and at 4:30 Ensign F. A. LaRoche was sent from the *Prairie* to inform her captain that Fletcher could not guarantee the ship's safety there after nightfall.[17] The Spanish captain took the hint and moved to join the other warships in the outer harbor. The *Florida* was directed to sweep the entrance to the inner harbor for any mines that might have been released during the day, and an officer was sent to San Juan de Ulúa to notify Commodore Cerisola that there must be no movement within the fortress during the night.[18]

By this time, Marine sharpshooters had driven away most of the snipers operating around the Terminal Station. One leatherneck was told to watch a building in which a particularly elusive sniper was believed to be at large. On a second-story balcony, a well-dressed Mexican sat reading a newspaper, apparently oblivious to the tumult in the streets below. After a few minutes, the Marine saw him fold the paper, raise a revolver from his lap and coolly fire towards the waterfront. The Mexican was reopening his newspaper when the Marine's bullet knocked him out of the chair. The Americans who reached the dying sniper recognized him as a prominent local businessman. A graduate of Cornell University, he had once taken tea with Fletcher on the *Florida*.[19]

In the early evening lull, Rush disposed the brigade for the night. Neville's men manned the perimeter around the railway yard and the barricades facing south and east on Montesinos. They had loopholed the Terminal warehouses during the afternoon.[20] Secure in these positions, the Marines did what they could to promote their creature comforts, though few were as discriminating as Captain Dyer, of the 18th Company, who managed to signal a friend aboard ship to bring him "fresh bread and butter, pickles, and a box of cigars between 4 and 5 A.M." [21]

The *Utah* battalion occupied the Customs House and Warehouse, the Juárez Light and adjacent private buildings. Wilkinson's *Florida* company remained at the Post Office. Lowry's company, which had suffered the heaviest losses, was placed in reserve. The First Section bivouaced on Pier Four, where Ensign Roy Dudley established his command post in an empty boxcar;[22] the Second Section slept beside Cresap's gunners in the Terminal Plaza. Lieutenant Jordan's company was put into the Marine line around the railway yard, Ensign Brownell's section being stationed with Ensign Withers' *Utah* section between the roundhouse and power plant, while Ensign Blandy's section held the power plant itself.[23] The *Utah* Support Section, under Ensign H. B. Lapham, was posted at the end of the causeway to San Juan de Ulúa.[24] The five prisoners taken during the day were sent aboard the *Prairie*.[25]

"As night fell on the city," wrote Consul Canada, "the firing became less frequent, although from time to time the rattle of an American machine gun and an occasional shot from a sharpshooter could be heard. The streets were entirely deserted by citizens and noncombatants, but the lights were kept burning. . . ." [26] Outside the American lines, the men from la Galera went on the rampage. Whatever chance there might have been of restraining the *rayados* had disappeared when the garrison withdrew. Drunk on rum from looted cantinas, the convicts swaggered down the streets, taking pot shots at anyone unwise enough to appear out-of-doors. "These stripers occasioned great alarm and committed a great many robberies during the night," reported the Veracruz newspaper, *La Opinión*. "One of these ferocious beasts fought with a husband for the possession of his wife and killed the husband and wounded the woman who resisted his brutal appetite." [27]

On Calle Doblado, a wildly drunken *rayado* carrying a Mauser with fixed bayonet accosted Felipe Carrillo, a portly and peaceable peon. Carrillo headed for the nearest house, the residence of don Salvador Campa, a prominent man of affairs. When Campa opened his door, Carrillo thrust his way inside, closely followed by the *rayado*. A number of well-to-do people had taken refuge at Campa's

U.S. Navy
Second Company, *Utah* battalion, in close quarters

R. M. Crosby
The Hamburg-American liner *Ypiranga*. The landing
at Veracruz was ordered to prevent her enormous cargo
of arms and munitions from reaching Huerta

during the day. Their efforts to calm the *rayado* were spectacularly unsuccessful. Covering them with his rifle, he called for *aguardiente,* a potent native liquor distilled from sugar cane. Finally, they gave him a bottle. He thrust the bayonet into his belt and set his rifle down to drink. While he guzzled the *aguardiente,* someone spirited the rifle into another room. A moment later, Carrillo darted out the door. In the stir of his exit, the *rayado* noticed that his Mauser had disappeared. Brandishing the bayonet in don Salvador's face, he demanded its return. Don Salvador swallowed hard and said that Carrillo had taken it. The *rayado* reeled off in pursuit. Don Salvador's guests were still congratulating him when they heard a burst of fire from the south. Losing his direction in the dim streets, the *rayado* had run headlong into the American lines.[28]

At 7:00 P.M., Fletcher radioed Badger of his decision to hold Pier Four for the night. "Desultory street firing continues," he reported. "You should be prepared to land infantry battalions and artillery immediately upon arrival under cover of darkness. Captain Huse or myself will repair on board on your arrival to advise you of the situation." [29]

While the first relief of sentries took their places at the barricades, Fletcher and his staff began to make plans for the morning. When all the vessels converging on Veracruz discharged their troops, there would be over four thousand men ashore.

The first ship to make port was the *San Francisco,* seventeen hours out of Tampico. She tied up at the Sanitary Wharf at 8:30 P.M. Fletcher called her captain, Commander William K. Harrison, to the *Prairie* and ordered him to put his troops ashore. The *San Francisco* anchored north of the flagship and, after a midnight snack of sandwiches and hot coffee, her battalion—nine officers and 116 men under Lieutenant W. J. Giles—landed on the south side of Pier Four. A circuitous advance brought the battalion into the Customs Zone around 1:00 A.M. Entering the line on the left of the *Utah* battalion, the *San Francisco* bluejackets were set to work constructing a barricade from the southeast corner of the central customs storehouse to the seawall. It was completed shortly before dawn.[30]

At 10:12 P.M., a Mexican naval officer from San Juan de Ulúa came aboard the *Prairie* to ask if some three hundred sailors and civilian laborers, at work in the fortress when the landing was made, could return to the mainland. This officer was a veteran at dealing with the United States Navy under adverse circumstances. Spanish by birth, he had been aboard the ill-fated *Don Juan of Austria* when that vessel went down before Dewey's guns in Manila Bay, sixteen years before. After a prolonged delay, he was permitted to see Admiral Fletcher, who denied his request; the workers would have to stay where they were until order was restored in the city. The Mexican left the *Prairie* a few minutes before midnight.[31]

The second ship to reach Veracruz was the scout cruiser *Chester*. Her captain was forty-four-year-old Commander William A. Moffett. An aristocratic South Carolinian, Moffett had served with the Asiatic Squadron during the Spanish-American War and recently completed a tour as executive officer of the flagship *Arkansas*. Generally recognized as a "daring, skillful seaman," he was also known as a difficult personality. "Unless he originated a suggestion," another officer wrote, "he seldom agreed with it."[32] Moffett had held the *Chester* at her full speed of twenty-one knots since leaving Tampico, ignoring the protests of her anguished engines.[33]

Nearing port, Moffett established radio contact with the *Prairie*. Fletcher warned him that the harbor lights were out, which would make navigating the eighty-six-foot-wide passage between the breakwaters into the inner harbor a hazardous undertaking. When Moffett asked for instructions, however, Fletcher left the matter to his discretion; if he wished, he could wait outside the breakwater until dawn. Moffett chose to run straight in, bringing the *Chester* through the narrow opening in a breath-taking display of seamanship and nerve. He dropped anchor off the Sanitary Wharf at 12:05 A.M. From the *Prairie,* Fletcher signaled, "Well done."[34]

In addition to her two seaman companies, the *Chester* carried a Marine company under Lieutenant H. W. Stone and Major Smedley Darlington Butler. At thirty-two, Smedley Butler was already the most controversial Marine of his generation. The genteelly-bred son of a Quaker Congressman, he had arrived in Cuba, a sixteen-year-old second lieutenant, in time to be the target for some of the last shots fired in the Spanish-American War. Since then he had proved his mettle against Boxers in China, Moros in the Philippines, bandits in Nicaragua, and superior officers throughout the world. A wiry little man, "140 pounds, soaking wet," with a sharp, perenially-boyish face, his outspoken criticisms of what he considered outmoded practices had earned him the enmity of the Navy Department, in which he was regarded as a flippant roughneck. Earlier in the year, Fletcher had sent him on a secret mission to

Mexico City, where as "Mr. Jones" he had sketched the defenses of Chapultepec and, with the inimitable Butler flair, achieved an invitation to the presidential palace. Neville, with whom he had been friends since the Boxer Rebellion, immediately placed him in charge of the companies around the railroad roundhouse.[35]

The *Chester* battalion, 137 men commanded by Lieutenant G. E. Lake, and Lieutenant Stone's eighty-eight Marines landed at Pier Four around 3:00 A.M. A detachment from the *Chester* relieved Blandy's *Florida* section at the power plant, while the Marines and the rest of Lake's men were posted to the right of the roundhouse, on Captain Breckinridge's flank.[36]

Thirty minutes after the *Chester* made port, the *Utah*'s lookouts saw a searchlight far at sea flashing the call letters of the *Arkansas,* Admiral Badger's flagship. The great, grey shapes of the battleships themselves were sighted minutes later. The *Arkansas* led the squadron into the outer harbor, followed by the *New Hampshire,* the *South Carolina,* the *Vermont* and, far astern, the *New Jersey.*[37] Around 2:00 A.M., April 22, Admiral Fletcher and Huse boarded the *Arkansas* to brief Admiral Badger. Fletcher offered to turn the conduct of operations over to him, but Badger generously replied that, as Fletcher was familiar with the situation, he preferred for him to remain in command.[38]

With that question settled, the admirals began to discuss the expanded organization of the Naval Brigade. In the end, it was decided to add the *Arkansas* battalion and its two guns to the First Seaman Regiment. The *New Hampshire, South Carolina, Vermont,* and *New Jersey* battalions, twelve hundred men with a 3-inch gun from each ship, would compose a Second Seaman Regiment commanded by the *New Hampshire*'s Captain E. A. Anderson. The three hundred Marines would be formed in a battalion under Major Albertus W. Catlin and assigned to Neville's regiment. A Third Seaman Regiment would be raised from the ships due to reach port later in the day.[39]

The plans to secure the city were simple. Initially, a final effort would be made to arrange a cease-fire with the Mexican authorities. Should the attempt be unsuccessful by 7:45 A.M., the advance would begin. The First Seaman Regiment would push south and west, clearing the area between Independencia and the waterfront to Calle Rayon, with Avenida Zaragoza as its axis of advance. The *Utah* battalion would take the lead, with the *Arkansas* and *Florida* battalions in support; the *San Francisco* and *Chester* battalions

ARTHUR J. SWEETMAN

Arthur J. Sweetman, who lived at the time of his enlistment at 1207 Light street, was in the landing party from the battleship New Hampshire when Vera Cruz was taken.

This is his second year in the navy and he is an expert signalman. He is a Queen Anne's countian, but lived and went to school for several years in Baltimore. A letter just received from his sister, Mrs. J. H. Row, of Chestertown, tells of his Mexican experience and brought the family the happiness of knowing that he was unhurt.

Arthur J. Sweetman

would remain in reserve around the Customs House. The *Utah*'s 3-inch gun, which had been landed at Pier Four around 2:30 A.M., was dragged to the Customs House to support the attack. Half an hour later, the *Florida*'s gun was drawn up beside it.[40]

The Second Seaman Regiment would move on the left flank of the First Regiment to enter Calle Francisco Canal, at which it would turn west to clear the blocks between that street and Calle Juárez to the outskirts of the city. The Marine Regiment would advance south from Montesinos to Juárez, keeping one block behind the seamen, on the streets parallel to Independencia. At Juárez, the Marines would swing west and push down the corridor between Montesinos and Juárez from Morelos to the sand hills. The city was divided into contiguous sectors several blocks square, to each of which a battalion was assigned. The battalions would halt upon arriving at the far boundaries of their respective sectors and the following units would move into the lead. A thorough search would be made of every building in the path of the advance.[41]

Veracruz remained relatively quiet through the night. A three-man *Utah* detachment under Boatswain's Mate First Class F. N. C. Overall patrolled the rooftops around the Juárez Light, preventing any sniping on the troops bivouaced in the streets below.[42] Fletcher's chief concern was that the Mexicans might try to bring artillery up against the vessels in the inner harbor. The *Utah* and *Florida* were ordered to be prepared to use their turret guns and vessels inside and outside the breakwater swept the city with their searchlights.[43] Bluejackets snatching a few minutes' sleep in the sandy waste of the railway yard awakened, with a sensation of extreme exposure, in the blinding glare of the beams.[44] On three occasions, the *San Francisco*'s lights picked up parties of men stealing across the breakwater from San Juan de Ulúa. A few shots fired into the air turned them back each time.[45]

Except for those trapped in the buildings on the flood-lit Plaza Constitución, from which they could not emerge without coming under American fire, most of the Mexican regular forces withdrew from the city. The movement originated around 8:00 P.M., when Commodore Azueta received the long-delayed order from General Maass to abandon Veracruz. Azueta relayed the message to Lieutenant Colonel Contreras, who had collected 170 men at the Church of the Ascension, with instructions to fall back to los Cocos and wait for the naval cadets. The evacuation of the Naval Academy required some ingenuity, as the entrances were covered by the ships' guns. Eventually, a hole was hacked in the rear wall, and the cadets slipped through one by one. Forming ranks in the street outside the San Sebastian Hospital, they marched down Zaragoza, turning south at the Parade Ground. Contreras' volunteers fell in behind them at los Cocos. The column reached Tejería around midnight.[46]

The regulars' retirement did not spell an end to resistance. The *rayados,* the civilian snipers, and a number of headstrong soldiers—such as Cadet Alasio Pérez of the 18th Battalion, killed at dawn at the intersection of Lerdo and Cortés [47]—remained at large outside the American lines. Any doubt of their determination would be dispelled in the first minutes of the advance.

Badger's ships began to discharge their troops shortly before daybreak. The battalions assigned to the First Seaman Regiment made for Pier Four, while those to form the Second Regiment converged on the Fiscal Wharf. The first two companies and stretcher-bearers of the *New Hampshire* battalion, together with the battalion and regimental staffs, landed around 4:10 A.M. The *Arkansas* and *South Carolina* battalions followed at 4:30, the Fleet Marines around fifteen minutes later. The *New Jersey* battalion came ashore at 6:15. The *New Jersey*'s troops had sat in their whaleboats at the ship's booms for nearly two hours, and after the initial excitement had passed, some of the men had begun to sing in a low key. Just as the chorus was picking up strength, it was interrupted by the pop-pop-pop of small arms fire from shore. From then on, there had been dead silence in the boats.[48] The *Vermont* battalion disembarked around 6:45, and the remaining two *New Hampshire* companies landed under scattered fire at 7:30.[49]

Once again, the junior officers were sent ashore without the benefit of a briefing. Ensign L. W. Comstock, one of the *Vermont* company commanders, was ordered to get his men aboard a towline of small boats. Comstock and a dozen men had boarded the motor launch while the rest of the company climbed into the whaleboats. It was pitch black. Comstock had no idea of who had given the coxswain the course to steer or where his company was to land. As the launch neared shore, a machine gun began to chatter in the blackness. Seconds later, Comstock's party heard the chilling sound of bullets striking in the water nearby. A young seaman began to cry. "I didn't come in the Navy to get killed," he sobbed. A petty officer growled, "Well, what the hell *did* you come in the Navy for?" The men were still laughing when the launch scraped alongside the pier.[50]

The troops from the Second Regiment assembled on the field

around the New Lighthouse. The sun's first rays revealed a medley of curiously-colored uniforms. To make themselves less conspicuous, the men had dyed their whites in vats infused with iron rust, iodine or, in one instance, coffee grounds, and their clothes had dried in an assortment of dingy, brownish hues.[51] One battalion's officers dressed in Marine uniforms, a decision which the volume of fire they attracted caused them to regret.[52]

Several other ships of the Atlantic Fleet reached port while the landing was in progress. The *Minnesota* and the *Hancock* stood in from Tampico at 6:06 A.M. The supply ship *Orion* appeared at 6:40, the battleship *Michigan* at 8:35, and the *Solace* at 11:45.[53]

At dawn, the snipers in the city resumed an intermittent fire. Around 4:30 A.M., machine guns in the *Utah* and *San Francisco* barricades began to spray the Hotel Oriente. The *San Francisco* bluejackets eventually succeeded in driving the snipers away from their front by the time-honored expedient of volley fire.[54]

Meanwhile, Consul Canada had been unable to locate any competent Mexican authority. "By eight o'clock," Fletcher recorded, "it was definitely ascertained that the firing of the enemy was not under organized control." [55] He then dispatched the following message to Captain Rush:

All efforts to get in touch with responsible authorities on shore have failed and efforts have been fruitless to have authorities stop firing.

I am well-informed that the regular troops have been withdrawn and the people now firing are irresponsible people under no control or authority.

You will advance at your discretion, and suppress this desultory firing, taking possession of the city and restore order, respecting as much as possible the hotels and other places where foreigners are lodged.

You are cautioned against the possible use by the enemy of machine guns and artillery.[56]

TEN: EVERY HOUSE WAS AN AMBUSH

The Commander in Chief desires you convey to wounded the following from Secretary of the Navy:

Quote—Your full telegrams with ample information answer demands for every item news.

People eager for every incident. All proud of the magnificent way the Navy has handled the situation.

Daniels to Badger, April 24[1]

At 7:45 A.M., the Second Seaman Regiment moved southwest, passing along the front of the *San Francisco* barricades. Mindful of the lessons of the previous day, Rush had cautioned the regimental commanders against bypassing possible pockets of resistance and instructed them to throw out "strong advance guards to develop the situation."[2] For some reason, however, the Second Regiment did not heed these wise counsels. The men marched in parade formation, a column of sections, with the safety locks on their rifles, and there was no advance guard. In the lead was Captain Anderson's own *New Hampshire* battalion, with himself and his staff at its head.[3]

Anderson was a veteran of thirty-two years' service. He was a handsome man, with a long, Highland face, bristly, grey mustache, and sea wrinkles at the corners of his eyes. His crew considered him "a pretty good old skipper." A story explicative of the esteem in which he was held concerned a bluejacket who had failed to present himself before Anderson to receive disciplinary action after being put on report. When the dilatory seaman was brought forward, Anderson asked sternly if he had not understood that he was on report. "Yes, sir," the bluejacket answered; "I knew it. I just thought I'd give myself a second chance." On many ships, he would have been rewarded by three days in the brig, but Anderson was amused and had simply sent the sailor on his way with a warning.[4]

A member of the Annapolis Class of 1882, Anderson had commanded the *Sandoval* during the Spanish-American War, wore the West Indies Medal with five bars, and had been advanced five places on the promotion list for extraordinary heroism under fire. But he

103

Captain E. A. Anderson, commander of the Second
Seaman Regiment

The attack on the Mexican Naval Academy, April 22, 1914

had never fought on land. Lieutenant (junior grade) T. Gordon Ellyson, the *South Carolina* artillery commander, begged Anderson to let him scout ahead, but his request was denied. Next Ellyson suggested that the regiment move in open order, with skirmishers well in advance. Anderson did not see the need of that, either. He had been assured that his route was clear of snipers.[5]

At the end of the Promenade, the regiment executed a column left, skirting the barren field, some 350 yards in width, between the New Lighthouse and the edge of town. Passing within pistol range of the New Market, the Naval Academy, and the Artillery Barracks, the column approached Calle Francisco Canal. At its entrance, Anderson gave a column right and led the regiment into the street.[6]

The foremost companies had completed the turn when they were hit by a sudden burst of rifle, machine gun and one-pounder fire from the Naval Academy and buildings nearby. Scattered shots had echoed through the city since dawn; it was not until they heard a sound like bees humming overhead that the men in the *New Hampshire*'s close-order ranks realized they were under fire.[7] If any orders were given, they were lost in the din and commotion. "Nobody said halt or take cover or defend yourselves, or anything," a young bluejacket recalled.[8] For a few seconds, the regiment plunged forward, like a befuddled boxer, into the fire. Solid shot from the Mexican cannon were clearly visible skipping across the plain after their initial impact.[9] "It was only due to the poor marksmanship of the Mexicans that the entire staff and battalion were not mowed down," a newsman asserted.[10] Lieutenant Ellyson would have agreed. "When the fire first opened I was at the head of the column talking to Captain Anderson," he wrote, "and as he didn't run I couldn't, but I sure did want to. . . . The worst of it was that we could see nothing to shoot at." [11] Men were falling now. Curses and screams of "My God! I'm hit, I'm hit!" rent the air.[12] The battalion began to waver, holding its ground for a moment as the neat files dissolved. Then it broke, and the leading companies streamed pell-mell back towards the waterfront.[13]

Rounding the corner into Calle Francisco Canal, the *South Carolina* battalion was swept away in the stampede. Ensign George S. Dale, a section leader in the First Company, was disconcerted by the sight of a mob of men pounding towards his formation. When they passed, Dale discovered that his section had vanished. Appalled, he drew his .45. Most of the shooting seemed to be coming from the Naval Academy. Doing what came naturally, he began firing at the Academy windows. After two or three shots, he remembered himself. Groups of men were still rushing past him on their way to the rear. Collaring a machine-gun crew, Dale made them lie down beneath a cart and set their gun up to cover the street. He had collected a number of riflemen behind a wall and was considering getting the machine gun to a roof when he noticed his company commander walking back towards the Promenade. The regiment appeared to be regrouping there, so Dale told his stragglers to rejoin their companies.[14]

An additional danger to the leading battalions was the wild fire from the rear of the regiment. Startled by the roar of rifles over his shoulder, Ensign Schuyler Mills of the *New Jersey* artillery whirled around and found himself staring into the frantic faces of a crowd of men who had climbed on a loading platform a few feet behind him and were shooting from the hip. Their bullets were passing within inches of his men's heads. Whenever one of their shots hit the side of a building, kicking up a cloud of dust, the men would shout "There he is!" and try to fire faster. Mills blew "Cease fire!" on his whistle until his ears ached, but the signal was drowned by the roar of the Springfields. Certain that at any moment he would stop a slug point-blank, he ran along the loading platform until he found an empty space to scramble up. Returning alongside the bluejackets, he managed to get them under control.[15]

Despite the confusion, the bluejackets retained enough presence of mind to carry off their casualties. The gallantry of the men who, resisting the contagion of panic, refused to abandon their dead and wounded comrades was one bright feature in an unseemly episode. Ensign Hugh Frazer, Boatswain's Mate Second Class Joseph H. Rissacher, Boatswain's Mate First Class J. P. Cush, Ordinary Seaman Emil Tyderic, and Surgeon Cary Langhorne pulled men off the field beneath a biting fire. Seaman George Bancroft was carrying a shipmate towards a nearby building when someone sniped at him from a window. Calling for assistance, Bancroft laid the man on the ground and began to return the enemy's fire. He kept the sniper pinned down until a litter team could pick up the casualty.[16]

Recoiling from the mouth of Calle Francisco Canal, the regiment had fallen back across the field, and along the edge of the Promenade, hundreds of men were milling about in apparent disorder. Lieutenant James P. Lannon, the *New Hampshire* battalion commander, had been shot through the body as he stooped to give a wounded bluejacket first aid.[17] From the bridge of the *Prairie,* Admiral Fletcher had a clear view of the mêlée. "The situation looked critical," [18] he wrote.

Unknown to Fletcher, part of the *New Hampshire* battalion was still defending itself in Calle Francisco Canal. When the Mexicans opened fire, Ensign J. P. Norfleet's company had swung back against the side of the Artillery Barracks. Someone had found a way inside and, as the battalion began to disintegrate, Norfleet's men had retired into the building, hauling their dead and wounded along. They could hear Mexicans firing from the roof, but the door to the stairway had been blocked with stores. Stationing a number of his men at the windows, Norfleet ordered the others to pull down the barricade. While they were working on it, Norfleet heard the report of an explosion. Hurrying to a window, he saw a round hole appear beneath the cupola of the Instituto Veracruzano, on the other side of the street. "My God," he thought, "they've got cannon up there." [19]

A moment later, he was relieved to realize his mistake. The Second Regiment's repulse had been observed aboard the ships in the inner harbor. As Anderson's bluejackets recrossed the field, gunners standing at the ready on the *Chester* and the *San Francisco* were ordered to open fire.[20] Waving his cap to attract attention, Norfleet led his men out of the building. As they moved towards the regiment, the sound of naval gunfire rolled across the harbor.[21]

For five minutes, the *San Francisco*'s 5-inch gun pounded the Naval Academy, while the *Chester* raked the Academy and the New Market with two 3-inch deck guns and her 5-inch bow chaser.[22] A near miss blew the roof off the residence of a prominent prostitute and another ignited a money exchange, but on the whole the ships' fire was remarkably accurate.[23] "Had the taxpayer at home witnessed the way those upper-story windows were put out by the *Chester*'s shells," Jack London wrote, "he would never again grudge the money spent of recent years in target practice." [24] At least forty rounds struck the second story of the Naval Academy, huge columns of red dust leaping upwards as each shot went home.[25] The fire from the building ceased within seconds.

At the beginning of the bombardment, snipers in the New Market turned their attention to the *Chester,* where one man was wounded in the forearm while loading the 5-inch gun and a coal passer, on deck to see the action, was hit in the foot. But when the cruiser shifted her fire to the New Market, the riflemen quickly retired.[26]

The Second Regiment was already regaining a semblance of order. The troops in the rear had not been seriously affected by the Mexican fire and the companies which had bolted rallied at the

Inside the Naval Academy after the bombardment. Commodore Azueta's office, showing the effect of the USS *Chester*'s shells

The scout cruiser *Chester*, which silenced the fire from the Academy

Looking south along Avenida Independencia towards the Parochial Church, whose steeple (right center) housed parties of snipers

The Mexican Naval Academy, a strongpoint of resistance in the fighting

seawall.[27] With a dauntless courage that would win him the second citation of his career for "extraordinary heroism in battle," Captain Anderson began to reform his command.[28] His efforts were complimented by those of his adjutant, Lieutenant Commander Rufus Z. Johnston, the *New Hampshire*'s executive officer. With Lieutenant Lannon down, Johnston took charge of the front of the regiment. Those in contact with him that day were unanimous in their praise of his leadership. Anderson commended Johnston's "zeal and . . . highly efficient service . . . under a very heavy fire," [29] and in a spontaneous personal letter, Lieutenant Commander H. E. Yarnell of the regimental staff told Johnston, "It is only on rare occasions, even in our profession, that the bearing and conduct of an officer can be ascertained under the supreme test of an enemy's fire. Your coolness and disregard of personal danger . . . set an example to officers and men, the good effects of which cannot be estimated." [30]

A skirmish line of riflemen and the regimental artillery went into action before the ships ceased fire. Within minutes, the Second Regiment was ready to resume the advance. This time the men crossed the plain in extended order. The battered shell of the Naval Academy and the Artillery Barracks were occupied by the *New Jersey* battalion. On entering the city, the companies deployed with a column on each sidewalk, covering the rooftops and windows on the opposite side of the street.[31]

The casualties were collected at the New Lighthouse. Among them the *New Hampshire* bluejackets were shocked to see the body of Seaman Frohlichstein, who had promised them he would be killed. He had been shot through the head.[32]

Promptly at 8:00 A.M., the *Utah* battalion jumped off from the barricades around the Customs House. Lieutenant Castle had given his company commanders their orders four hours earlier; they had been studying their objectives through field glasses since dawn.[33] The Mexican fire, intermittent through the morning, commenced with redoubled fury when the bluejackets appeared in the open.[34]

"Being an excellent marksman and notably cool," Chief Turret Captain de Somer was sent ahead in the point where, in Admiral Fletcher's words, he was of more value than a whole squad.[35] De Somer's performance was rivalled by that of Seaman George J. Smith, a machine gunner. During the advance, Smith discovered that the short struts fitted to his Benet-Mercier gun were totally unsuited for cobblestone streets. Their uneven surface threw the gun off level, making accurate aiming impossible. Finally, Smith stood up, grasping the gun by the barrel and butt, and began to fire from the hip.[36]

Emerging on the Plaza Constitución, the *Utah* sections swept across the square. Ensign Foster's company, assembled at the intersection of Lerdo and Zaragoza, rushed the Municipal Palace. It was occupied with rather less resistance than Foster had expected. He sent his best shots to the tower to open fire on the Mexicans in the Hotel Diligencias and the Parochial Church, while the other men searched the building for snipers.[37]

The company assigned to take the Diligencias was led by twenty-three-year-old Ensign Oscar C. Badger, the son of the commander of the Atlantic Fleet. The hotel was defended by two lieutenants with a detachment of forty or fifty soldiers on the roof. From this position they had directed a spirited fire on the bluejackets advancing through the streets below. The Mexicans suffered several losses of their own as Americans began to appear on nearby rooftops, but they stayed in action until one of the lieutenants was killed and the other wounded. With both their officers down, the men became demoralized. Few remained in the Diligencias when Badger's men, side-stepping the knot of bodies on the veranda, burst through the great, nail-studded oaken doors. On the roof the bluejackets found only piles of empty Mauser shells, ammunition boxes, and discarded uniforms. The American women who had been caught in the hotel were unharmed. They had occupied themselves caring for the Mexican wounded, a mission they did not allow their liberation to interrupt.* [38]

A section under Ensign Laurence Townsend, the machine-gun officer, broke into the Parochial Church. Pistol in hand, Townsend charged up the narrow, iron stairway to the steeple. It was deserted, but dozens of empty cartridge cases on the window ledge and floor gave mute evidence of the purpose it had served. Afterwards, there was a rumor on the *Utah* that as he dashed into the church, "Duke" Townsend glimpsed the figure of a man crouched in a dusky corner. When the man ignored his challenge, Townsend blasted him with his .45. Advancing to investigate, he discovered his shadowy adversary to be a carving of Christ bent beneath the Cross.[39]

By 9:30 A.M., the Plaza Constitución was under control of the *Utah* battalion. Its position was considered so secure, in fact, that when the *Chester*'s troops appeared in the area somewhat behind schedule they were ordered back to the Terminal Plaza.[40]

---

* Ensign Badger was cited for this action in Consul Canada's report to the State Department, the only junior officer mentioned by name.

Vice Admiral Paul F. Foster, USNR, (Ret.)
Bluejackets in the portales of the Plaza Constitución.

Lieutenant Commander Arthur B. Keating's *Arkansas* battalion took the lead from the Plaza Constitución, advancing down Zaragoza into the market area. South of Calle Arista, resistance stiffened. Snipers in a house midway in the first block south of the corner of Zaragoza and Calle Francisco Canal caught the bluejackets in the intersection.[41] A rifle cracked and Ordinary Seaman Fried pitched forward on his face. Fried was dead before he could finish the word which had sprung to his lips, but the startled boy behind him heard enough to know that it was "Mother!" [42]

The battalion adjutant was burly Lieutenant (junior grade) Jonas H. Ingram, whose turret division had set a world's record for speed and accuracy at the Guantánamo gunnery exercises in 1913. When the column halted, he rushed the Colt machine gun forward. Its fire failed to dislodge the snipers and one of the gun crew was killed. Gunner's Mate First Class Johan Svenson carried his body to cover under heavy fire. The ensign in charge of the nearest field piece had been called away, but Chief Boatswain's Mate Augustin O'Neill brought the gun into action. A few rounds over open sights disposed of the snipers, and the advance was resumed.[43]

A block further, at the intersection of Calle Rayon, the battalion was ordered to fall back to Francisco Canal while the *Chester* shelled the Military Barracks, at which a concentration of Mexican troops had been reported. A machine gun near the Juárez Memorial in the Presidente Díaz Park and the Instituto Veracruzano were shelled around the same time. Some firing was reported from old Fort Santiago, but whoever had occupied the structure withdrew before it became necessary to bombard it. After the shelling, the battalion took possession of the Instituto Veracruzano and prepared to defend the line of Calle Rayon.[44]

As the fighting spread into the heart of the city, numbers of women and youths took up arms. Glancing towards a house he was passing, Ensign Lowry saw an odd sight. In an open window a Mexican woman was standing with her back to the street, firing a gun over her shoulder.[45] Later in the afternoon, several shots were fired from the pilot office on the end of the Fiscal Wharf. From the bridge of the *Prairie*, Ensign E. S. R. Brandt sprayed the building with a machine gun and after a few moments the snipers signaled that they wished to surrender. When they filed out of the office, the waiting bluejackets were surprised to find that one was a woman.[46]

Chivalry became even more of a strain as snipers overrun by the

American advance began putting on women's clothing to improve their chances of escape. A man dodging out of a house in front of the *New Hampshire* battalion tripped and sprawled on the paving to reveal the trousers underneath his skirt. It was a fatal mishap. Thereafter, *New Hampshire* bluejackets tended to turn a suspicious eye towards women appearing in their path.[47]

Along the waterfront, bluejackets came under fire from Mexican sailors aboard ships in the inner harbor. Around 8:00 A.M., the *Chester*'s lookouts reported snipers in evidence on the *Haakon VII,* a merchantman flying the Norwegian flag. At 8:30, the *Chester* signaled the *Haakon:* "If we see you firing at us we will sink you." Suspicious activity continued to be observed on board the steamer, and the message was repeated at 8:40 and 8:47. A few minutes later, Captain Anderson semaphored that the *Haakon* was shooting at the Second Regiment. The *Chester* then ordered her to leave the inner harbor; she stood out around 9:00 A.M.[48]

Firing was also reported from the Mexican freighter *El Gubernador.* At 9:00 A.M., the *Chester* sent a party under Lieutenant A. D. Turnbull to board and search her. All Turnbull found was one revolver, but two-and-a-half hours afterwards, Ensign Fuller of the *Vermont* battalion signaled that snipers on the *Gubernador* had wounded two of his men. At that moment, the *Gubernador* was in the act of steaming out of the harbor. She was intercepted by an armed launch from the *Florida* and her ten-man crew was taken aboard the *Chester.*[49]

At the same time, snipers resumed fire from the *Sonora,* which still lay beside the Fiscal Wharf. Soon the volume became so heavy that the refugee ship *Esperanza* was obliged to leave the inner harbor. Ensign Elder, in charge of the reserves and pioneers around Pier Four, was ordered to seize the *Sonora.* Advancing along the route Lowry's *Florida* company had taken the preceding day, Elder's men approached the steamer. Once again, the crew ceased fire when the bluejackets reached the Fiscal Wharf. But the ruse would not work twice, and the forty men aboard were marched away as prisoners.[50]

The scow *Verano* was also reoccupied by snipers. A few shells from the *Chester*'s 3-inch guns sufficed to set it awash and send the Mexicans hurrying ashore. Despite the presence of American patrols, however, it was not until mid-afternoon that the waterfront grew quiet.[51]

To the north, Neville had broadened the front of the Marine regiment, sending Butler's and Reid's battalions across the railway tracks to extend his left flank. Major Catlin's Fleet Marines were placed in reserve a block behind the front lines. As the two seamen regiments moved down the waterfront, the Marines began to push south from Montesinos.[52] "We fought like hell," said Smedley Butler. "Since the Mexicans were using the houses as fortresses, the Marines rushed from house to house, knocking in the doors and searching for snipers. Just as two of my men were smashing through one door, they were mysteriously shot in the stomach from below. The house was deserted, but from the angle of the bullets, the Mexicans were obviously under the floor. We poured a volley through the floor and then ripped up the boards. There they were, two dead Mexicans dangling between the cross beams."[53] By 10:30 A.M., the Marines had reached Calle Juárez and Captain Dyer's company was clearing the block south to Miguel Lerdo.[54]

Though they were not involved in the fighting around landmarks such as the Naval Academy or the Municipal Palace, the Marines saw ample action. Their canny tactics could not prevent an occasional surprise and sometimes men wounded from ambush were caught under the enemy's fire. Privates Cohen and Leddick rescued a comrade from an exposed position, and Private Lee Mahr figured in two episodes. In the first, he and Hospital Apprentice First Class B. W. Claggett of the *Florida* brought in two Marines, and in the second, Mahr and Hospital Apprentice First Class John Henry Hendrickson, also of the *Florida,* pulled a fallen Marine to cover.[55]

By now, the Second Seaman Regiment had reached Calle Francisco Canal and turned west. "Much time was lost in beating the doors of houses," wrote Captain Rush, "as in many instances, the inhabitants were too scared to open them up. A thorough search of each room and every male person . . . was made, and whenever arms were found they were destroyed and the men were marched to the Terminal Station as prisoners."[56] A newsman reported, "Scores of prisoners were taken, most of them protesting, many hysterically, that they were not guilty of any unfriendliness to the Americans. Accustomed as the Mexicans are to their own . . . forces shooting immediately all prisoners, the captured men could not believe that they would receive less drastic treatment from the Americans."[57]

No major strong points were encountered in the regiment's advance to the sand hills, but many buildings were defended by

Marine officers at Veracruz. Front row, left to right: Lieutenant Colonel Wendell C. Neville, Colonel John J. Lejeune, Brigadier General Littleton T. Waller, Major Smedley Darlington Butler, Major Randolph C. Berkeley, unidentified

A Marine outpost beyond Veracruz

snipers. Ensign W. A. Lee of the *New Hampshire,* a member of the Navy Rifle Team, went ahead, engaging in a competition in which there were no return matches. During a halt, a friend saw him sitting on a curb, a borrowed rifle across his knees, deliberately inviting a sniper to shoot at him.[58] Lee's tactic was as reasonable as it was risky, for the bluejackets rarely glimpsed their enemies. "They wouldn't show themselves," Quartermaster Sweetman said. "All you'd would see would be a rifle barrel or a hand holding a pistol out a window or over the edge of a roof." [59]

Several houses were shelled. The *Utah* and *Florida* field pieces had been added to the four guns of Lieutenant John Grady's regimental artillery,[60] and no less than six gunners received citations. The one awarded Boatswain's Mate Second Class Harry Smith, an Englishman aboard the *New Hampshire,* was typical. "He was assiduous in instructing the men in the proper handling of the piece while under fire," Lieutenant Grady wrote. "Due to the intense heat, the men appeared to become exhausted dragging the heavy field piece over railroad tracks and through soft earth; . . . I personally noticed this petty officer . . . assisting and making light of the difficulties." [61] Smith was uniquely fitted to instruct in the proper handling of the gun. A career man who had been up and down the ranks several times, he was the only member of the *New Hampshire* artillery who had ever even seen a 3-inch field piece fired. The effects of the first round, which had been gotten off without his assistance, had been almost as dangerous to the gunners as to their target. The spade supposed to secure the piece had not been fully imbedded in the ground and instead of recoiling on its carriage, the whole gun bucked backwards, bowling over the gunners and scattering the shells.[62]

Ensign R. B. Hammes of the *South Carolina* artillery was also singled out for praise. "His work was superb," Lieutenant Ellyson recorded. "A puff of smoke would come from some window and five seconds later he would put a 3″ shot through that place, which was the end of whoever happened to be there and not once during the day did he miss a shot." [63] One of Hammes' hits shattered the ammonia coils in the ice plant; the fumes dislodged the enemy as effectively as the shells.[64]

Reaching the outskirts of the city south of Calle Díaz Aragon, the Second Regiment turned up three parallel streets to Avenida Libertad and occupied the Military Barracks. Captain Anderson established his headquarters in the Mexican Commandancia Militar. A *South Carolina* company and a gun were left at the Barracks under Lieutenant Ellyson while the remainder of the battalion, led by Lieutenant Adolphus Staton, and the regimental artillery continued towards the sand hills. The artillery halted beside the railway track near the Waters-Pierce Refinery; the bluejackets advanced a mile further down the track. Later they were joined by troops from the *New Hampshire*.[65]

"Opposed," as Richard Harding Davis wrote, "by an enemy they could not see, in the streets of a strange city where every house was an ambush and every church tower had a fighting top," the bluejackets developed a tendency to shoot first and ask questions later.[66] Admiral Badger commented, "I rather think that as increasing numbers of our men were killed or wounded, it fared rather badly with those discovered with arms in hand on the spot from which the shooting came." [67] For its part, *La Opinión* protested, "The precautions observed by the American forces in order to stop possible aggressions have reached, in some of these cases, the very limit which legally could be permitted armies of occupation belonging to a civilized nation. . . . There were patrols which exercised their functions to the very extremity, pointing their guns at passers-by, saying 'Hands up,' which many of our inhabitants did not understand and subjecting them to death for unjustifiable lack of knowledge of a strange language." [68]

Ensign Roy Dudley, who questioned the morality of the landing, remembered the difficulties he had maintaining fire control over his section. Moving along the waterfront, his men suddenly began to blaze away at a small, brick building. After he had succeeded in stopping the firing, Dudley opened the door and was horrified to find a large family of Mexicans, with many small children, huddled inside. All were unarmed and obviously innocent of any sniping. Miraculously, no one had been wounded. "After that," Dudley declared, "I had better fire discipline." [69]

An incident with more serious consequences occurred shortly after dark, when the *Minnesota* battalion became involved in a brisk firefight with a *New Hampshire* outpost. Landing south of Pier Four around 5:45 P.M., the *Minnesota*'s troops were sent to join the Second Regiment. "I reported to the staff of Captain Anderson," the *Minnesota* commander wrote, "and received orders to march to the 'end' of the Alameda,* turn right one block, and support the artillery section stationed there under Lieutenant Grady.

"I proceeded to the circle at the south end of the Alameda, went

* Parade ground.

column right, and had just sent the first section of the first company into line of skirmishers when two shots came from cars to the left and one from right ahead. The order was given to 'Lie down' and all of the front column obeyed. One gun was discharged by accident while lying down and other shots were fired by someone in the front. The order to 'Cease firing' was given immediately, but several men got excited and fired at the flashes and drowned the orders. Ensign Haines blew his whistle but it could not be heard. A large number of shots were fired at our battalion from Calle Laguna through a picket fence across a pasture lot. Either at this time or when fired upon a minute later, one man was wounded in the leading company 'A' and one officer and three men in the last company 'C.' A man in the second company 'B' was also wounded, but it has been established that the man shot himself accidentally while lying down. The last company, special details, and two squads of company 'C' rushed back to the circle at the end of the Alameda and took station behind the concrete seats.

"By this time I, with the help of Ensign Haines, Ensign Wolfard, and Ensign Howell, had stopped the firing of the first two companies. Two other men and myself went ahead and found a *New Hampshire* picket stationed as outpost one block outside of Calle Laguna. While talking to this picket the firing was resumed by the men in Calle Laguna against our men in the circle of the Alameda, at which time I heard a 3-inch field gun fired. Our men in the circle returned the fire but Company 'A' and 'B' did not fire. I returned on the run to the Alameda and advanced to the circle ordering 'Cease firing,' but could not stop all the firing until I reached the circle. I then formed companies as soon as possible, leaving the wounded to be attended by the ambulance party and carried out the orders received at this moment from Lieutenant Commander Johnston of Captain Anderson's staff, to retire one block north along the Alameda and then turn west on Calle Laguna to the railroad, where I took station supporting the guns." [70]

Colonel John J. Lejeune, commanding the Marines aboard the *Hancock,* came ashore around 11:00 A.M. Fletcher put him in charge of all Marine forces in Veracruz. Improvising a brigade organization, Lejeune ordered Lieutenant Colonel C. G. Long to disembark the *Hancock* regiment and prepare to advance along the area between Juárez and Francisco Canal, moving west from Independencia. Neville would remain in command of the first regiment. [71] It was a good plan, but it was too late. At that moment, the forces already ashore were completing the occupation of Veracruz.

ELEVEN: TIMES WERE DIFFICULT FOR ALL

Bulletin No. 25   *April 25*

To the Governor of the State—

The Governor of the State of Veracruz informs me today by tele-graph that which follows:

General Rubio Navarrete marched from—[?] to Veracruz in which there are 165 men of the Government under Colonel Vigil. The invading forces disembarked 7,000 infantry and marines and 8 bat-teries—advance guards to Vergora 4 kilometers from Veracruz. Americans do not give any signs of taking offensive. Jefes Politicos advise me that there are no disembarkations of troops in any part. All of which I send you for your information.

Minister of Gobernacion
ALEOCER
Intercepted Mexican radio transmission [1]

At noon," wrote Consul Canada, "it was possible with some risk to go out into the streets. The Plaza presented a gruesome sight, as many dead Mexicans were still lying on the sidewalks." [2] Collecting these bodies was among the first tasks to which Rush put his men after the firing ended. Everyone assumed that Maass would counterattack upon receipt of reinforcements, which made the rapid restoration of order in Veracruz a matter of utmost importance: the brigade must secure its base. While the Marines and Second Seaman Regiment entrenched their lines along the sand hills, the troops inside the city began to clear away the wreckage of the fight.[3]

Collier's correspondent Arthur Ruhl managed to get ashore in the midafternoon. The city was in a turmoil. "People were trying to get into their houses, to do a thousand little necessary things," he wrote, "and puzzled bluejackets, under orders, and with nerves strung to the breaking point by the knowledge that they might at any time be shot from ambush, were stopping them. One very respectable-looking old gentleman with his grown son was trying to get from the street corner to his house a few doors away. The sentry would not let them by, and, searching the old man, found two bottles in his inside pocket. They were medicine, he said, for his daughter, frightened to death by the firing, but the conscientious young bluejacket, thinking, doubtless, they were poison, hurled them to the pavement.

"One broke. The son, stooping excitedly to pick up the other to show that it contained only ether, contrived to throw the contents into his eyes. Howling with pain, he dashed round in a circle, the old gentleman raised despairing arms, women peeping through barred windows began to wring their hands. I finally got both father and son to their house. The son, pointing out each in turn, explained that they were all really and truly the same family—that his wife, this mother . . . , and so on.

"I took off my hat, but they would not hear of such condescension and insisted I keep it on. I explained that it was hot and I preferred it off—no, I must 'cover myself'—and the old gentleman proceeded to do it for me. It was all very quaint and amusing—yet not so amusing either. A few moments later the battalion from our ship marched up Independencia . . . and almost at the very corner of the old gentleman and his ether bottle, Boswell, chief gunner's mate, was killed by a shot from a doorway." [4]

Fletcher had been able to avoid a wholesale bombardment; the 5-inch guns on the *Chester* and the *San Francisco* were the heaviest used against the city, and they had fired only at selected targets. Nevertheless, Veracruz bore many scars of battle. "Everywhere are the marks of bullets along the once-peaceful streets," observed an American woman; "quaint cornices chipped; electric street globes destroyed; pink façades looking as if there was a design in white where the shots had taken off the color." [5] Barricades thrown up the preceding afternoon and power lines broken by the shelling made some streets almost impassable.

The most concentrated destruction had occurred at the Naval Academy, where "every conceivable disorder was evident—cadets' uniforms lay with sheets, pillows, books, broken furniture, heaps of mortar [and] plaster." [6] Newsmen poked through the debris, looking for material for human-interest stories. The luckiest found a series of love letters, excerpts of which would be included in his next dispatch. In one room, a pile of blood-soaked pillows, mattresses and sheets had been thrown over an ankle-deep litter of collars, gloves, letters, brushes, combs and the like.[7] On the blackboard, someone had chalked: *Mueran los Gringos*.[8] Nearby, Jack London noted another inscription: "Captured by the USS *New Hampshire*, April 22, 1914." [9]

"The Mexicans killed the first day . . . were still lying where they had fallen," Ensign Lowry recalled. After twenty-four hours in the tropical sun, some were in a bad state.[10] Several collection points were established and unclaimed corpses were carried there to be buried or burned before dark. Medical considerations made it imperative to dispose of the dead in the most expedient manner. In the sector assigned the *New Hampshire* battalion, corpses were stacked on creosote-impregnated railroad ties and set afire. No one present ever forgot the sight or the smell of it. Some men took surreptitious snapshots, despite orders that none should be made. Other photographs were taken of bluejackets posed in the big game hunter's classic stance, rifles grounded at their sides, with the bodies of snipers replacing the lions and tigers usually featured in the foreground of such pictures.[11]

The exact number of Mexican casualties will never be known. Twenty-seven bodies were removed from the *portales* of the Plaza Constitución alone. Captain Rush's initial estimate was that 230 Mexicans had been killed and at least as many wounded. The *Washington Post* correspondent wrote of "wounded by the scores . . . found in doorways and out-of-the-way corners where they had crawled for refuge." [12] The First Seaman Regiment, assisted by the Mexican White Cross, was officially credited with burying ninety-four bodies, fifty-eight of which the *Florida*'s First Company laid in one long trench. Twenty-five corpses were interred in a mass grave near the Fiscal Wharf, and two others had been buried near the Terminal Station on the night of April 21/22. The most painstaking attempt to determine the Mexican losses was made by a Navy surgeon on April 23–24. Basing his report upon a census of the city's hospitals, the doctor arrived at a total of 126 killed and 195 wounded, an aggregate of 321. But as he failed to take into account the considerable number that were buried without passing through a treatment facility, there is little doubt that his figure was too low.[13]

When their last casualty had been suffered, the American forces would have lost seventeen killed and sixty-three wounded.[14]

Admiral Fletcher came ashore at 1:55 P.M. to confer with Captain Rush. Returning to the *Prairie* around 4:15, he asked Admiral Badger to request that the Naval Brigade be relieved by the Army at the earliest practicable moment.[15] "Relations between Mexico and the United States and conditions existing in Mexico are such that in all probability we will be unable to relinquish military control [of

The Plaza Constitución, showing the *Florida* battalion outside the Municipal Palace arcades, where the Provost Marshal later set up office

Mexicans lining up for provisions after the fighting

Veracruz] for some time," Fletcher observed, and he warned that the prolonged detachment of large numbers of seamen to shore duty must adversely affect the efficiency of their ships.[16] His argument was incontrovertible, and on April 23, the War Department ordered Brigadier General Frederick Funston, commanding the Second Division at Texas City, Texas, to embark for Mexico. Funston sailed with the Fifth Reinforced Brigade * the next day.

The municipal government of Veracruz had collapsed the instant the first shot was fired. That was to be expected. What was alarming was that it showed no signs of reviving now that the affray had ended. Into the vacuum, Ensign Paul Foster was surprised to find himself thrust.[17] The manner in which law enforcement in Veracruz came to rest with Foster illustrates the adage that war is the province of chance.

When Foster's men had searched the Municipal Palace for snipers, someone had discovered a supply of detailed maps of Veracruz. "None of us on the *Utah* had ever seen a map of Veracruz," Foster related, and it occurred to him that these maps would prove very helpful. "I immediately dispatched messengers with rolls of these maps with orders to deliver them to any battalion and regimental commanders they could find and to inform them that additional copies, if needed, could be supplied by Ensign Foster of the *Utah*, then occupying the Municipal Palace. This action had the most unexpected results; somehow the recipients of the maps erroneously concluded that I had been appointed Provost Marshal with headquarters in the Municipal Palace. Soon messengers began arriving with requests for more maps and information and within a few hours we began receiving prisoners for safekeeping. . . . Many of the prisoners who were turned over to me were accused of being snipers. Usually they were in custody of a junior officer and carried instructions to the effect that I was to give them a court-martial and shoot them." [18]

As Foster had neither the "inclination nor the authority" [19] to obey such instructions, it was not long before he had accumulated more prisoners than he had a place to put. To make room, he released the criminal prisoners he had inherited in the jail to the rear of the Municipal Palace. After the cells had been filled, new arrivals were confined in the offices on the upper floors of the Palace itself. Finally, Foster formed the prisoners into fatigue details and sent them out under guard to remove the dirt and debris from the Plaza Constitu-

---

* Consisting of the 4th, 7th, 19th, and 28th Infantry Regiments.

ción. By nightfall, he had over two hundred of these Mexicans on his hands.[20]

"I reported the situation that was then developing to my battalion commander, Lieutenant Castle," Foster wrote. "He told me simply to carry on and use my best judgment. By Thursday morning I was receiving requests for working parties from all over the city as well as requests to get the street cars running, to get the power and light service in operation, and a score of minor requests made on the assumption that I was Provost Marshal and as such had the unlimited authority and manpower to accomplish all of the near-miracles requested. Additionally, scores of Mexicans began coming to the Municipal Building and were referred to my office, which was a table and chair on the sidewalk under the portales, . . . with the kind of requests that I assume the citizens of Veracruz had for years been making to . . . authorities in the Municipal Building. I remember granting permission to hold marriages, to hold funerals, to go fishing, and acting as a municipal judge in the settling of a wide variety of disputes between Mexican citizens and, of course, all complaints on the part of Mexicans against our bluejackets and Marines." [21]

While ashore, Admiral Fletcher issued a proclamation urging merchants to resume business as usual, confident of every protection.[22] Reviving the commerce of the city would be prerequisite to persuading the *Veracruzanos* to return to their normal occupations. The hotel and cantina owners complied at once. The proprietors of retail stores were more cautious, but as hours passed they began to reopen their doors. A free food distribution point was set up for the people, many of whom had gone hungry since the landing, and late in the afternoon, the *Florida*'s band gave the customary concert in the Plaza Constitución.[23] By then, things seemed to be going so smoothly that a correspondent ventured to predict, "Tomorrow Veracruz will almost be her sleepy self again." [24]

In reality, Veracruz was still far from her sleepy self. An undercurrent of resistance survived. One of these incidents in which this spirit was revealed had occurred while the Mexican casualties were being collected. A bluejacket sentry on the corner of Independencia and Zaragoza observed a party of Mexicans approaching the intersection. Two men were carrying a stretcher on which lay a body draped by a bedsheet; a third man walked ahead with a White Cross flag. As they passed, the sentry noticed something curiously like a rifle barrel sticking out from under the sheet. Springing forward, he snatched the sheet away. On the stretcher was an able-bodied Mexican soldier with a loaded rifle at his side. Thanks to the sentry's quick wits, the Mexicans were made prisoner before anyone was harmed.[25]

Other acts of hostility were less covert. The scattered firing which had persisted through the afternoon grew heavier after dark. When the *Michigan* battalion, landing at dusk, marched down Independencia to join the Second Regiment at the Military Barracks, it was fired upon intermittently all along its route. Before the battalion reached its destination, a chief petty officer had been killed and the advance guard claimed to have hit at least five snipers.[26]

The firing did not die down until around ten o'clock the next morning, by which time a Marine from the *Vermont* had been killed and an *Arkansas* bluejacket wounded. Even then, the sound of an occasional shot could be heard in the city. Shortly before noon, Ship's Cook Revetti of the *Michigan,* at work on the Sanitary Wharf, saw an armed man in a window of a building from which there had been some shooting during the night. Ducking behind a water tank, Revetti drew his service revolver and killed the sniper at a range in excess of one hundred yards, a feat of marksmanship his battalion commander deemed worthy of inclusion in his official report.[27]

Admiral Fletcher transferred his headquarters to the Hotel Terminal at 9:00 A.M. Thursday, April 23. Once ashore, he embarked upon an earnest attempt to restore the municipal government of Veracruz. A rude shock awaited him. In a lengthy conference with the mayor, the collector of customs, and the chief of police, Fletcher discovered that these officials were unwilling to return to their duties while Veracruz remained under American control. A law dating from the French invasion of 1862 made it a federal offense for a Mexican citizen to hold office under a foreign power occupying Mexican soil. "The attitude of these Mexicans was amicable . . . but restrained," Fletcher reported, "and no definite promise could be obtained that [they] would . . . lend their cooperation in reestablishing the old order of affairs." [28] This meant that unless he could persuade the native authorities to change their minds, Fletcher would be forced into the administrative nightmare of establishing a military government.

That afternoon, in Mexico City, Edith O'Shaughnessy was attending a ceremony at which her presence seemed unusual: the wedding of Major Victoriano Huerta, the president's son, and Señorita Concepción Hernandez. On the steps of the cathedral, Mrs. O'Shaughnessy paused to embrace the elder Señora Huerta, for whom she felt a real affection. As their eyes met, Edith O'Shaughnessy burst into tears. Then she turned, still weeping, and hurried to the limousine in which her escort, naval Flag Lieutenant Stephen C. Rowan, sat waiting. In the car, Mrs. O'Shaughnessy apologized for having lost her composure. "Don't worry," Rowan reassured her; "the Mexicans will understand the tribute, and all your sadness and regret." [29] The last three days had been the most trying of Edith O'Shaughnessy's life.

The State Department had not deigned to advise Nelson O'Shaughnessy of the decision to land at Veracruz. He did not learn of the fighting until the afternoon of April 21, when he was informed by the Mexican government—"a most embarrassing way to get the news," [30] as Mrs. O'Shaughnessy said. Since then, the American Embassy had existed in a virtual state of siege. Weeks earlier, as the horizon had begun to darken, O'Shaughnessy had laid in a supply of arms and ammunition. Captain Burnside, commanding the Marine Guard, had taught the diplomatic staff how to work the two machine guns O'Shaughnessy procured and Admiral Fletcher sent Flag Lieutenant Rowan to assist. Cradock detailed Lieutenant Strawbensie to act in a similar capacity at the British Embassy, and the French cruiser commander did the same.[31] By the time negotiations finally foundered, the diplomatic community had begun, almost subconsciously, to think in terms of the defense of the legations at Peking.

Nothing quite so dramatic occurred. Huerta appeared at the American Embassy late on April 21, not long after O'Shaughnessy had received word of the landing. "You have seized our port," he told O'Shaughnessy. "You have the right to take it if you can, and we have the right to try to prevent you. *Sua Excelencia el Señor Presidente* Wilson has declared war unnecessarily, on a people that ask only to be let alone, to follow out their evolution in their own way, though it may not seem to you a good way." [32] Huerta showed no bitterness towards the O'Shaughnessys, and left them convinced that he was still their friend. Another Mexican friend, Eduardo Iturbide, Governor of the Federal District, sent a guard of one hundred mounted gendarmes, and a volunteer "auto-squad," composed of the more martially-inclined American residents, was permitted to patrol the streets around the Embassy that evening. Demonstrators waving Mexican flags and shouting "things not flattering to *los Gringos"* appeared on schedule, but their demeanor was not unduly alarming.[33] Though stones were thrown through a few windows and the United States shield was torn off the Embassy gates, the situation seemed so much less menacing by then that Mrs. O'Shaughnessy, who had spent the afternoon thinking: "We might all be massacred," found the crowd rather inoffensive.[34]

More spirited rioting took place elsewhere in the city. Porter's Hotel, "The Meeting Place for Americans," was assailed by a mob which, finding the plate-glass windows protected by iron shutters, forced its way into the lobby to smash them. An American-owned antique store was looted; the American Club was threatened by a mob harangued by a member of the Mexican Chamber of Deputies; and the office of the *Mexican Herald,* the capital's English-language newspaper, was stoned. "Practically all the windows in the front of the building were broken by the stones and half bricks were loudly called for petroleum witch to found made the rooms," stammered the *Mexican Herald,* badly shaken. "The crowd set fier to the building but has this was not forthcoming they grew tired of waiting and pased on." [35]

Other demonstrations followed on April 22. A mob of women paraded through the city, methodically trampling a large American flag, and in the evening a bronze statue of George Washington, presented to the people of Mexico City by the American colony, was wrenched from its pedestal and dragged behind automobiles to the foot of the Juárez Memorial. A bust of Hidalgo was set in its place.[36]

Nor were the disturbances confined to the capital. The American Consulate at Mazatlán was stoned and the houses of Americans pillaged. At Monterrey, civilians led by a Federal army officer ransacked the Consulate, kidnapped the consul, and burned all the American flags on the premises.[37] Public opinion was inflamed and exhilarated by the wildly inaccurate reports of the Mexican press. In the days after the landing, Mexican newspaper readers were informed that Veracruz's defenders had sunk several American battleships; that General Joaquín Maass, the brother of the Maass of Veracruz, was leading an army of 20,000 men into Texas, and that Pancho Villa had captured El Paso.[38] Provincial officials encouraged mob action by posting patriotic proclamations, a fair sample of which was copied by a fleeing American engineer:

To arms, citizens of Córboda! Kill, yes, and throw to the buzzards the meat of the damned Yankees, who, in cowardly fashion, have invaded our sacred soil of Mexico; God and Justice are on our side.

We will imitate the example of our forefathers in defending the country until we conquer or die. Kill in whatever way you can; this will be our revenge! Viva Mexico! [39]

Such admonitions made a sharp contrast to the Federal government's laconic communiqué:

TO THE REPUBLIC

In the port of Veracruz we are sustaining with arms the national honor.

The offense the Yankee government is committing against a free people, such as this Republic is, has always been, and will ever be, will pass into history—which will give to Mexico and to the government of the United States the place each merits.

V. HUERTA [40]

The worst outbreaks occurred in Tampico, where anti-American feeling had become increasingly virulent in the weeks since the now famous Incident. On the afternoon of April 21, General Zaragoza proclaimed a *levée-en-masse* and made no effort to curb the demonstrations which inevitably ensued. Consul Miller, whose communications from the Consulate were relayed to Admiral Mayo via the radio on the yacht *Wakiva* at the Huasteca Oil Company dock, promptly asked Mayo to reenter the Pánuco River to receive American refugees. Mayo declined, stating, "Any move on our part now would increase disturbances and aggravate situation." [41] Then, in the midst of another message from Miller, the *Wakiva*'s wave length went dead. Officers from the Mexican gunboat *Zaragoza* had cut the telephone wire from the Consulate and ordered the *Wakiva* to cease transmission, but Mayo leaped to a more dire conclusion: the rioters were running wild. He must enter the Pánuco at once.

Though Mayo was prepared to use force, he asked Captain H. M. Doughty of HMS *Essex* to inform General Zaragoza that his purpose was peaceful. Doughty was certain that the Mexicans would interpret the appearance of Mayo's ships as the commencement of hostilities. Would not Mayo let him try to bring the refugees out first? Mayo agreed and, assisted by German officers from the *Dresden*, Doughty proceeded to commandeer every private vessel in sight. Then he led them, bedecked with British and German flags, into the Pánuco. The Mexicans allowed the convoy to pass, and by dark Doughty had embarked all the foreigners who wished to leave Tampico. Consul Miller was the last, delaying his own departure until he was satisfied that everyone else had been taken aboard. [42]

Huerta called at the American Embassy for the last time on the evening of April 22. Mrs. O'Shaughnessy went to meet him. His dress was informal, which seemed to her "suitable to events." [43]

"I led him into the drawing room," she wrote, "where, to the accompaniment of stomping hoofs outside, of changing arms and footsteps coming and going, we had a strange and moving conversation. I could not . . . speak the endless regret that was in my heart for the official part we had been obliged to play in the hateful drama enacted by us to his country's undoing. He greeted me calmly—'Señora, how do you do? I fear you have had many annoyances.' Then he sat back, quietly, in a big arm chair, impersonal and inscrutable. I answered as calmly as I could that the times were difficult for all, but that we were most appreciative of what he had done for our personal safety and that of our nationals, and asked him if there was nothing we could do for him. He gave me a long, introverted, and at the same time piercing look, and, after a pause, answered:

" 'Nothing, Señora. All that is done I must do for myself. Here I remain. The moment has not come for me to go. Nothing but Death could remove me now.' " [44]

Chargé O'Shaughnessy entered the room a second later, and Huerta explained the object of his visit. Under the circumstances, he could not allow the Embassy to remain in operation. O'Shaughnessy would be expelled. A special train, escorted by troops under General Corona, the Chief of Staff, was scheduled to carry the Embassy staff to Veracruz. It would leave Mexico City at 9:30 in the evening of April 23. At the moment, Huerta continued, he must ask O'Shaughnessy to surrender his arsenal. O'Shaughnessy could scarcely refuse and, as the conversation continued, a detail of well-mannered Mexican soldiers removed the weapons—two machine guns, 250 rifles and 85,000 rounds of ammunition. When their official business had been concluded, Huerta told the O'Shaughnessys that their invitation to his son's wedding, issued weeks earlier, was still good. Their presence would do his family great honor.

At the doorway, Huerta put his hand on O'Shaughnessy's shoulder. "I hold no rancor towards *Sua Excelencia el Señor Presidente* Wilson," he said. "He has not understood." [45]

"It was the first and last time I ever heard him speak the President's name," Mrs. O'Shaughnessy wrote. "I gave him my hand . . . and knew that this was indeed the end. I think he realized that my heart was warm and my sympathies outrushing to beautiful, agonizing Mexico, for as he stood at the door he suddenly turned and made me a deep reverence. Then taking N[elson].'s arm, he went out into the starry, perfumed night." [46]

The Embassy train pulled out of Mexico City shortly before midnight, April 23. After a sixteen-hour ride across the sweltering, hostile countryside, it came to a halt at the rail break at Templadora, six kilometers from Veracruz. Chargé O'Shaughnessy stepped outside to investigate. Mrs. O'Shaughnessy remained in the stateroom. Just as she was becoming anxious at the length of time that had elapsed since her husband's departure, the door opened to admit "big, agreeable, competent" Captain Huse, Admiral Fletcher's chief of staff.

"Mrs. O'Shaughnessy," he said, "I am glad to see you safely arrived and welcome you to our lines."

Actually, Huse was anticipating. The O'Shaughnessys had to hike the mile-long break in the railroad and ride a few miles further before they were within American lines, but the journey was accomplished without incident. When her excitement began to subside, Mrs. O'Shaughnessy addressed Captain Huse: "Are we at war with Mexico?"

"I don't know," he answered. "They say not; but when one armed force opposes another armed force, and many are killed, we are rather of the opinion that it is war." [47]

TWELVE: A TALE OF THREE CITIES

In Washington

Mediation, meditation,

Parleying, procrastination,

Hesitation, pacification,

Anything for mollification.

In Mexico

Indignation, detestation,

Agitation, lamentation,

Laceration, destination,

Conflagration, strangulation,

Threatening assassination,

Ever-spreading desolation.

In Veracruz

Perspiration, heat prostration,

Cuss words and exasperation,

Jubilation, aviation,

Vaccination, sanitation,

Occupation, expectation.

N.A.J.
From the *Mexican Herald* [1]

Explaining the situation to Edith O'Shaughnessy at Templadora, Captain Huse believed that the bloodshed at Veracruz
meant war. His opinion was shared throughout the United States.
The first news of the fighting had been released to the Washington
press services at 6:00 P.M., April 21. The next morning, the nation

awoke to headlines typified by those of *The New York Times:*

MARINES, AIDED BY PRAIRIE'S SHELLS, TAKE VERACRUZ; LOSE FOUR
KILLED, TWENTY WOUNDED; KILL 200 MEXICANS; LANDING ORDERED BY
WILSON TO STOP IMPORT OF ARMS; STILL BATTLING AT 10 P.M.

The country responded with a wave of patriotic demonstrations. In
Topeka, Kansas, a group of high-school boys compelled a dozen,
presumably Mexican railroad workers to salute the American flag; [2]
Teddy Roosevelt threatened to raise, not merely a regiment, but a
brigade of Rough Riders; [3] Lawrence College students held a torch-
light parade through Appleton, Wisconsin, beating drums and
chanting "Avenge the flag!"; [4] the Egbert J. Jones Camp, United
Confederate Veterans, of Huntsville, Alabama—"100 strong and of
average age 73, still game and fit for the fight of our lives"—wired
the White House to offer their services to their country; [5] and near
City Hall, in New York, police were forced to rescue two I.W.W.*
orators who had called Fletcher's men murderers, from an outraged
crowd shouting "Lynch them!" and "Kill the reds!" [6]

Though the public generally was firm for intervention, a few
sturdy souls challenged the consensus. Their outlook was expressed
by Cyrus L. Sulzberger, a prominent New York businessman. In a
letter to the New York *Evening Post,* Sulzberger attacked the premise
that the people must back up the admiral. "Why must we back up
the admiral?" he demanded. "Who charged him with the responsibility of our international relations? The people of the United
States elected Woodrow Wilson to attend to that job. . . . How can
any demands made [by Mayo] bind us? We are as free to reject them
as any principal is free to disavow the unauthorized action of his
subordinate." As long as the backing-up theory was followed, said
Sulzberger, "there is no reason why we should not get into war with
every country having a seaport." [7]

At the other end of the spectrum were those who wished to
extend intervention to annexation. Colonel McCormick's *Chicago
Tribune* ran a map of the United States, with Utah, Arizona,
California, New Mexico, and Nevada shaded to show "What We
Got from Mexico After the Other War" and asked: "Aren't all the
people in this territory, both American and Mexican, better off
because we annexed this region?" [8] At Philadelphia, the Ward Line
steamer *Morro Castle* was chartered to transport a second regiment
of Marines to Veracruz, and governors moved hurriedly to put their
National Guards on a war footing.[9] Editors across the land advised

* International Workers of the World.

their readers that armed conflict, under whatever name, was a certainty, and warned them to expect a long and bitter struggle.[10]

The European press was inclined to agree, though it viewed the prospect with even more misgivings. To English commentators, "The Mexican Muddle" exemplified American diplomacy at its worst. "The war into which the United States has wandered in a casual, somnambulistic sort of way, threatens to be a very bad sort of war, indeed," observed the *London Standard*. "The events of the last few days . . . show the impossibility of conducting hostilities on the limited liability principle. A philosopher from Mars . . . might appreciate the distinction drawn by the American President between war against Mexico and a person named Huerta, but to expect the Mexicans themselves to look on the matter with complete detachment is to show an extraordinary lack of imagination." [11]

Unassailable as was the logic upon which these predictions were based, events were to prove them in error. There would be no war. Despite the bloodshed at Veracruz, the Democratic majority in the United States Senate forced the passage of the original version of the resolution Wilson had requested authorizing him to intervene in Mexico. "It is never too late to declare war," said Senator Shively, acting chairman of the Foreign Relations Committee, in support of the resolution. "It can easily become too late . . . to preserve peace." [12] Opposing the measure, the Republicans contended that Veracruz had increased the need for the broader resolution Lodge had prepared. "We learn tonight that Veracruz has fallen," said Senator Elihu Root; "that four American marines [sic] lie dead in that city; that twenty-one lie suffering from wounds. Is there nothing but this dispute about . . . a salute to justify the sacrifice of these American lives? It is intervention technically but it is war in its essence that we are to justify tonight. Men will die . . . because of the action we approve tonight. . . . American children will go through life fatherless because of the action that we . . . approve tonight, and when these children, grown to manhood . . . learn for what cause their fathers died, are they to find that it was about a quarrel as to the number of guns or the form and ceremony of a salute . . . ? Oh, Mr. President, how inadequate! How can we justify ourselves if we have no justification but that? . . . But, Mr. President, that is not all. There is a justification. . . . It is that lying behind this insult to our flag . . . are years of violence and anarchy in Mexico; lying behind it are hundreds of American lives sacrificed, millions of American property destroyed, and thousands of Americans reduced to poverty. . . . Lying behind it is the condition which

makes it impossible to secure protection for American life and property in that country by diplomatic means. . . . We omit from the
resolution all reference to . . . the justification for action." [13]

Root's speech forms a reasonable critique. Wilson's curious, legal-
istic insistence upon advancing the Tampico Incident as the single
cause for intervention compromised his conduct throughout the
encounter. The fact that the United States had very real grievances
in Mexico, upon which a strong case could be made for intervention, was obscured by the astonishing appearance that Wilson was
willing to go to war over a disagreement as to the precise method of
firing a twenty-one-gun salute. This was as obvious to astute contemporary observers as it is today. Yet the response to the Senate roll
call was strictly along party lines,[14] and at 2:25 A.M., Thursday,
April 23, Wilson's resolution was approved, unchanged in any important respect:

> In view of the facts presented by the President of the United States
> in his address, delivered to the Congress in joint session on the 20th day
> of April, 1914, in regard to certain affronts and indignities committed
> against the United States in Mexico, be it
>
> Resolved, That the President is justified in the employment of the
> armed forces of the United States to enforce his demands for unequivocal
> amends for affronts and indignities committed against the United States;
> be it further
>
> Resolved, that the United States disclaims any hostility to the Mexican
> people or any purpose to make war upon them.[15]

The House accepted the measure with a minimum of debate
when it convened later in the morning, and a copy was sent to
Wilson for his signature. Brought face to face with the realities of
war, the legislators were considerably less exuberant than they had
been when Wilson had addressed them four days earlier. "There
was no suggestion of either patriotic enthusiasm or a thirst for war
in the deliberation of the House," the *New York Herald* reported.
"Denunciation of war by Representative James R. Mann, of Illi-
nois, and a patriotic appeal by Representative Henry D. Flood of
Virginia, telling of 'unfurled battle flags,' met with the same cold
reception." [16]

Regardless of its shortcomings, the resolution possessed what
Wilson regarded as the cardinal virtue of an escape clause. It did
not commit the United States to a definite course of action in
Mexico. A front-page profile in the *Washington Post* for April 23
was titled: "President Sad, Disillusioned and Weary," and the adjec-
tives were apt. Everyone familiar with the Washington scene real-

ized that Wilson was trying desperately to brake the drift towards war. Visiting the White House that afternoon, Henry Cabot Lodge found Wilson "very much disturbed" and came away convinced that all he wanted was "to get out of the trouble in any way possible." [17]

In addition to the revulsion Wilson felt towards more killing, he was worried by the attitude of the Constitutionalists. Contrary to his expectations, Carranza did not applaud the occupation of Veracruz. In fact, the First Chief made it uncompromisingly clear that should the American forces advance into the interior, his men would help the Federals fight them.[18] Of the Constitutionalist leaders, only Pancho Villa, the least reputable of the lot, professed himself pleased. "Why," he laughed, throwing his arm around George Carruthers, another of Wilson's innumerable agents, "all Europe would laugh at us if we went to war with you. They would say 'that little drunken Huerta has drawn them into a tangle at last.' . . . Honest, I hope the Americans bottle up Veracruz so tight they can't even get water into it. Your administration is doing something it would have taken us a long time to accomplish, if we could have accomplished it at all." [19]

Fortunately for Wilson's purposes, a way out was forthcoming. On April 24, the ministers of the ABC Powers—Argentina, Brazil, and Chile—joined in an offer to mediate the dispute between Mexico and the United States. Wilson accepted it at once.[20] Orders were sent to the forces at Veracruz not to undertake offensive operations.

At that moment, offensive operations were among the least of Admiral Fletcher's concerns. On the whole, the situation at Veracruz was well in hand. A Third Seaman Regiment, commanded by Captain Roy Simpson, had been formed from the battleships *Louisiana, Michigan, Minnesota,* and *North Dakota,* and the Naval Division—for such it had been renamed—now numbered over 5,800 men: 3,300 bluejackets and 2,500 Marines. Twenty U.S. naval vessels lay at Veracruz and nineteen off Tampico. Entrenched lines had been thrown out as far as the Veracruz-Vergara Road, and Marine battalions guarded the pumping stations at Tejar and El Garto, which supplied Veracruz with water.[21]

A regular routine had been established for the troops within the city: reveille at 6:00 A.M., roll call at 6:15, police call from 6:20, breakfast at 8:00, guard mount at 9:00, a band concert at 10:00, battalion formation, inspection and drill from 10:30 and dinner at 12:00; unit activities from 1:00 P.M., dress parade at 4:00, another concert at 5:00, supper at 6:30, and tattoo and taps at 9:00.[22] "The men look happy, proud and pleased . . . in the novel excitement of

. . . conquest," wrote Mrs. O'Shaughnessy.[23] Down near the rail-roads tracks, off-duty Marines were teaching the Mexican children how to play baseball,[24] while a company of bluejackets had trained a snappy, green parrot to cry "Look out for the snipers!"[25] Best of all, from Fletcher's viewpoint, Funston's brigade was on the way.

But beneath this well-ordered exterior, Fletcher had problems aplenty. The apparent impossibility of aiding American citizens in the interior, of whose mistreatment Fletcher was receiving greatly exaggerated reports, was acutely distressing. Two even more immediate irritants were the continued sniping and the refusal of the Mexican officials to participate in a government for Veracruz. And aside from matters of such magnitude, there were a host of petty difficulties to whose solution Fletcher was forced, if only in passing, to give his attention. Thus, in the opening days of the occupation, his headquarters issued orders which allowed author-ized correspondents to carry sidearms for their own protection; enjoined junior officers to exercise tact in evicting the occupants of buildings being searched for snipers; granted permission for Chief of Police Villavenecio, who, "in the execution of the duties of his office, . . . has naturally aroused the enmity of a class of people . . . now at large to carry firearms . . . night and day"; and apologized to the incensed French consul for the failure of an American forma-tion to return his salute.[26]

Everything imaginable was done to suppress the sniping. Armed sentries were stationed at each intersection twenty-four hours a day and a vigorous patrol system was initiated. Still the sniping per-sisted. During the night of April 23/24, a *Michigan* outpost at los Cocos exchanged shots with five men who appeared in the brush outside its lines and several patrols were fired on in the city.[27]

The sniping ceased at sunrise April 24, when the Mexicans began to hold their funerals. Throughout the day, processions wound through the streets of Veracruz to the Campo Santo Cemetery, just south of the American entrenchments. Late in the afternoon, a bluejacket reported that he had seen three suspiciously large proces-sions set out from the same house. The third was followed to Campo Santo. As the cortege neared the canvas-covered grave, the sailors rushed forward and pried open the coffin, revealing a pile of new Mausers. Others tore the tarpaulin off the grave. It contained three Mexican soldiers, all very much alive, and stacks of arms and ammu-nition brought out by the preceding processions. After the arms were recovered, the grave was given a legitimate purpose.[28]

Firing broke out again after nightfall. One of Rush's patrols fought a brisk skirmish at the corner of Zaragoza and Francisco Canal, in the heart of the city, and in the course of the evening two snipers were killed and another was wounded and captured.[29]

The next morning, April 25, the British, French, German, and Spanish consuls called on Rush to make the fatuous request that he take "all possible measures" to stamp out the sniping. Testily, Rush informed them that he was already taking all the measures that had occurred to him; but that he would be glad to receive any suggestions. The consuls produced several, all of which, wrote Rush, with evident satisfaction, were either impractical or had already been put in effect. There was one exception, which was to have the admiral issue a proclamation stating that no one would be allowed on the roofs after 7:00 P.M. on penalty of being shot, and that all people hearing men upon their roofs should report the same to the nearest patrol. Rush transmitted the idea to Fletcher, and the proclamation was published.[30]

Fletcher conferred with the municipal authorities again that afternoon. Though the federal and state officials were obviously hopeless, he still hoped to induce the local men to reconsider. His anger and exasperation show through the normally restrained language of his report. "I informed them of the shooting at our men during the previous night, and told them that it must stop," he wrote; "that martial law would be proclaimed, all inhabitants disarmed, and more severe measures adopted; that if a shot was fired from any house it would be surrounded by our troops and the inhabitants removed, or if fired from any block in the city, the whole block would be surrounded and men found there would be taken away. I informed them that . . . furthermore, I regretted for their own interests that they had not been able to resume the government of their city, and advised them to make another attempt. They were notified that if they failed to establish a government themselves, I would be obliged to establish one for them which would probably not suit them as well as their own." [31]

On this occasion, Fletcher enjoyed the assistance of Robert J. Kerr, an American attorney who had been returning to his practice in Mexico City from a lecture tour in the United States at the time of the landing. The author of the definitive English translation of the Mexican civil code, Kerr was recognized as an expert on Mexican law.[32] The effect of his contributions cannot be determined, but at the close of the interview it was apparent that Mayor Díaz and the

Ayuntamiento * had seen the light. After leaving Fletcher, they voted unanimously to resume office and carry on the affairs of the city of Veracruz.[33]

The same day, Fletcher issued an order requiring the citizens of Veracruz to surrender all arms and ammunition to the Provost Marshal. "Within hours there were literally hundreds of Mexicans lined up in front of my desk turning in all kinds of rifles, carbines, revolvers, duelling pistols, etc.," Ensign Foster related. "I can remember some individuals coming in with clothesbaskets of revolvers and pistols of all descriptions. As I had no secretarial help except a yeoman with one typewriter, I had to improvise an exceedingly brief and probably inaccurate receipt form acknowledging only that a certain number of firearms had been turned over to me. These I signed and dated and the firearms were carried into the Municipal Building and stacked like cordwood until office after office was filled to overflowing." [34] In all, over 11,000 small arms and 133,000 rounds of ammunition were collected.

As usual, there was firing in several sections of the city during the night.

With no alternative, Admiral Fletcher proclaimed martial law on the morning of April 26. Civilians were not allowed on the streets after 7:30 P.M. without a pass, to be presented to sentries at each intersection, and other restrictions of a similar nature were imposed. Combined with the confiscation of firearms and an intensified patrol system, this measure proved decisive. For the first time in five days, the sound of gunfire did not echo through Veracruz after dark.[35]

The city remained tranquil throughout April 27, and on April 28, Fletcher lifted the curfew. "It is gratifying to note that all business is resumed in Veracruz and that good order prevails," he announced. "Citizens may pass freely in the streets, both night and day, and resume their usual customs." [36]

The most delicate of Fletcher's problems—assisting Americans in the interior to reach Veracruz—was solved, not without some friction, under British auspices. The first intimation of its outcome was received around 9:30 P.M. April 22, when Admiral Cradock advised Fletcher that a refugee train accompanied by Mr. Hohler, First Secretary of the British Legation in Mexico City, was expected to arrive on the following day. Fletcher put the only operative locomotive in Veracruz at Cradock's disposal, and on the morning of April 23, Captain Watson of HMS *Essex* took it out to the rail break to meet

---

* City council.

the refugees. He returned with nearly 600 persons—58 British, 75 German, 150 American and some 300 Mexican.[37]

That afternoon, Hohler asked Fletcher to lend him the train again the next day. He had promised to bring General Maass' family—which had remained in Veracruz—to the Mexican lines. Fletcher granted his request a few hours before receiving the telegram in which O'Shaughnessy announced that the Embassy train would arrive at the rail break the same morning. There could be no question of meeting the Chargé d'affairs in a train under British colors. Fletcher had no choice but to tell Cradock that he would need the train himself. Hohler and Maass' family would be welcome aboard, but Captain Huse would be in charge.[38]

Cradock did not take the news kindly. As far as Sir Christopher was concerned, Fletcher had reneged on alerting him to the approach of hostilities. Now Fletcher was trying to renege on the use of the train. Firing an angry note to Admiral Badger, Cradock insisted that the locomotive had been promised to Hohler. Badger upheld Fletcher, of course, suggesting, as a compromise, sending the train out displaying both British and American flags. Cradock was unappeased: for the second time, he had been promised something he did not get. There was not a great deal he could do about it, however, and on April 25 the train pulled out of Veracruz under two flags. Approximately four hundred refugees, including the O'Shaughnessys and the fifty members of their staff, returned with it to Veracruz.[39]

In conference with General Corona, who had escorted the Embassy train, Captain Huse arranged to run a train out to the rail break daily. Lieutenant Frank Jack Fletcher, who had distinguished himself on the *Esperanza*, was made train commander. Thereafter the flow of refugees proceeded fairly smoothly. There were a few tight moments; the Mexicans had mined the track and occasionally they became obstreperous, but Lieutenant Fletcher surmounted each incident by a combination of forcefulness and tact.[40]

Jack London went along with one of the Navy trains and wrote a vivid description of the Mexican soldiery it met. "Two miles beyond our last outpost we came to the break," he related. "Here . . . was a blockhouse of advanced Federal outposts. Under a white Turkish towel, carried by a sailor, Lieutenant Fletcher . . . conferred with the Mexican lieutenant in charge. The latter was a small, stupid-tired, and a greatly embarrassed sort of man. . . . It was patent that he was mostly Indian. Even more of the Indian was in the ragged, leather-sandalled soldiers under him. They were short, squat, pa-

Vice Admiral Paul F. Foster, USNR (Ret.)

Ensign Paul F. Foster, Acting Provost Marshal (seated), hearing charges
against a sniper from Ensign T. S. Wilkinson. War correspondent Richard
Harding Davis called Foster the "Boy Pooh-Bah of Veracruz"

tient-eyed, long-enduring. . . . One could not help being sorry for these sorry soldiers, who slouched awkwardly about while our Lieutenant scanned the far track across the break in the hope of some sign of our countrymen fleeing the capital—sorry Indian soldiers they truly were. . . . And yet one must not forget that each of these sorry soldiers bore a modern rifle, the cartridges for which . . . are capable of propelling a bullet a mile and further, and, at close range, to perforate the bodies of two or three men." [41]

A nasty situation arose when Huerta, misinformed that Mexicans who wished to leave Veracruz were being held against their will, threatened to halt the movement of foreign refugees. On April 26, Commander Hugh J. Tweedie, R.N., of the *Essex,* was sent to Mexico City to assure him that anyone who wanted to depart Veracruz was free to go. Several hundred Mexicans had already been carried to the rail break. Tweedie was also supposed to expedite the evacuation of foreigners remaining in the capital. He was successful on both counts. Acting with the unrequited courtesy he always accorded Americans, Huerta took no steps to interfere with their departure. The morning train of April 27 carried 21 American, 31 British, and 92 Mexican refugees. Tweedie returned on April 28, bringing 206 Americans who had been detained and insulted but unharmed at Soledad and Córdoba. His party was the last large group of Americans to enter Veracruz.[42]

"They were a bedraggled-looking bunch," Quartermaster Sweetman recalled. "It was hot as blazes. Most of the women had worn high-heeled shoes. After walking a mile or so in the cinders and gravel along the railroad track, they didn't have any shoes left and their feet weren't in very good shape, either. We gave them most of our water, and we were on one canteen a day." [43] *Collier's* Arthur Ruhl met a group from a land-development colony in Oaxaca. "They were typical American prairie farmers," he wrote; "lean, sun-baked, patient, quizzical, with tired-looking wives and incredible numbers of tow-headed children—just the sort of queer, hopeful fish who jam the home-seekers' trains to some Government land opening in the Northwest. They had come to the tropics just as they had gone to Texas and Oregon before, learned the new ways, got used to the climate, put in their oranges and pineapples, and were just getting ready to make a little money when the order came to go. One man told me that he and his family had four hours to pack up and get out. A squad of federal soldiers . . . told them it was not thought safe for them to stay. 'It's a fine country,' he said; 'ain't a richer country nowhere.' " [44]

The office of the Provost Marshal was one of the few areas which did not cause Admiral Fletcher any trouble. Ensign Foster's resourceful, highly individual brand of justice met general approbation. When, on April 25, Commander David F. Sellers was appointed Provost Marshal,[45] Foster was retained as Deputy Provost Marshal and he and Ensign Junkin continued to discharge the routine duties of the office. In one of his Veracruz articles, Richard Harding Davis described Foster's activities under the title "Boy Officer as Pooh-Bah." [46] "When I heard about it," Foster said, "I didn't know whether to shoot him or buy him a drink." [47]

"For six days," wrote Davis, "Foster, who is but twenty-four years old, was in a city of 40,000 Mexicans and 5,000 Americans, chief of police, provost marshal, lord chief justice and executioner." Davis exaggerated at the end, for Foster condemned no one to death. "Before this terrible judge . . . ," Davis continued, "came murderers, snipers, thieves, and denizens of the red-light district. He dispensed punishment according to his own ideas. Rich young Mexicans brought before him for creating disorder, to whom a fine would have meant nothing, he made sweep the streets, while their friends sat under the portales and laughed at them. Murderers he placed under guard and forced to dig graves for the dead." Davis told of the night Foster was informed that Admiral Fletcher wanted an automobile for a tour of inspection within the hour. Foster hurried to the "bull pen," where convicted criminals were awaiting sentence. "If any of you can get back here in less than an hour with an automobile," he announced, "he needn't come back again." The admiral got his car.[48]

The Naval Division was extraordinarily well-behaved throughout the occupation. In his First General Order, Captain Rush had stated, "Drinking, destruction of property, public or private, looting or maltreatment of inhabitants is expressly forbidden, and will be considered a general court martial offense," [49] and he was taken at his word. "I cannot recall any incidents or allegations of crimes or serious misbehavior against our sailors or Marines," Foster related. "There were remarkably few incidents of overindulgence in intoxicants, and there was not a single incident involving mistreatment of Mexican women by our men. The only incident involving a Mexican woman occurred around 2 A.M. one morning when a cab driver pulled up in front of my sidewalk office and complained that he had picked up the passenger from what he said was a house of ill-repute, and had taken her to her destination. The passenger had said she had no money to pay the fare, and so he had driven immediately to lodge a complaint with the Provost Marshal. I settled this case to what appeared to be their mutual satisfaction by suggesting that the fare be taken out in trade." [50]

"Among the bluejackets from the *Utah*," wrote Richard Harding Davis, ". . . only one man was charged with looting. A German claimed that in searching his home for snipers one of the men . . . had helped himself to a safety razor. He could not identify the offender. But when the German made the charge the man happened to be on duty. 'Why, Lieutenant,' he volunteered to Castle, 'I took that safety razor. . . . I hadn't had a shave in two days, and I wasn't going dirty any longer.' " [51]

Only thirty-one claims arising from the destruction or theft of private property were presented to the Office of Military Government during the occupation. Most were for goods damaged during the fighting. Three cases involved what might be termed legitimate larceny. The items in question consisted of an expensive camera, a herd of pigs, and, in a single instance, cash.[52]

Writing in the spring of 1965, Foster recalled a rather unusual claim which had come to his attention in 1916. "I received through official channels from my Commanding Officer a formidable stack of papers with all kinds of government seals and ribbons attached," he related. "The basic letter in this file was from a Spanish citizen then living in Mexico City and was addressed to the Spanish Ambassador in Mexico City who forwarded it to his Foreign Ministry in Madrid, which in turn forwarded it to our Secretary of State in Washington. The Secretary of State had forwarded this accumulated correspondence to the Secretary of the Navy, who had forwarded it to the Commander in Chief of the U.S. Atlantic Fleet. Then it had gone on down the line until it reached me with a request that I provide information for the basis of an appropriate reply.

"In brief, the Spaniard's story was that he had arrived in Veracruz by steamship from Spain a few days before we seized the city. While he was temporarily living in a small hotel on the second night of the occupation, some American sailors broke into his room on the pretext of searching for concealed firearms. He claimed that they had smashed open the trunk in which he was carrying an exceedingly valuable collection of postage stamps. . . . The bluejackets had seized these postage stamps and then disappeared. A few hours later he said he located the Provost Marshal, Ensign Paul Foster, and . . . described the crime in detail. The Spaniard alleged that Ensign Foster told him to 'write a letter to the Pope about his

Captain Roy Dudley, USN (Ret.)

Ensign Roy Dudley (second from right, seated) and his section at the
rail break, awaiting the refugees

National Archives

A section of the U.S. Navy's aviation camp established at Veracruz

U. S. Marine Corps

The American flag is raised over Veracruz, April 27, 1914

loss' and move on so that he could hear the next case. The Spaniard said that he had indeed written to the Pope and had gotten word back that this was a matter to be taken up with temporal authorities and accordingly he was sending his complaint to the Spanish government with a demand for the return of his property. The answer I gave my Commanding Officer was that I had no recollection whatsoever of the incident but that in the context of conditions prevailing at that time and in view of the fact that Ensign Junkin and I had been on duty continuously for about three days with little or no sleep, it was not inconceivable that I had in truth told the Spaniard to write the Pope about his lost postage stamps. I might say that I have heard nothing further of this complaint in the last forty-eight years." [53]

San Juan de Ulúa was occupied by a company of Marines from the *North Dakota* on April 26. Its garrison capitulated with undisguised relief; they had been living on black bean soup since the landing. The formal occupation occurred two days later. At that time, de Ulúa was found to contain 443 prisoners, 325 of whom were held for no charge—presumably for attempting to escape conscription. The prisoners in this category were immediately released, while the criminal prisoners were moved to the mainland.[54]

"Now the Stars and Stripes floats over the frowning walls and another chapter in the thrilling history of the fortress has been written," effused the *New York Herald*'s Hamilton Peltz, in a dispatch typical of the reportage produced at Veracruz. "American sentries now pace up and down . . . flagstones worn by the feet of soldiers of Spanish kings, of Iturbide, of Maximilian, of Napoleon the Third, . . . and of all the presidents and dictators of Old Mexico. When this morning dawned, and the grey mist withdrew from the spot, it was still, quiet, wrapped in peace and a mantle of memories. . . . The cells are empty, the prisoners gone. San Juan de Ulúa is deserted except by the Americans who guard it." [55]

One of the last reinforcements Fletcher received was a novel organization known as the Aeroplane Section. It consisted of four hydroplanes—two each in the 1st and 2nd Aero Sections—under Lieutenants J. H. Towers and P. N. L. Bellinger. Leaving the United States aboard the USS *Birmingham* and *Mississippi* on April 20, the aircraft arrived at Veracruz on April 28. A primitive field was constructed along the beach south of the city, and soon the pilots were flying reconnaissance missions inland from Veracruz.

Their patrols were the first ever made over enemy territory by American naval avaitors. Meticulous reports of troop movements, road conditions, and other matters of military interest, generally investigated at an altitude well under one thousand feet, led Admiral Fletcher to commend the performance of these "flying machine scouts." [56] Few dreamed that in little more than a decade the successors to these fragile craft would be able to sink a battleship.

The American flag was raised over Veracruz on April 27. "The ceremony was simple but most impressive," wrote Consul Canada. "All the troops who had landed on 21st April . . . were formed in the open space in front of the Terminal Hotel. . . . Promptly at 2 P.M., the flag was raised by Captain DeLano, of the Marine Corps, and Ensign McDonnell of the Navy, assisted by a first class quartermaster from the *Utah* and a sergeant of the Marine Corps, the band playing the 'Star Spangled Banner' and the *Minnesota*, in the inner harbor, firing a salute of twenty-one guns." [57]

✠✠

THIRTEEN: THIS GOVERNMENT IS TOO PIOUS

This is a hell of a war.

Marine sentry to Jack London [1]

The army transports *Kilpatrick, Meade, Sumner,* and *McClellan* appeared off Veracruz shortly before midnight April 27.[2] The next morning, General Funston met Admiral Fletcher and Captain Huse to discuss the transfer of control of the city. The thorniest problem to confront them was the formation of a municipal government. After deliberation, they decided to install Robert Kerr as Governor; Fletcher liked the way Kerr had handled himself in the conference with the Mexican authorities. Two other American civilians, Charles H. Stewart and William F. Buckley, were named Treasurer and Administrator of Justice. Commander Stickney was appointed Inspector of the Port and Collector of Customs, and Commander J. F. Luby was named Postmaster.[3]

The next matter Fletcher and Funston considered was not so amicably resolved. It concerned the control of the Marine brigade, which would soon amount to nearly half the Corps. Fletcher and Badger thought that as the Marines belonged to the Navy, a naval officer should be in charge. Funston disagreed, asserting that the command of the forces of occupation should be unified under the Army. The argument went all the way to a cabinet meeting, at which Wilson decided in favor of the Army. The Marines would take orders from Funston.[4]

In the meanwhile, the details of the transfer of Veracruz had been arranged. The *Kilpatrick* moved beside the Ward Line Pier at 8:00 A.M., April 30. Richard Harding Davis was aboard to record the event. "The troops on the *Kilpatrick* . . . found waiting to greet them here a force consisting of exactly five persons," he wrote; "four Mexican stevedores, supported by one moving picture man. Into the eager faces of the 3,000 soldiers swarming the ratlines of the transport the four stevedores yawned." [5]

The disembarkation was indeed anticlimatic. "The arrival of the Fifth Brigade . . . finds Veracruz tranquil, with no signs of disorder," wrote Hamilton Peltz. "The streets are clean and the inhabitants . . . gaze upon the men of the American Army with a look that is stoical, indifferent. . . . The disembarkation occurred . . . when the sun hung overhead like a red ball of fire. The thermometer

War correspondent Jack London
and his wife at Veracruz

War correspondent Richard Harding Davis on left;
Lt. P. N. L. Bellinger, naval aviator, on right

registered 100 degrees. . . . A slight breeze from the Gulf of Mexico swept over the waterfront and found a way through the narrow streets, but the heat was almost intolerable." [6]

The ceremony marking the transfer of the city was held in front of the New Lighthouse, at the foot of the Sanitary Wharf, at 2:00 that afternoon. Richard Harding Davis compared the site to the aviation field at Governor's Island, New York. "The reviewing party faced the asphalt promenade at the water's edge," he related. "Behind them, in companies, were the Marines . . . and the 28th Regiment. The Navy officers wore white gloves, side arms, and stiff-necked tropical blouses. The Army, being on field service, made a contrast with khaki flannel shirts. It was distinctly a family party, informal and heartily cordial. Very few Mexicans were present, and some of those, when the colors passed, having their sombreros knocked off by enthusiastic refugees . . . retired to cantinas. The sun shone brilliantly on the white uniforms, the gold braid, and the national colors, and the American spectators applauded continuously. . . . When the review ended, the Marines just arriving cheered their brother Marines of the landing party. Major Lindsay of the 28th Infantry jumped on a bench and led the cheers for the Navy bluejackets, who cheered the Army while the bands played 'Auld Lang Syne.' At this the Mexicans, taking the song to be the national anthem, hastily uncovered." [7]

Writing for family newspapers, Davis neglected to mention that its approach route led the Naval Division through the red-light district. Recognizing some old acquaintances, the girls dashed into the ranks, throwing their arms around furious, red-faced bluejackets who riveted their eyes upon the necks of the men in front. For a while, the girls' laughter and cries of *"Mi dulce corazón!"* threatened to drown out the band. They had been shaken off before the formation reached the reviewing party, but the commotion had lasted long enough to cause at least one amused ensign to wonder what those august gentlemen thought.[8]

The Naval Division turned column right at the Promenade, the bands still playing at its head. Rain had fallen that morning and there were muddy puddles at the edge of the pavement. A handful of curious curs trotted beside the marching men, nipping at their heels. Four tugs and a fleet of launches were waiting to carry the sailors back to their ships. Ensign Roy Dudley was in charge of a beach guard at a landing to the north. From his position, Dudley could see the formation wheel towards the waterfront, but intervening buildings blocked his view of the disembarkation. As battalion after battalion vanished, it seemed as though they had marched into thin air.[9]

Among those remaining in Veracruz were Jack London and Richard Harding Davis. The two best-paid and most widely-read American authors of the day, their own fame far exceeded that of any of the soldiers whose activities they had come to chronicle. Davis represented the Wheeler Syndicate; London was one of the team sent by *Collier's Magazine.* In their mid-forties, Davis and London looked much alike: both were broad-shouldered, athletic men, handsome in a brusque, straightforward way, with large, cleft chins, massive foreheads, short noses and deep, rather wide-set eyes. They thought alike, too. Though Davis had always held conventional convictions, in earlier years London had gained—somewhat fortuitously, true—the reputation of a rabid socialist. General Funston had not been inclined to recognize him as a correspondent on account of "The Good Soldier," [10] an anonymous article generally attributed to London which had vilified the military several months before. It had been necessary for Davis to exert all his considerable influence to obtain accreditation for London. But London had long since recanted. The imperialistic fervor of the articles he wrote in Mexico would equal any of Davis's efforts.

Finding all quiet at Veracruz was an enormous disappointment. It was Dick Davis who had made the war correspondent a figure of romance and glamour. Since the day he had grabbed a carbine and followed Teddy Roosevelt up San Juan Hill to fame, Davis had reported wars enough to wear two rows of ribbons on his expansive chest. Never easily discouraged, in the weeks to come he would do his best to whip up still another war. The day after Wilson agreed to mediation, Davis headlined his dispatch: "Six Thousand Sturdy Men in Khaki, Fit to Have Marched on Mexico City, Doomed to Idleness that May Cost Many Lives by Disease." [11] ("Not," he wrote, "that I want to catch bullets in my teeth, but I *did* expect quick action and something to write about." [12]) But Davis alone could not keep the pot boiling, and at length he was compelled to conclude: "It looks to me that *nothing* will induce Wilson to go to war." [13]

Jack London was even more disconsolate. He had gone to the Orient to cover the Russo-Japanese conflict of 1904–1905, but the Japanese had refused to cooperate with correspondents and all he had seen of battle was a smattering of smoke on the Manchurian horizon. The Mexican assignment was to have been his first opportunity to really report a war. Amoebic dysentery and an all-night crap game in which he broke his fellow newsmen and the French and Spanish consuls were sad substitutes for the excitement he had expected.[14]

Davis lingered in Veracruz for six weeks, the leading light of the host of reporters who had converged on the city. He held court at a permanently-reserved table on the sidewalk café of the Hotel Diligencias, at which, from time to time, he could be seen chatting with General Funston, Colonel Lejeune, and other high-ranking officers. A stack of telegraph blanks was kept near at hand to deter unwelcome callers. Afterwards, his less-sophisticated colleagues would remember him as the only man in Veracruz who dressed for dinner every night.[15]

Though Davis failed to find much news in Veracruz, he did contrive to make some. In the middle of May, he set out with two other correspondents, Frederick Palmer and Medill McCormick, on a secret attempt to reach Mexico City and interview Huerta. The trio was imprisoned overnight at Paseo de Macho. Palmer was escorted back to Veracruz, but Davis and McCormick talked their way to the capital, where they were arrested for a second time. The British ambassador obtained their release after twenty-four hours, but Huerta refused to see them. At the end of the week, Davis and McCormick returned to Veracruz. There they discovered that Palmer's story of their first arrest had aroused such fears for their safety that they themselves had been front-page news for days.[16]

Ironically, the *Ypiranga* and her guns were almost forgotten in the aftermath of the landing. On April 23, Commander Stickney advised Captain Bonath that he could discharge his cargo at Veracruz. Bonath indicated that he would prefer to carry the arms back to Germany, a decision which delighted everyone involved. Bryan thanked von Bernstorff for the cooperation of the German government, and on May 3, the *Ypiranga* left Veracruz. At Tampico, she took on a number of American refugees and carried them to Mobile. From Mobile she proceeded to Puerto Mexico, where, to the intense disgust of the veterans of the landing, she unhurriedly unloaded the arms. Then, with staggering *sang-froid*, Bonath returned to Veracruz. He had pressed his luck too far. Making use of a Mexican law which prohibited the landing of goods at a port other than that to which consigned, Commander Stickney imposed a fine of nearly 900,000 pesos on the Hamburg-American Line. The *Ypiranga* was not permitted to sail until Hamburg-American agents posted a bond in the amount of the fine. But Wilson was fearful of alienating the

Germans, and the assessment was revoked.[17] It was just as well. Huerta's army was disintegrating; the arms had come too late to do him any good.

On May 1, Funston learned that the plans he and Fletcher had made for governing Veracruz had been disapproved. In Washington, Robert J. Kerr was *persona non grata*. While in the United States, Kerr had charged that Wilson's Mexican policy favored "the government or the set of individuals, or the political party, or the mob of bandits, pledged, if they get into power, to do things which will be favorable to the Standard Oil interests." [18] It was useless for Funston to protest that he and Fletcher had attached no more importance to Kerr's politics than to the color of his hair.[19] The governor had to go.

The ostensible reason for the change was the reluctance of the War Department to place a civilian in charge of a foreign city under military occupation. It was asserted that the Army, which had received considerable experience in civil affairs during the Philippine Insurrection, could govern the city itself. The municipal administration would be composed as largely as possible of Mexican personnel, with American officers at the head of each department.[20]

In practice, it was a workable arrangement. At no time in Mexican history had a local government acted with the honesty and efficiency of the Office of Military Government of Veracruz. Graft and corruption were eliminated from the customs and police. A conscientious public school system was organized; rents and taxes were collected, and innumerable administrative reforms were put into effect.[21]

The most herculean tasks accomplished under the Military Government were those performed by the Department of Public Works. To this department was assigned the awesome responsibility of establishing and maintaining sanitary conditions in Veracruz. The success of its campaign was reflected in the remarkably low incidence of disease among the six thousand men of the army of occupation and, no less significantly, by the departure of the throngs of vultures which formerly had feasted in the streets.

The *Veracruzanos'* utter indifference to considerations of hygiene was most evident in the New Market, where the bulk of the food consumed within the city was sold. The odor emanating from the market was so offensive, an American officer wrote, that "it was almost unbearable for a white person to remain in the vicinity." [22] Laid out in the last days of Díaz, the market had not reached completion at the outbreak of the revolution and had since fallen into an appalling state of disrepair. The urinals were never cleaned, and small animals were permitted to wander through the area at will. Food displayed in unscreened stalls became black with flies the moment it was uncovered. The tiled floors had cracked, and maggots writhed in the offal-clogged crevices. The tiles themselves were barely visible beneath a festering meringue of dried blood, fish scales, chicken feathers, entrails, putrid produce, and excrement.[23]

The Department of Public Works went to work with a will. The New Market was scrubbed clean; fly-screens were installed in the concessions, and the floors were hosed down with sea water each day. Ashes from the coal-burning battleships were carried ashore to resurface the roads. The entire population was vaccinated for smallpox. GI cans were distributed at over 1,000 locations throughout the city and 69,000 gallons of crude oil were poured on stagnant watercourses to combat malaria. Platoons of bewildered peons were deployed as street sweepers and the rules of hygiene were rigidly enforced.[24]

Prostitution was brought under strict supervision. Mexican prostitutes were required to undergo careful medical examinations twice weekly. Foreign prostitutes were deported, and American officers were forbidden to enter the red-light district in uniform. Despite such precautions, the profession continued to present an occasional problem. "To illustrate," wrote an appalled Red Cross official, "a Mexican girl, thirteen years of age, ran away from her home in Orizaba to see the American Army. Apparently she was an innocent and unsophisticated girl. But she was absolutely without funds and soon succumbed to temptations offered by the lower class of Mexicans and, it must be added, also by some Americans. According to her own confession, nearly every night from the time of her arrival was spent in the company of some man or boy. Twice she was treated in the women's hospital for gonorrhea and twice for intermittent fever; finally the American authorities arrested her as a common prostitute and ordered her deported from the American lines. Before she could be deported, however, she required treatment for syphilis and was found to be three months advanced in pregnancy. Under direction of American Army officers, the Red Cross director and a nurse, with the aid of the state police of Veracruz, took her to her family in Orizaba." The writer did not relate the details of this happy homecoming, but as if doubtful of its outcome, he added: "Other women liable to succumb to temptations were given transportation before it was too late." [25]

Though no one was unlucky enough to suspect it, the United States Army would remain in Veracruz for seven singularly dull months. When they had disembarked, many of Funston's men hoped to see fighting. "It was good, some of them told me, to feel land beneath their feet again," a correspondent wrote; "to go from the dull monotony of camp life at Galveston to the field of active service." [26] But the prospects of active service were already fading. No one still believed that General Maass intended to attack; all he had attempted was a half-hearted blockade of the city, and Wilson's acceptance of the ABC offer had put the kiss of death on the plans for an offensive on Mexico City. Huerta had wired his agreement to mediation to Washington on the afternoon the Army came ashore. If the idea of defying the United States had ever been in his mind, it had been discarded. The only action in which the members of the army of occupation would engage was at the end of a shovel.

To men like Smedley Butler, it was a revolting development. Butler made Mrs. O'Shaughnessy think of "a hungry man who has been given thin bread and butter when he wants beefsteak and potatoes." Visiting his battalion headquarters, a derailed boxcar on the outpost line, she found Butler snorting: "In the good old days in Nicaragua, it was otherwise. You *took* what you *needed*. This government . . . is too pious . . . to suit me." [27]

The only soldier to find adventure at Veracruz was an aristocratic young captain attached to the intelligence section of Funston's staff. His name was Douglas MacArthur. Early in the occupation, MacArthur was asked to determine the number of railroad engines at the disposal of the Mexican forces outside Veracruz. The information would be useful in the unlikely event that the Army were ordered to advance. Convinced that accuracy could be assured only through personal observation, MacArthur decided to slip through the Mexican lines and count the engines himself. He did not submit his plan to Funston's headquarters for fear it would be disapproved. He did advise his immediate superior, but their understanding was that the project was strictly unofficial. If MacArthur were captured, he would be disavowed.

Procuring two Mexican guides of questionable loyalty, MacArthur left Veracruz under cover of darkness. He reached the Mexican stations and counted the engines without running into trouble. The return was another story. Riding along the railway track in a hijacked handcar, MacArthur's party attracted the attention of a band of Mexican cavalry. In the running gunfight which ensued, MacArthur downed the better-mounted Mexicans with his .45. Outdistancing the remainder, he abandoned the handcar and struck out through the brush. One of his guides had been wounded and the need to help him over rough ground held MacArthur's pace to a crawl. It was dawn before they stumbled into an American outpost. For a while it was unclear whether MacArthur would be recommended for the Medal of Honor or a court martial. The alternatives canceled each other, and in the end no official notice was taken of the incident.[28]

Several weeks were spent settling the details of the mediation conference. It was May 21 before, at the Clifton House in Canadian Niagara Falls, the representatives of Argentina, Brazil, and Chile held their first session. "The Niagara Conference," as it came to be called, was a fiasco from fumbling start to faltering finish. Though Wilson had assented to mediation, he declined to accredit American delegates, declaring that the object of the conference was simply to arrive at a solution to Mexico's internal problems. The Constitutionalists, who had also been expected to attend, adopted an attitude similar to Wilson's. Carranza approved the proceedings "in principle" but refused to participate because he did not acknowledge the right of foreign powers to arbitrate Mexican affairs. In the outcome, both Wilson and Carranza sent observers, but their contributions were invariably negative. The ABC ministers persevered until the end of June when, having arrived at no solution acceptable alike to Wilson, Huerta, and Carranza, they adjourned. They never reconvened.[29]

Less than three weeks later, however, the object of Wilson's Mexican policy was attained. On July 15, in the face of a new Constitutionalist offensive, Huerta resigned the provisional presidency of Mexico. Luckier than Madero, he made it to Puerto Mexico, gaining asylum aboard His Germanic Majesty's cruiser *Dresden*. Its officers put on their dress uniforms to receive him.

Wilson was as jubilant as his self-esteem would allow. When Carranza installed himself in Mexico City, Wilson assumed it would only be a matter of weeks before he called for free elections.

Alas for Wilson's expectations, Carranza demonstrated that he had no intention of doing any such thing. It was not the first time, nor the last, that the invincible idealism of an American President would allow him to be duped by the leader of a purportedly democratic revolution against an autocratic but friendly régime.

Wilson's previous experience had taught him nothing; in July, 1913, he had sent John Lind, an aggressive Protestant, to a government allied with the Catholic Church; now, in August, 1914, he promptly dispatched another special agent, Paul Fuller, a devout Catholic, to a government of anticlericals. Predictably, Fuller was no more effective with Carranza than Lind had been with Huerta. While Fuller extolled free elections, Carranza insisted on the evacuation of Veracruz. The Constitutionalist victory had removed the moral grounds upon which Wilson felt able to justify the retention of the city, and on September 16, he informed Carranza that the American forces would be withdrawn. All Wilson asked in return was the appointment of a responsible authority to receive control of the municipal administration. Carranza stated that General Cándido Aguilar had been so designated. Upon this basis, Wilson announced that the evacuation would begin.[30]

That was easier said than done. Funston advised the Secretary of War that he would need at least four weeks to transfer control of the city. Having labored so diligently to create a model government for Veracruz, the Army did not wish to see it collapse into confusion. Before this problem could be solved, one far more important arose. The Constitutionalists outside Veracruz began to proclaim their intention to impose harsh punishment upon all Mexicans who had served the Military Government and upon the *Huertista* refugees who had sought sanctuary in the city. Furthermore, the Constitutionalist spokesmen asserted that the merchants who had paid customs duties to the American administration would be required to pay them again after the city changed hands.

Funston requested that the State Department obtain assurances that no reprisals would be taken against Mexican personnel of the Military Government or the refugees, and that the customs duties would not be imposed a second time. Wilson evinced scant concern for the refugees, but he did direct Acting-Secretary of State Robert Lansing to inform Carranza that guarantees of the safety of the Mexican employees would be required. Carranza balked, stalling through September and October, while Funston's unhappy men lived in breathless anticipation of orders to evacuate.

Eventually, dissention in the Constitutionalist ranks forced Carranza to concede. Villa and Zapata, with whom Carranza's relations had never been cordial, rose in open revolt against the First Chief. At the beginning of November, it was apparent that Mexico was about to be embroiled in another civil war. Carranza was obliged to retire from Mexico City. Gaining control of the customs revenues of Veracruz was imperative if he was to continue the struggle. Accordingly, on November 9, he issued a general amnesty for the employees of the Office of Military Government and promised not to levy new taxes on imports whose duties had already been collected. On November 13, Secretary of State Bryan stated that the evacuation of Veracruz would begin in ten days.

Carranza would not keep his word. Persons who had worked for the Americans would be dismissed from their posts and subjected to harassment and discrimination. But such affairs were of little interest to Funston's men, who eagerly awaited the end of a tedious and irksome tour. As the Army prepared to depart, many refugees and ex-employees booked passage out of Mexico. Funston chartered several ships for those who could not afford to pay their own way. The evacuation was accomplished in an orderly manner on the morning of November 23.[31]

FOURTEEN: THE PUBLIC GAZE

The public gaze rested for a day or two . . . and then, having
heard a few scattered stories of Veracruz, marvelled, digested and
tired of them, it shifted to other fields of springtime interest.

The *Brooklyn Daily Eagle*, May 23, 1914

W hen towards noon, November 23, ·1914, the vanguard of
Cándido Aguilar's Constitutionalist division reached the
seawall, in time to see the last of Funston's transports steam over the
horizon, the landing at Veracruz had already slipped into the obli-
vion of history. On June 28, Franz Ferdinand, Archduke of Austria,
had been assassinated in Serajevo, the capital of a backward Balkan
province of the empire to which he was heir. The safety valves of
European diplomacy had failed to stem the pressures generated by
his death, and the governments of the great powers had watched in
helpless horror as the irresponsible élan of the Austrian foreign
office drew them into a war no one wanted. In the dark of an August
night, the European warships disappeared from Mexican waters,
heading for distant war stations on the high seas. American soldiers
were still marking time in Veracruz the day Sir Christopher Cradock
died at Coronel, lost with all hands when his flagship was destroyed
attacking a German squadron against heavy odds.

By November, 1914, the miracle of the Marne was already a
legend, and the Franco-German race to the sea had ended in
Flanders' flooded fields in a stalemate which would endure until the
spring of 1918. Compared to the battles on the Western Front, the
landing at Veracruz was no more than a skirmish. It had not made
the headlines since the bodies of the men killed in action were
carried to the Brooklyn Navy Yard by the battleship *Montana*.

The memorial service was held in New York on May 13. The
Mayor laid a wreath of orchids on the coffin of one of the three
sailors from the city, and thousands of onlookers stood bareheaded
as the flag-draped caissons rumbled past. President Wilson was
present to deliver the funeral oration; conscience-stricken by the
bloodshed at Veracruz, the administration had resolved to pay all
honor to those who had died or distinguished themselves there. In
his address, Wilson reiterated the purposes which guided his Mexican policy. "We have gone down to Mexico to serve mankind if we

163

can find out the way," he said, almost plaintively. "We do not want to fight the Mexicans. We want to serve the Mexicans. . . . A war of aggression is not a war in which it is a proud thing to die, but a war of service is . . . a proud thing [in which] to die." He promised that "these lads" would not have laid down their lives in vain.[1]

For its part, Congress amended the regulations governing the award of the Navy Medal of Honor, previously restricted to enlisted men, to include officers; and, in the largest distribution ever made for a single engagement, bestowed fifty-five Medals of Honor—thirty-seven to officers and eighteen to enlisted men—for the landing at Veracruz.* [2] Major Smedley Butler sent his Medal of Honor back to the Navy Department, explaining that he did not feel entitled to the nation's highest decoration. The Department returned it with a stiff endorsement stating that he would not only keep but wear it.[3] The home towns of a few of the fallen servicemen raised monuments to their memories and, its duty done, the nation forgot.

For the United States, there was no apparent sequel to the occupation of Veracruz. Prefacing one of the last feature stories on the landing with the quotation which opens this chapter, a reporter summed it up. By the summer of 1914, the public gaze had shifted from Veracruz, never to return. Today the landing is so little known that a query to the Marine Corps historical section produced a list of references to the Mexican War of 1846–47. Even students of history, as a whole, are unaware that American troops landed under fire in Mexico in this century.

Small wonder. Wilson's experiment at Veracruz was in noways satisfactory. At a glance, it might seem otherwise. The immediate object for which he had ordered the landing was attained: Huerta was effectively deprived of the *Ypiranga*'s cargo; and the loss of the customs' revenues of Veracruz, his principal source of income, certainly accelerated his downfall, inevitable though that may have been. But the elimination of Huerta failed to produce the results Wilson had expected. Peace and good order did not return to Mexico. Rather was the country plunged into a savage war between the rival Constitutionalist chiefs.

In 1916, the conflict lapped over the border. Desperate for supplies, Pancho Villa raided Columbus, New Mexico, and Wilson was forced to intervene again. This time, a punitive expedition of

---

* None of the decorations comprising the Armed Forces' "Pyramid of Honor" had been established at this time; before 1918, American servicemen won the Medal of Honor or nothing at all.

United States cavalry under Brigadier General John J. Pershing was sent on a fruitless chase across the sun-baked plateaus of northern Mexico. When the cavalry clashed with Carranza's troops, 150,000 National Guardsmen were rushed to the border. For a while, war with Mexico seemed nearer than it had in the week following Veracruz. But interest in the Mexican issue receded as the thunder-clouds of the European war drifted over the United States, and in February, 1917, the American forces were unconditionally withdrawn.

The lingering anticlimax that was the Pershing expedition marked the end of Wilson's crusade for moral uplift in Mexican public life. Its failure could not have been more complete. Far from teaching the Mexicans to elect good men, Wilson taught a generation of Mexicans to regard the policies of the United States with cynical distrust. The seizure of Veracruz alienated everyone who would hold political power in Mexico for thirty years to come. It was with the ill will originating at Veracruz in mind that in 1917, German Foreign Minister Zimmermann would send his famous telegram, offering Mexico the recovery of her "lost provinces" of Texas, Arizona, and New Mexico in reward for an offensive alliance with Germany should the United States join the Allies.[4]

The record Wilson made in Mexico may be evaluated on the Presidential scorecard he himself prepared. His "earnestness of purpose" and "courage of conviction" could not have been bettered. From the hour of his inauguration until the instant he ordered the landing at Veracruz, the immutable aim of Wilson's Mexican policy had been to engineer the overthrow of Victoriano Huerta. As for "force of character" and "instinct and capacity for leadership," the Mexican episode did not provide a conclusive test of Wilson's abilities. With a strong majority in Congress and a nation aching for martial exercise, he had encountered no significant opposition to the decision to intervene. What the Republicans contested was the style, not the substance, of his program. Yet in clinging so stubbornly to the Tampico Incident as the sole cause for intervention, Wilson first revealed that doctrinaire attitude which would finally cost him the support of Congress and the rejection of the League of Nations, his life's most cherished work.

It was in "grasp of intellect," "clearness of vision," and "readiness of resources"—qualities in which Wilson was expected to excel—that his conduct was questionable. The philosophy with which Wilson had approached the Mexican problem was basically unsound. Nations are no more amenable than individuals to the intrusions of third parties, however nobly motivated, in their domestic affairs. Because Wilson did not recognize this homey truth, the means he had employed were sadly unsuited to the ends he desired. But the lesson was not lost. After Veracruz, Wilson abandoned his intention of reshaping the political mores of Latin America. Though he would send American troops into action in the Caribbean again, they would go in support of established régimes. Wilson realized that for all practical purposes, the Philistines of dollar diplomacy had been right. The disappearance of Huerta, "the only strong man," threw Mexico into the chaos they had foreseen and feared. Eventually, after six more years of struggle, the Mexican revolution would wind its bloody way to an outcome which Wilson approved. Whether the same result could have been attained, over a longer but less painful period, will never be known.

Ironically, it was only from a military standpoint that much pride could be taken in the seizure of Veracruz. Confronted with widely divergent objectives, Admiral Fletcher had reconciled them in a manner which kept their conflict to a minimum. There was never any doubt that the Naval Brigade could capture the city; the problem was to restrict the hostilities to the smallest scale necessary to insure success. Fletcher's solution had been both efficient and humane. It is difficult to imagine what he could have done to keep the cost in lives, Mexican or American, lower.

Tactically, the engagement was hardly illuminating. The mechanics of street fighting—the deadly, monotonous business of clearing a city, house-by-house and block-by-block—have not changed appreciably since Vespasian stormed Jerusalem in 69 A.D. At Veracruz, the confusion inherent in this type of action was heightened by the inadequate staff work of an improvised organization. Considering how hasty that improvision had been, there were remarkably few bad moments. The worst, of course, was the Second Regiment's setback before the Naval Academy, when Captain Anderson led his men forward in a formation more appropriate to a parade-ground "pass in review." It pointed to nothing more startling than the fact that good sailors do not necessarily think like good infantrymen. In every other encounter, the caution and prudence of the senior officers had complemented the dash and initiative of their juniors. When all the circumstances were taken into account, there could be only one conclusion: thrown into a nasty and unfamiliar job, the Atlantic Fleet had earned a resounding "Well done."

EPILOGUE

Though it arrived too late to take part in the fighting, the Army could also be proud of its record at Veracruz. The achievements of the Office of Military Government surpassed anything that could have been asked. The operation of the Military Government is, in fact, the only aspect of the occupation about which many historians find a kind word to say. Unfortunately, its accomplishments were altogether transitory. After the Army departed, the *Veracruzanos* resumed their old ways. The screens in the New Market rusted to powder; the streets deteriorated; and the drainage ditches choked with debris. Heaps of refuge reappeared throughout the city and in the restaurants it again became impossible to separate the food from the flies. Soon the *zopilotes* returned. In a few years, there was no evidence that an American Army had ever ruled Veracruz.

Mexico needs no reminders of Veracruz. The event that is only an awkward footnote in American history is a dramatic chapter in the epic of the struggle from which modern Mexico emerged. And if Huerta himself held no rancor towards *Sua Excelencia el Señor Presidente* Wilson, his example has been ignored. Despite the altruism of Wilson's well-publicized intentions, Mexico remembers the landing at Veracruz as a kind of Caribbean Pearl Harbor.

Several memorial ceremonies have been held in Veracruz since the landing. In 1936, a medal was presented to the veterans of the fighting. The mothers of Lieutenants Azueta and Gutiérrez received posthumous awards to their sons.[1] A few years later, a monument was dedicated to the defenders of 1847 and 1914. It stands near the waterfront, a granite column topped by a bronze figure of Mexico as a young mother holding her child. An honor guard of Mexican marines marches around it twice daily.[2] Curiously, the invasion of 1847, a barefaced smash-and-grab affair, has been forgiven; but the air of moral superiority with which Wilson seized Veracruz continues to rankle in Mexican minds. It is really not so strange—this preference, from the Mexican standpoint, for the highwayman over the fraud; yet it seems unlikely that Wilson would have understood. Perhaps that was the problem.

APPENDIXES

Appendix One: Panorama of Veracruz, Mexico, 1914

Hospital San Sebastian

Artillery Barracks

Instituto Veracruzano

Ice Plant   Naval Academy   New Market

Parochial Church

New Market   Hotel Buena Vista   Hotel Diligenc

unicipal Palace   Juárez Light

         Customs Storehouse   Customs Storehouse

Post Office	Terminal Hotel	Power Plant
Customs Storehouse	Terminal Station	Fiscal Wharf

R. M. Crosby

Terminal Wharf (Pier Four)

Fiscal Wharf

Appendix Two: Organization of the Naval Brigade

HEADQUARTERS [1]

REAR ADMIRAL FRANK F. FLETCHER, Commanding U.S. Naval Forces on Shore

CAPTAIN HENRY MCL. HUSE, Chief of Staff

LIEUTENANT (jg) GEORGE M. COURTS, Aide (Personal)

ENSIGN MARK L. HERSEY, JR., Aide

ENSIGN H. DODD, Aide and Signal Officer

LIEUTENANT FRANK J. FLETCHER, Aide (Detached)

BRIGADE STAFF

CAPTAIN WILLIAM R. RUSH, Brigade Commander

LIEUTENANT GERALD HOWZE, Adjutant

LIEUTENANT (jg) F. COGSWELL, Aide

ENSIGN EDWARD O. MCDONNELL, Signal Officer

SURGEON MIDDLETON S. ELLIOTT, Brigade Surgeon

CHIEF BOATSWAIN JOHN MCCLOY, Beachmaster

FIRST SEAMAN REGIMENT
(57 Officers and 1,146 Men)

LIEUTENANT COMMANDER ALLEN BUCHANAN, Commanding [2]

ARKANSAS BATTALION
(17 Officers and 313 Men)

LIEUTENANT COMMANDER ARTHUR B. KEATING, Commanding

LIEUTENANT (jg) JONAS H. INGRAM, Adjutant

ENSIGN W. A. RICHARDSON, Aide

1st Company
(3 Officers and 53 Men)

LIEUTENANT W. E. EBERLE, Commanding

ENSIGN MEEK, Chief of Section

ENSIGN WEBB, Chief of Section

2nd Company
(3 Officers and 54 Men)

LIEUTENANT C. H. DAVIS, Commanding

ENSIGN HATCH, Chief of Section

ENSIGN HULL, Chief of Section

---

1. Many additional positions and special staff functions were created during the occupation.
2. Captain John H. Gibbons assumed command after the action, and Lieutenant Commander Buchanan became chief of staff to Captain Rush.

3rd Company
(3 Officers and 54 Men)
LIEUTENANT (jg) R. W. CLARK, Commanding
ENSIGN SANBORN, Chief of Section   ENSIGN DUNN, Chief of Section

4th Company
(3 Officers and 53 Men)
LIEUTENANT (jg) J. W. W. CUMMING, Commanding
ENSIGN TIMBERLAKE, Chief of Section   ENSIGN GILLESPIE, Chief of Section
Special Details: 99 Men

FLORIDA BATTALION

(13 Officers and 272 Men)
LIEUTENANT RICHARD WAINWRIGHT, JR., Commanding
ENSIGN W. L. AINSWORTH, Aide

1st Company
(2 Officers and 55 Men)
ENSIGN GEORGE M. LOWRY, Commanding
ENSIGN ROY DUDLEY, Chief of Section   CHIEF TURRET CAPTAIN WARD, Chief
of Section

2nd Company
(2 Officers and 55 Men)
ENSIGN T. S. WILKINSON, Commanding
ENSIGN DAVIS, Chief of Section   CHIEF TURRET CAPTAIN R. SEMPLE,
Chief of Section

3rd Company
(3 Officers and 54 Men)
LIEUTENANT (jg) L. S. JORDAN, JR., Commanding
ENSIGN W. H. P. BLANDY, Chief of Sec-   ENSIGN J. A. BROWNELL, Chief of Section   tion

4th Company [3]
(3 Officers and 53 Men)
ENSIGN JAMES MCD. CRESAP, Commanding
ENSIGN GREENE, Chief of Section   ENSIGN WEEKS, Chief of Section (Ma-
(Artillery)   chine guns)
Special Details: 53 Men

UTAH BATTALION

(17 Officers and 367 Men)
LIEUTENANT GUY W. S. CASTLE, Commanding
ENSIGN H. B. GROW, Adjutant   ASSISTANT SURGEON W. E. EATON, Sur-
geon

1st Company
(2 Officers and 52 Men)
ENSIGN OSCAR C. BADGER, Commanding
ENSIGN C. WITHERS, Chief of Section

---

3. Artillery.

2nd Company
(3 Officers and 48 Men)
LIEUTENANT ARCHIBALD G. STIRLING, Commanding
ENSIGN J. M. KATES, Chief of Section   ENSIGN OTTO M. FORSTER, Chief of Section

3rd Company
(2 Officers and 53 Men)
LIEUTENANT (jg) PHILIP SEYMOUR, Commanding
ENSIGN G. M. TISDALE, Chief of Section

4th Company
(2 Officers and 54 Men)
ENSIGN PAUL F. FOSTER, Commanding
ENSIGN GEORGE B. JUNKIN, Chief of Section

Machine Guns
ENSIGN LAURENCE TOWNSEND, Commanding
ENSIGN S. H. GREER, Chief of Section

Artillery Detachment
(Including Machine Gun Detachment, 4 Officers and 60 Men)
LIEUTENANT (jg) W. P. WILLIAMSON, Commanding
ENSIGN E. D. LAPHAM, Adjutant
Special Details: 100 Men

CHESTER BATTALION
(2 Officers and 79 Men)
LIEUTENANT G. E. LAKE, Commanding
CHIEF QUARTERMASTER ORMSTRON, Adjutant

1st Company
LIEUTENANT G. E. LAKE, Commanding

2nd Company
ENSIGN F. S. STEINWACHS, Commanding
Special Details: 23 Men

SAN FRANCISCO BATTALION
(8 Officers and 118 Men)
LIEUTENANT W. J. GILES, Commanding
ENSIGN R. MARTIN, Adjutant   CHIEF GUNNER R. M. O'CONNOR, Gun Cotton Party

1st Company
(1 Officer and 37 Men)
ENSIGN R. D. GATEWOOD, Commanding
CHIEF BOATSWAIN D. J. O'CONNELL, Chief of Section

2nd Company
(1 Officer and 44 Men)
ENSIGN C. RIDGLEY, Commanding
GUNNER A. B. MCCRARY, Chief of Section
Special Details: 36 Men

Appendix Two

SECOND SEAMAN REGIMENT
(64 Officers and 1,301 Men)
CAPTAIN E. A. ANDERSON, Commanding

LIEUTENANT COMMANDER RUFUS Z. JOHNSTON, Adjutant

LIEUTENANT (jg) THEODORE G. ELLYSON, Ordnance Officer

ENSIGN T. G. BERRIEN, Signal Officer

LIEUTENANT COMMANDER H. E. YARNELL, Quartermaster

SURGEON CARY DEV. LANGHORNE, Surgeon

ENSIGN C. K. OSBORNE, Aide

ENSIGN C. J. PARRISH, Aide

NEW HAMPSHIRE BATTALION
(14 Officers and 356 Men)
LIEUTENANT JAMES C. LANNON, Commanding [4]

ENSIGN L. A. DAVIDSON, Adjutant

ASSISTANT SURGEON C. C. WILSON, Surgeon

1st Company
(2 Officers and 68 Men)
ENSIGN C. H. WRIGHT, Commanding

ENSIGN C. L. PEARCE, Chief of Section

CHIEF MASTER-AT-ARMS JAMES GLAVIN, Chief of Section

2nd Company
(3 Officers and 70 Men)
ENSIGN W. A. LEE, Commanding

ENSIGN HANS ERTZ, Chief of Section

ENSIGN JEROME A. LEE, Chief of Section

3rd Company
(2 Officers and 69 Men)
ENSIGN J. P. NORFLEET, Commanding

ENSIGN O. W. BAGBY, Chief of Section

CHIEF GUNNER'S MATE COX, Chief of Section

4th Company [5]
(3 Officers and 72 Men)
ENSIGN J. A. SAUNDERS, Commanding

ENSIGN B. H. LINGO, Chief of Section (Artillery)

ENSIGN P. HENDREN, Chief of Section (Machine guns)

Special Details: 74 Men

VERMONT BATTALION
(12 Officers and 308 Men)
LIEUTENANT J. C. TOWNSEND, Commanding
ENSIGN S. B. MACFARLANE, Adjutant

1st Company
(2 Officers and 55 Men)
ENSIGN C. G. WEST, Commanding

---

4. Succeeded by Lieutenant I. C. Johnson after being wounded.
5. Artillery.

177

ENSIGN O. L. DOWNES, Chief of Section   CHIEF TURRET CAPTAIN HARRISON, Chief of Section

2nd Company
(2 Officers and 55 Men)
LIEUTENANT (jg) J. R. BEARDALL, Commanding

ENSIGN D. DETREVILLE, Chief of Section   TURRET CAPTAIN J. T. MCCARTHY, Chief of Section

3rd Company
(2 Officers and 55 Men)
ENSIGN J. A. FLETCHER, Commanding

ENSIGN W. MASEK, Chief of Section   GUNNER'S MATE PETERSON, Chief of Section

4th Company
(2 Officers and 55 Men)
ENSIGN L. W. COMSTOCK, Commanding

ENSIGN L. P. BISCHOFF, Chief of Section   CHIEF BOATSWAIN'S MATE ENGLEHART, Chief of Section

Artillery Section
(1 Officer and 33 Men)
ENSIGN LIGON B. ARD, Commanding
Special Details: 55 Men

SOUTH CAROLINA BATTALION
(15 Officers and 319 Men)
LIEUTENANT ADOLPHUS STATON, Commanding
ENSIGN L. L. HUNTER, Adjutant

1st Company
(3 Officers and 51 Men)
LIEUTENANT CHARLES C. HARTIGAN, Commanding

ENSIGN H. C. FRASER, Chief of Section   ENSIGN G. S. DALE, Chief of Section

2nd Company
(2 Officers and 55 Men)
ENSIGN J. T. MELVIN, Commanding

ENSIGN D. R. LEE, Chief of Section   CHIEF TURRET CAPTAIN HANSEN, Chief of Section

3rd Company
(2 Officers and 53 Men)
ENSIGN E. W. HANSON, Commanding

ENSIGN CONGER, Chief of Section   CHIEF TURRET CAPTAIN SNYDER, Chief of Section

4th Company
(2 Officers and 55 Men)
ENSIGN V. C. GRIFFIN, Commanding

ENSIGN D. F. PATTERSON, Chief of Section   MACHINIST MAYNARD, Chief of Section

Appendix Two

Artillery Section
(1 Officer and 27 Men)
ENSIGN R. B. HAMMES, Commanding

Machine Gun Section
(1 Officer and 18 Men)
ENSIGN B. F. POE, Commanding
Special Details: 69 Men

NEW JERSEY BATTALION
(19 Officers and 322 Men)
LIEUTENANT FREDERICK V. MCNAIR, Commanding

ENSIGN C. E. VAN HOOK, Adjutant   ENSIGN F. K. ELDER, Battalion Engineer

ASSISTANT SURGEON J. T. BORDEN, Surgeon   ENSIGN F. M. HARRIS, Aide

1st Company
(3 Officers and 64 Men)
ENSIGN G. C. FULLER, Commanding

ENSIGN E. BUCKMASTER, Chief of Section   ENSIGN C. P. MCPEATERS, Chief of Section

2nd Company
(3 Officers and 64 Men)
ENSIGN S. R. CANINE, Commanding

ENSIGN L. R. BROWN, Chief of Section   ENSIGN H. W. PILLSBURY, Chief of Section

3rd Company
(3 Officers and 64 Men)
ENSIGN G. W. HEWLETT, Commanding

ENSIGN E. S. MCCAWLEY, Chief of Section   ENSIGN L. L. BABBITT, Chief of Section

4th Company [6]
(3 Officers and 54 Men)
ENSIGN S. S. KENNEDY, Commanding

ENSIGN SCHUYLER MILLS, Chief of Section   ENSIGN W. H. BURTIS, Chief of Section

Special Details: 76 Men

ARTILLERY BATTALION [7]
(Personnel of this battalion are included in the totals of the ships' battalions from which they were detached.)
LIEUTENANT JOHN GRADY, Commanding
ENSIGN J. A. SAUNDERS, Adjutant

---

6. Artillery.
7. Consisting of four 3-inch field guns and six machine guns.

SECOND PROVISIONAL REGIMENT, ADVANCED BASE BRIGADE, USMC
(28 Officers and 715 Men)
LIEUTENANT COLONEL WENDELL C. NEVILLE, Commanding

CAPTAIN FREDERICK H. DELANO, Adjutant   CAPTAIN JETER R. HORTON, Quartermaster

JACOB STEPP, Surgeon

1st Battalion
(10 Officers and 299 Men)
MAJOR RANDOLPH C. BERKELEY, Commanding
FIRST LIEUTENANT RALPH L. SHEPARD, Adjutant

15th Company *

1st Company
(2 Officers and 100 Men)
CAPTAIN JOHN A. HUGHES, Commanding
SECOND LIEUTENANT LESTER S. WASS

16th Company *

2nd Company
(3 Officers and 99 Men)
CAPTAIN WALTER N. HILL, Commanding

FIRST LIEUTENANT ALFRED MCC. ROBBINS   SECOND LIEUTENANT ROLLAND E. BRUMBAUGH

17th Company *

3rd Company
(3 Officers and 99 Men)
CAPTAIN ELI T. FRYER, Commanding

FIRST LIEUTENANT WOOLMAN G. EMORY   SECOND LIEUTENANT CHARLES G. SINCLAIR

3rd Battalion [8]
(6 Officers and 164 Men)
MAJOR SMEDLEY DARLINGTON BUTLER, Commanding
FIRST LIEUTENANT EDWARD A. OSTERMANN, Adjutant

8th Company *

7th Company
(2 Officers and 79 Men)
CAPTAIN JESSE F. DYER, Commanding
SECOND LIEUTENANT ARTHUR J. WHITE

10th Company *

8th Company
(2 Officers and 82 Men)
FIRST LIEUTENANT HOWARD W. STONE, Commanding
SECOND LIEUTENANT ALEXANDER A. VANDEGRIFT

---

* Actual unit designations; company numbers in italics were temporarily assigned.

8. The Second Battalion, consisting of 9 officers and 350 men, was formed of personnel who arrived after the action.

Appendix Two

THIRD PROVISIONAL REGIMENT, ADVANCED BASE BRIGADE, USMC

(20 Officers and 608 Men)

MAJOR ALBERTUS W. CATLIN, Commanding

CAPTAIN RICHARD B. CREECY, Adjutant

FIRST LIEUTENANT JOSEPH A. ROSSELL, Quartermaster

ALLEN STUART, Surgeon

1st Battalion

(8 Officers and 295 Men) [9]

MAJOR GEORGE C. REID, Commanding

FIRST LIEUTENANT JOSEPH D. MURRAY, Adjutant

Company A: Utah Marines
(2 Officers and 61 Men)

CAPTAIN JAMES C. BRECKINRIDGE, Commanding

SECOND LIEUTENANT WILLIAM B. SULLIVAN

Company B: Florida and Minnesota Marines
(2 Officers and 124 Men)

CAPTAIN WILLIAM C. HARLLEE, Commanding

SECOND LIEUTENANT ALBERT R. SUTHERLAND

Company C: New Jersey and Michigan Marines
(2 Officers and 110 Men)

CAPTAIN FRANK F. ROBARDS, Commanding

SECOND LIEUTENANT CHARLES D. BARRETT

2nd Battalion

(9 Officers and 309 Men) [10]

CAPTAIN LOUIS M. GULICK, Commanding

SECOND LIEUTENANT EDMOND H. MORSE, Adjutant

Company D: Arkansas Marines
(1 Officer and 76 Men)

SECOND LIEUTENANT DAVID S. BARRY, Commanding

Company E: Vermont and Louisiana Marines
(3 Officers and 119 Men)

CAPTAIN ARTHUR T. MARIX, Commanding

FIRST LIEUTENANT ALPHONSE A. RACICOT

SECOND LIEUTENANT FREDERICK R. HOYT

Company F: New Hampshire and South Carolina Marines
(3 Officers and 114 Men)

CAPTAIN ROBERT B. FARQUHARSON, Commanding

FIRST LIEUTENANT ANDREW B. DRUM

SECOND LIEUTENANT HARRY L. SMITH

---

9. This total includes 110 men (60 from the *Minnesota* and 50 from the *Michigan*) who arrived after the action.

10. This total includes 68 *Louisiana* Marines who arrived after the action.

Appendix Three: United States Naval and Marine Personnel Killed in Action or Died of Wounds at Veracruz

Compiled from "Casualties since Landing of U.S. Naval Forces Vera Cruz, Mexico," U.S. Atlantic Fleet, Flagship *Arkansas,* Veracruz, Mexico, April 24, 1914. Naval Records Collection, The National Archives.

Name	Rank/Rate	Organization	Date
POINSETT, GEORGE	Ordinary Seaman	*Florida*	April 21
SCHUMAKER, JOHN F.	Coxswain	*Florida*	"
PERCY, RUFUS E.	Private, USMC	*Utah* Marines	"
MARTIN, SAMUEL	Private, USMC	16th Company, 2nd Regiment, Advanced Base Brigade	"
HAGGERTY, DANIEL A.	Private, USMC	8th Company, 2nd Regiment, Advanced Base Brigade	"
DELOWRY, FRANCIS P.	Ordinary Seaman	*New Hampshire*	April 22
FISHER, ELZIE C.	Ordinary Seaman	*New Hampshire*	"
FROHLICHSTEIN, ESAN H.	Ordinary Seaman	*New Hampshire*	"
LANE, DENNIS J.	Seaman	*New Hampshire*	"
SMITH, CHARLES E.	Ordinary Seaman	*New Hampshire*	"
DEVORICK, FRANK	Ordinary Seaman	*South Carolina*	"
STREAM, ALBIN E.	Ordinary Seaman	*New Jersey*	"
DEFABBIO, GABRIEL A.	Gunner's Mate Third Class	*New Jersey*	"
FRIED, LOUIS O.	Ordinary Seaman	*Arkansas*	"
WATSON, WILLIAM L.	Ordinary Seaman	*Arkansas*	"
BOSWELL, LOUIS F.	Chief Gunner's Mate	*Michigan*	"
SUMMERLIN, RANDOLPH D.	Private, USMC	*Vermont* Marines	April 23

Appendix Four: Medal of Honor Recipients,
Veracruz

Name	Rank/Rate	Vessel	Position in which Serving
ANDERSON, EDWIN A.	Captain, USN	*New Hampshire*	Commanding Officer, 2nd Seaman Regiment
BADGER, OSCAR C.	Ensign, USN	*Utah*	Company Commander, *Utah* battalion
BEASLEY, HARRY C.	Seaman, USN	*Florida*	Rifleman, *Florida* battalion
BERKELEY, RANDOLPH C.	Major, USMC		Commanding Officer, 1st Battalion, 2nd Provisional Regiment, Marine Brigade
BISHOP, CHARLES F.	Quartermaster Second Class, USN	*Florida*	Brigade Signal Section
BRADLEY, GEORGE	Chief Gunner, USN	*Utah*	In Charge of Special Details
BUCHANAN, ALLEN	Lieutenant Commander, USN	*Florida*	Commanding Officer, 1st Seaman Regiment
BUTLER, SMEDLEY D.	Major, USMC		Commanding Officer, 3rd Battalion, 2nd Provisional Regiment, Marine Brigade
CASTLE, GUY W. S.	Lieutenant, USN	*Utah*	Commanding Officer, *Utah* battalion
CATLIN, ALBERTUS W.	Major, USMC		Commanding Officer, 3rd Provisional Regiment, Marine Brigade
COURTS, GEORGE M.	Lieutenant, USN	*Florida*	Aide-de-camp to Admiral Fletcher
CREGAN, GEORGE	Boatswain's Mate Second Class, USN	*Florida*	Rifleman, *Florida* battalion
DECKER, PERCY A.	Boatswain's Mate Second Class, USN	*Florida*	Rifleman, *Florida* battalion
DE SOMER, ABRAHAM	Chief Turret Captain, USN	*Utah*	Section leader, *Utah* battalion

Name	Rank/Rate	Vessel	Position in which Serving
DRUSTRUP, NIELS	Chief Turret Captain, USN	*Utah*	Section leader, *Utah* battalion
DYER, JESSE F.	Captain, USMC		Commanding Officer, 8th Company, 2nd Provisional Regiment, Marine Brigade
ELLIOTT, MIDDLETON S.	Surgeon, USN	*Florida*	Brigade Surgeon
FLETCHER, FRANK F.	Rear Admiral, USN	*Florida*	Commanding U.S. Naval Forces
FLETCHER, FRANK J.	Lieutenant, USN	*Florida*	Acting-Captain, *Esperanza*
FOSTER, PAUL F.	Ensign, USN	*Utah*	Company Commander, *Utah* battalion
FRAZER, HUGH C.	Ensign, USN	*South Carolina*	Section leader, *South Carolina* battalion
FRYER, ELI T.	Captain, USMC		Commanding Officer, 17th Company, 2nd Provisional Regiment, Marine Brigade
GISBURNE, EDWARD A.	Electrician Third Class, USN	*Florida*	Brigade Signal Section
GRADY, JOHN	Lieutenant, USN	*Arkansas*	Commanding 2nd Seaman Regiment artillery
HARNER, JOSEPH G.	Boatswain's Mate Second Class, USN	*Florida*	Rifleman, *Florida* battalion
HARRISON, WILLIAM K.	Commander, USN	*San Francisco*	Captain, *San Francisco*
HARTIGAN, CHARLES C.	Lieutenant, USN	*South Carolina*	Company Commander, *South Carolina* battalion
HILL, WALTER N.	Captain, USMC		Commanding Officer, 16th Company, 2nd Provisional Regiment, Marine Brigade
HUGHES, JOHN A.	Captain, USMC		Commanding Officer, 15th Company, 2nd Provisional Regiment, Marine Brigade
HUSE, HENRY MCL. P.	Captain, USN	*Florida*	Chief of Staff to Admiral Fletcher
INGRAM, JONAS H.	Lieutenant (jg), USN	*Arkansas*	Adjutant, *Arkansas* battalion
JARRETT, BERRIE H.	Seaman, USN	*Florida*	Brigade Signal Section
JOHNSTON, RUFUS Z.	Lieutenant Commander, USN	*New Hampshire*	Adjutant, 2nd Seaman Regiment

Name	Rank/Rate	Vessel	Position in which Serving
LANGHORNE, CARY DEV.	Surgeon, USN	*Vermont*	Surgeon, 2nd Seaman Regiment
LANNON, JAMES P.	Lieutenant, USN	*New Hampshire*	Commanding Officer, *New Hampshire* battalion
LOWRY, GEORGE M.	Ensign, USN	*Florida*	Company Commander, *Florida* battalion
MCCLOY, JOHN	Chief Boatswain, USN	*Florida*	Beachmaster
MCDONNELL, EDWARD O.	Ensign, USN	*Florida*	Brigade Signal Officer
MCNAIR, FREDERICK V., JR.	Lieutenant, USN	*New Jersey*	Commanding Officer, *New Jersey* battalion
MOFFETT, WILLIAM A.	Commander, USN	*Chester*	Captain, *Chester*
NEVILLE, WENDELL C.	Lieutenant Colonel, USMC		Commanding Officer, 2nd Provisional Regiment, Marine Brigade
NICKERSON, HENRY N.	Boatswain's Mate Second Class, USN	*Utah*	Rifleman, *Utah* battalion
NORDSIEK, CHARLES L.	Ordinary Seaman, USN	*Florida*	Brigade Signal Section
REID, GEORGE C.	Major, USMC		Commanding Officer, 1st Battalion, 3rd Provisional Regiment, Marine Brigade
RUSH, WILLIAM R.	Captain, USN	*Florida*	Commanding the Naval Brigade
SCHNEPEL, FRED J.	Ordinary Seaman, USN	*Florida*	Brigade Signal Section
SEMPLE, ROBERT	Chief Gunner, USN	*Florida*	Section leader, *Florida* battalion
SINNETT, LAWRENCE C.	Seaman, USN	*Florida*	Rifleman, *Florida* battalion
STATON, ADOLPHUS C.	Lieutenant, USN	*South Carolina*	Commanding Officer, *South Carolina* battalion
STICKNEY, HERMAN O.	Commander, USN	*Prairie*	Captain, *Prairie*
TOWNSEND, JULIUS C.	Lieutenant, USN	*Vermont*	Commanding Officer, *Vermont* battalion
WAINWRIGHT, RICHARD, JR.	Lieutenant, USN	*Florida*	Commanding Officer, *Florida* battalion
WALSH, JAMES A.	Seaman, USN	*Florida*	Brigade Signal Section
WILKINSON, THEODORE S.	Ensign, USN	*Florida*	Company Commander, *Florida* battalion
ZUIDERVELD, WILLIAM	Hospital Apprentice First Class, USN	*Florida*	Aid-man, *Florida* battalion

NOTES

Preface

1. Ted C. Hinckley, "Wilson, Huerta, and the Twenty-One Gun Salute," *The Historian: A Journal of History*, Vol. XXII, No. 2 (February, 1960).

Chapter One

1. Josephus Daniels, *The Life of Woodrow Wilson*, p. 75.
2. Lieutenant Colonel Roscoe Arnett, USMC (Ret.), to the author.
3. Herbert Croly in *The New Republic*, November 21, 1914.
4. Arthur S. Walsworth, *Woodrow Wilson: American Prophet*, I, 241.
5. Daniels, *op. cit.*, p. 132.
6. *Ibid.*
7. *Ibid.*, p. 133.
8. *Ibid.*, p. 134.
9. Henry B. Parkes, *A History of Mexico*, p. 286.
10. Ernest H. Gruening, *Mexico and Its Heritage*, p. 560.
11. Francesco Bulnes, *El Verdadero Díaz*, p. 299.
12. Ramon Prida, *De la Dictadura a la Anarquia*, pp. 555–56.
13. *Ibid.*, p. 613.
14. Department of State, *Papers Relating to the Foreign Relations of the United States, 1913*, p. 721.
15. Daniels, *op. cit.*, p. 192.
16. Department of State, *Foreign Relations 1913*, File 812.001/6277, 6347, 6325.
17. Daniels, *op. cit.*, p. 177.

Chapter Two

1. David R. Loth, *Woodrow Wilson*, p. 101,
2. J. B. Moore, "Memorandum on the Mexican Situation," May 14, 1913. State Department Papers, The National Archives.
3. Walsworth, *op. cit.*, I, 358.
4. Ray Stannard Baker, *Woodrow Wilson, Life and Letters*, IV, 248.
5. W. B. Hale, "Affairs in Mexico," July 9, 1913. State Department Papers, The National Archives.
6. William Jennings Bryan and Mary Baird Bryan, *The Memoirs of William Jennings Bryan*, II, 357.
7. Baker, *op. cit.*, IV, 273.
8. Gerald Langford, *The Richard Harding Davis Years*, p. 287.
9. Department of State, *Foreign Relations 1913*, File 812/6271.
10. Walsworth, *op. cit.*, I, 360.
11. W. B. Hale to B. G. Davis, June 3, 1913. State Department Papers, The National Archives.
12. Joseph Tumulty, *Woodrow Wilson as I Know Him*, p. 146.

13. Charles W. Thompson, *Presidents I've Known and Two Near Presidents,* p. 261.
14. Department of State, *Foreign Relations 1913,* pp. 820–23.
15. *Ibid.*
16. *Ibid.*
17. *The New York Times,* August 9, 1913.
18. O'Shaughnessy to Bryan, August 27, 1913. State Department Papers, The National Archives.
19. *Ibid.*

Chapter Three

1. Baker, *op. cit.,* IV, 55.
2. Department of State, *Foreign Relations 1913,* pp. 820–23.
3. *New York Herald,* August 28, 1913.
4. Lind to Bryan, August 27, 1913 (in Arthur S. Link, *Woodrow Wilson, The New Freedom,* p. 362).
5. Bryan to Lind, August 27, 1913. State Department Papers, The National Archives.
6. O'Shaughnessy to Bryan, September 13, 1913. *Ibid.*
7. *The New York Times,* September 12, 1913.
8. Baker, *op. cit.,* IV, 273.
9. Link, *op. cit.,* p. 379.
10. Bryan to the American Embassy, November 1, 1913. State Department Papers, The National Archives.
11. Secretary of State Circular of September 24, 1913. State Department Papers, The National Archives.
12. Burton J. Hedrick, *The Life and Letters of Walter H. Page,* I, 204.
13. Link, *op. cit.*
14. Edith O'Shaughnessy, *A Diplomat's Wife in Mexico,* p. 260.

Chapter Four

1. Tumulty, *op. cit.,* p. 147.
2. Lowell Thomas, *Old Gimlet Eye: The Adventures of Smedley Darlington Butler,* p. 170.
3. *Ibid.*
4. Chief Radio Engineer John Robert Johnson, USN (Ret.), to the author.
5. *Ibid.*
6. *Ibid.*
7. Thomas, *op. cit.,* p. 176.
8. Mr. Arthur J. Sweetman to the author.
9. "News From Veracruz," *The Fleet Review,* March, 1913.
10. Jack London, "Our Adventurers at Tampico," *Collier's Magazine,* Vol. LIII (June 27, 1914).
11. O'Shaughnessy, *op. cit.,* pp. 96, 136.
12. Rear Admiral Sir Christopher Cradock, RN, "Second Attack by Rebels in Tampico 26th March to 14 April and their subsequent retirement. Incident of Demand by United States Rear Admiral Mayo for Salute

to the United States Flag." April 14, 1914. Admiralty File 1/8374, Public Records Office, London.
13. *The New York Times,* April 10, 1914.
14. Rear Admiral Frank F. Fletcher to Secretary of the Navy Daniels, April 19, 1914. Naval Records Collection, The National Archives.
15. General Morelos Zaragoza in the Mexico City *Excelsior,* December 6, 1933.
16. This account is a synthesis of those contained in the following works: Robert E. Quirk, *An Affair of Honor: Woodrow Wilson and the Occupation of Veracruz,* pp. 19–23; Justino M. Palomares, *La Invasión Yanqui en 1914,* pp. 255–264; and various reports in the Naval Records Collection, The National Archives.
17. "With Mayo at Tampico," *The Literary Digest,* Vol. XLVIII (May 2, 1914).
18. Department of State, *Papers Relating to the Foreign Relations of the United States 1914,* p. 448.
19. *Ibid.,* pp. 474–76.
20. S. G. Blythe, "Mexico: The Record of a Conversation with President Wilson," *Saturday Evening Post,* Vol. CLXXXVI (May 23, 1914).
21. Tumulty, *op. cit.,* p. 158.
22. "President Wilson on His Foreign Policy," *World's Work,* Vol. XXVIII (October, 1914).
23. Department of State, *Foreign Relations 1914,* p. 449.
24. Cradock, *loc. cit.*
25. Department of State, *Foreign Relations 1914,* p. 462.
26. O'Shaughnessy, *op. cit.,* p. 53.
27. *Ibid.,* p. 66.
28. O'Shaughnessy to Bryan, April 14, 1914. State Department Papers, The National Archives.
29. *The New York Times,* April 12, 1914.
30. Quirk, *op. cit.,* p. 49.
31. Fletcher to Daniels, April 13, 1914. Naval Records Collection, The National Archives.
32. Fletcher to Daniels. Naval Records Collection, The National Archives.
33. O'Shaughnessy to Bryan, April 12, 1914. State Department Papers, The National Archives.
34. Department of State, *Foreign Relations 1914,* pp. 474–76.
35. *Ibid.*
36. Hinckley, *loc. cit.*
37. Quirk, *op. cit.,* p. 73.
38. *Washington Post,* April 21, 1914.

Chapter Five

1. Cradock, *loc. cit.*
2. Daniels to Fletcher, April 20, 1914. Naval Records Collection, The National Archives.
3. Vice Admiral Paul F. Foster, USNR (Ret.), and Rear Admiral George M. Lowry, USNR (Ret.), to the author.

4. Mr. Arthur J. Sweetman to the author.
5. Vice Admiral Paul F. Foster, USNR (Ret.), to the author.
6. Cradock, *loc. cit.*
7. Rear Admiral Frank F. Fletcher, "Seizure and Occupation of Vera Cruz, April 21–30, 1914." May 13, 1914. Naval Records Collection, The National Archives.
8. *Ibid.*
9. *Ibid.*
10. *Ibid.*
11. Quirk, *op. cit.*, pp. 70–71.
12. Fletcher, *loc. cit.*
13. Quirk, *op. cit.*, pp. 8–9; Chief Radio Engineer J. R. Johnson, USN (Ret.), to the author.
14. Fletcher, *loc. cit.*
15. *Ibid.*
16. *Ibid.*
17. *Ibid.*
18. *Ibid.*
19. *Ibid.*
20. Consul Clarence Miller, "Political Conditions at Tampico." May 21, 1914. State Department Papers, The National Archives; Post Records (Tampico).
21. *Ibid.*
22. *Ibid.*
23. Fletcher, *loc. cit.*
24. *Ibid.*
25. Canada to Bryan, April 20, 1914. State Department Papers, The National Archives.
26. This conversation is reconstructed from those contained in Daniels, *op. cit.*, pp. 182–83 and Tumulty, *op. cit.*, pp. 152–53; Tumulty confuses Fletcher with Mayo. A slightly different version appears in Barbara W. Tuchman, *The Zimmermann Telegram,* pp. 49–50.
27. Tumulty, *op. cit.*, p. 153.
28. *Ibid.*
29. Fletcher, *loc. cit.*

Chapter Six

1. Fleet Order No. 17–24, U.S. Atlantic Fleet, Veracruz, April 26, 1914. Naval Records Collection, The National Archives.
2. Fletcher, *loc. cit.*
3. Rear Admiral G. M. Lowry, USNR (Ret.), to the author.
4. Matt Hensley, "Notes, Comments and Discussion: USS *Florida* at Veracruz," *United States Naval Institute Proceedings,* Vol. 87, No. 11 (November, 1961).
5. Fred T. Jane (ed.). *Fighting Ships* (1914), p. 168.
6. Fletcher, *loc. cit.*; Rear Admiral G. M. Lowry, USNR (Ret.), to the author.
7. Mr. Henry N. Nickerson to the author.
8. Lieutenant Gerald Howze, "Journal of the Commander of the Naval

Brigade Operating on Shore at Vera Cruz, Mexico, April 21–30, 1914."
Naval Records Collection, The National Archives. The organization
was prescribed by Brigade Orders Nos. 1 and 2 of April 13 and 20, 1914.

9. Fletcher, *loc. cit.*
10. *Ibid.*
11. *Ibid.*
12. *Ibid.*
13. *Ibid.*
14. *Ibid.*
15. Consul W. W. Canada, "Report of the Occupation of Vera Cruz by the
American Forces, April 21st and 22nd, 1914," August 11, 1914. Naval
Records Collection, The National Archives (another copy is filed with
the State Department Papers).
16. Log of the *Prairie*, April 21, 1914. Records of the Bureau of Naval
Personnel, The National Archives.
17. Thomas, *op. cit.*, p. 177.
18. These were: *Sporting Notes from the East* (1884), *Wrinkles in Seamanship* (1894), and *Whispers from the Fleet* (1907).
19. O'Shaughnessy, *op. cit.*, pp. 72–74.
20. Thomas, *op. cit.*, p. 177.
21. O'Shaughnessy, *op. cit.*, pp. 137–38.
22. Fletcher, *loc. cit.*
23. *Ibid.*
24. *Ibid.*
25. Log of the *Prairie*, April 21, 1914, *loc. cit.*
26. *Ibid.;* topedo tubes noted in *Washington Post*, April 24, 1914.
27. Fletcher, *loc. cit.*
28. *Ibid.*
29. *Ibid.*
30. *Ibid.*
31. Mr. Ralph M. Crosby to the author.
32. Canada, *loc. cit.*
33. *Ibid;* cf. Quirk, *op. cit.*, pp. 90–91.
34. Canada, *loc. cit.*
35. *Ibid.*
36. *Ibid.*
37. *Ibid.*
38. Quirk, *op. cit.*, pp. 90–91.
39. O'Shaughnessy, *op. cit.*, pp. 135; 305–06.
40. Quirk, *op. cit.*, p. 91.
41. *Ibid.*
42. Palomares, *op. cit.*, pp. 92–93.
43. *Ibid.*
44. Quirk, *op. cit.*, p. 92.

Chapter Seven

1. *Washington Post*, April 22, 1914.
2. Fletcher, *loc. cit.*
3. *Washington Post*, May 1, 1914.

4. Hamilton Peltz in the *New York Herald,* April 22, 1914.
5. *Washington Post,* April 22, 1914.
6. *The New York Times,* April 22, 1914.
7. *Ibid.*
8. Fletcher, *loc. cit.;* Quirk, *op. cit.,* p. 93.
9. "Vera Cruz: A Crusade for Decency." *Outlook,* Vol. 107 (July 4, 1914).
10. Thomas, *op. cit.,* p. 170.
11. Charles Jenkinson, "Vera Cruz: What American Occupation Has Meant to a Mexican Community." *Survey,* Vol. XXX (November 7, 1914).
12. Quirk, *op. cit.,* pp. 81–83.
13. The description of this and other landmarks is based primarily upon a study of contemporary photographs.
14. "Vera Cruz: A Crusade for Decency," *loc. cit.*
15. *The New York Times,* April 22, 1914; *Washington Post,* April 30, 1914.
16. O'Shaughnessy, *op. cit.,* p. 233.
17. Howze, *loc. cit.*
18. Thomas, *op. cit.,* p. 20.
19. Canada, *loc. cit.*
20. Lieutenant Colonel W. C. Neville, "Report of Operations of the 2nd Advanced Base Regiment from April 21, 1914 to 8:00 P.M. April 26, 1914." Headquarters, 1st Advanced Base Brigade, Veracruz, April 27, 1914. Naval Records Collection, The National Archives.
21. *Ibid.*
22. *Washington Post,* April 22, 1914.
23. Fletcher, *loc. cit.*
24. Rear Admiral George M. Lowry, USNR (Ret.), to the author.
25. Howze, *loc. cit.*
26. Fletcher, *loc. cit.*
27. Rear Admiral George M. Lowry, USNR (Ret.), to the author.

Chapter Eight

1. *Brooklyn Daily Eagle,* May 24, 1914.
2. Palomares, *op. cit.,* pp. 32–33, 40, 90–96; Quirk, *op. cit.,* p. 95.
3. Canada, *loc. cit.*
4. Fletcher, *loc. cit.*
5. Palomares, *op. cit.,* pp. 90–96.
6. *Ibid.,* pp. 97–98.
7. Fletcher, *loc. cit.*
8. Neville, *loc. cit.*
9. *Washington Post,* April 22, 1914.
10. Matt Hensley, *loc. cit.*
11. Palomares, *op. cit.,* 98.
12. *Mexican Herald,* April 26, 1914.
13. "Heroism at Vera Cruz," *Our Navy,* Vol. VIII, No. 3 (July, 1914), quoting Admiral Fletcher's report of commendations; Palomares, *op. cit.,* p. 96. There seems little doubt that the incident to which these sources refer is the same.
14. *Mexican Herald,* April 26, 1914.
15. Rear Admiral George M. Lowry, USNR (Ret.), to the author.

16. *Ibid.*
17. *Ibid.*
18. *Ibid.*
19. *Mexican Herald,* April 26, 1914.
20. General Order No. 101, June 15, 1914. Naval Records Collection, The National Archives.
21. General Order No. 116, August 9, 1914. Naval Records Collection, The National Archives.
22. Rear Admiral George M. Lowry, USNR (Ret.), to the author.
23. Neville, *loc. cit.;* Subcommittee of Veterans' Affairs of the Committee on Labor and Public Welfare, United States Senate, *Medal of Honor Recipients, 1863–1963,* pp. 761, 765; Palomares, *op. cit.,* p. 210.
24. Palomares, *op. cit.,* pp. 99–100; Commander John A. Brownell, USN (Ret.), to the author.
25. Fletcher, *loc. cit.*
26. *Ibid.*
27. Vice Admiral Paul F. Foster, USNR (Ret.), to the author.
28. Log of the *Utah.* April 21, 1914. Records of the Bureau of Naval Personnel, The National Archives.
29. Fletcher, *loc. cit.*
30. *Washington Post,* April 23, 1914.
31. *Mexican Herald,* April 26, 1914; Fletcher, *loc. cit.;* Howze, *loc. cit.;* "Heroism at Vera Cruz," *loc. cit.*
32. Log of the *Utah,* April 21, 1914, *loc. cit.*
33. Quirk, *op. cit.,* p. 98.
34. Fletcher, *loc. cit.*
35. Palomares, *op. cit.,* p. 90.
36. *Ibid.;* Fletcher, *loc. cit.*
37. Rear Admiral G. M. Lowry, USNR (Ret.), to the author.
38. Subcommittee of Veterans' Affairs, *op. cit.,* p. 742.
39. "Heroism at Vera Cruz," *loc. cit.;* Fletcher, *loc. cit.*
40. Log of the *Prairie,* April 21, 1914, *loc. cit.*
41. Palomares, *op. cit.,* pp. 91, 96.
42. Written at Veracruz, May 31, 1914. Naval Records Collection. The National Archives.
43. Howze, *loc. cit.;* "Heroism at Vera Cruz," *loc. cit.*
44. Fletcher, *loc. cit.*
45. Vice Admiral Paul F. Foster, USNR (Ret.), to the author.
46. Howze, *loc. cit.*
47. Copeland's narrative appeared in the *Brooklyn Daily Eagle,* May 24, 1914.
48. "Heroism at Vera Cruz," *loc. cit.*
49. Vice Admiral Paul F. Foster, USNR (Ret.), to the author.
50. *Ibid.;* Fletcher, *loc. cit.*
51. "Heroism at Vera Cruz," *loc. cit.;* Mr. H. N. Nickerson to the author.
52. "Heroism at Vera Cruz," *loc. cit.*
53. Rear Admiral George M. Lowry, USNR (Ret.), to the author.
54. *Ibid.*
55. *Ibid.*
56. Howze, *loc. cit.*

57. Palomares, *op. cit.,* pp. 274–78.
58. Canada, *loc. cit.*
59. Fletcher, *loc. cit.*
60. *The New York Times,* April 22, 1914.
61. Palomares, *op. cit.,* pp. 98–99.
62. Howze, *loc. cit.;* "Heroism at Vera Cruz," *loc. cit.*
63. *Mexican Herald,* April 25, 1914.
64. Vice Admiral Paul F. Foster, USNR (Ret.), to the author.
65. Captain H. B. Grow, USN (Ret.), to the author.
66. Mr. Arthur J. Sweetman to the author.
67. *Ibid.*

Chapter Nine

1. Records of the Bureau of Naval Personnel, The National Archives.
2. Fletcher, *loc. cit.*
3. *Ibid.*
4. *Ibid.*
5. Canada, *loc. cit.*
6. *Ibid.*
7. Subcommittee of Veterans' Affairs, *op. cit.,* p. 143.
8. Fletcher, *loc. cit.*
9. Baker, *op. cit.,* IV, 330.
10. Walsworth, *op. cit.,* I, 373.
11. Quirk, *op. cit.,* pp. 98–99.
12. Canada, *loc. cit.*
13. *Ibid.*
14. Fletcher, *loc. cit.*
15. "Heroism at Vera Cruz," *loc. cit.*
16. Log of HMS *Essex,* April 22, 1914. Admiralty File 53/41085, Public Records Office, London.
17. Log of the *Prairie,* April 21, 1914, *loc. cit.*
18. Fletcher, *loc. cit.*
19. Captain Roy Dudley, USN (Ret.), to the author.
20. Neville, *loc. cit.*
21. Naval Records Collection, The National Archives.
22. Captain Roy Dudley, USN (Ret.), to the author.
23. Howze, *loc. cit.*
24. Captain E. B. Lapham, USN (Ret.), to the author.
25. Howze, *loc. cit.*
26. Canada, *loc. cit.*
27. Veracruz *La Opinión,* April 22, 1914.
28. Palomares, *op. cit.* pp. 134–35.
29. Fletcher, *loc. cit.*
30. "Operations of the *San Francisco* in connection with the occupation of Vera Cruz," May 9, 1914. Naval Records Collection, The National Archives.
31. Fletcher, *loc. cit.;* log of the *Prairie,* April 21, 1914, *loc. cit.*
32. Thomas, *op. cit.,* p. 177.
33. *Ibid.*

34. Log of the *Chester,* April 21, 1914. Records of the Bureau of Naval Personnel, The National Archives; transcripts of messages exchanged between Fletcher and Moffett, Naval Records Collection, The National Archives.
35. A wonderfully vivid portrait of Butler emerges from Thomas' *Old Gimlet Eye.*
36. Fletcher, *loc. cit.*
37. Logs of the *Florida* and *Utah,* April 21, 1914, *loc. cit.*
38. Fletcher, *loc. cit.*
39. *Ibid.*
40. *Ibid.*
41. Howze, *loc. cit.*
42. "Heroism at Vera Cruz," *loc. cit.*
43. Fletcher, *loc. cit.*
44. Commander John A. Brownell, USN (Ret.), to the author.
45. "Operations of the *San Francisco,*" *loc. cit.*
46. Palomares, *op. cit.,* pp. 95–96; Canada, *loc. cit.*
47. Palomares, *op. cit.,* pp. 96–97.
48. Captain Schuyler S. Mills, USN (Ret.), to the author.
49. Logs of the *Arkansas, New Hampshire,* and *Vermont,* April 22, 1914. Records of the Bureau of Naval Personnel, The National Archives.
50. Captain Lewis S. Comstock, USN (Ret.), to the author.
51. *Washington Post,* April 24, 1914; Lieutenant Commander J. F. Peck, USN (Ret.), and Mr. R. M. Crosby to the author.
52. Captain R. B. Hammes, USN (Ret.), to the author.
53. Logs of the *Arkansas, Florida, Prairie,* and *Utah,* April 22, 1914, *loc. cit.*
54. Lieutenant W. J. Giles, "Narrative of Events, Vera Cruz, April 21–30, 1914." Naval Records Collection, The National Archives.
55. Fletcher, *loc. cit.*
56. *Ibid.*

Chapter Ten

1. Naval Records Collection, The National Archives.
2. Howze, *loc. cit.*
3. *Washington Post,* May 10, 1914; Lieutenant (jg) T. Gordon Ellyson, "Letter" to Mrs. Ellyson, May 4, 1914, Naval Historical Foundation; Rear Admiral L. L. Hunter, USN (Ret.), Mr. Arthur J. Sweetman and others to the author.
4. Mr. Arthur J. Sweetman to the author.
5. Ellyson, "Letter," *loc. cit.*
6. This reconstruction of the Second Regiment's advance, not clearly stated in official records, has been developed from information contained in the following references: Giles, "Narrative of Events," *loc. cit.;* logs of the *Chester* and *Prairie,* April 22, 1914, *loc. cit.;* Ellyson, "Letter," *loc. cit.;* and statements by Mr. Arthur J. Sweetman, Commander James P. Norfleet, USN (Ret.), and Lieutenant Commander George S. Dale, USN (Ret.), to the author.
7. Mr. Arthur J. Sweetman to the author.
8. *Ibid.*

9. Chief Radio Engineer J. R. Johnson, USN (Ret.), to the author.
10. *Washington Post,* May 10, 1914.
11. Ellyson, "Letter," *loc. cit.*
12. Mr. Arthur J. Sweetman to the author.
13. It is interesting to compare the official reports of Fletcher and Howze, which convey the impression that the regiment retired in fairly good order, with the log entry of HMS *Essex* ("landing party broke back to the sea front"), *loc. cit.,* and the recollections of the men who were present in the action, upon which this account is based.
14. Lieutenant Commander George S. Dale, USN (Ret.), to the author.
15. Captain Schuyler S. Mills, USN (Ret.), and Rear Admiral L. L. Hunter, USN (Ret.), to the author.
16. "Heroism at Vera Cruz," *loc. cit.*
17. Ellyson, "Letter," *loc. cit.*
18. *Ibid.*
19. Commander James P. Norfleet, USN (Ret.), to the author.
20. Fletcher, *loc. cit.*
21. Commander James P. Norfleet, USN (Ret.), to the author.
22. Logs of the *Chester,* April 22, 1914, *loc. cit.;* "Operations of the *San Francisco,*" *loc. cit.*
23. Chief Radio Engineer J. R. Johnson, USN (Ret.), to the author; Fletcher, *loc. cit.*
24. Jack London, "With Funston's Men," *Collier's Magazine,* Vol. LII (May 23, 1914).
25. *Washington Post,* April 24, 1914.
26. Log of the *Chester,* April 22, 1914, *loc. cit.*
27. Fletcher, *loc. cit.*
28. Subcommittee of Veterans' Affairs, *op. cit.,* p. 758.
29. Letter, subject: "Lt. Cdr. Rufus Z. Johnston: Appreciation of Services Rendered," USS *New Hampshire,* May 8, 1914. Naval Records Collection, The National Archives.
30. Aboard the *New Jersey,* May 12, 1914. Naval Records Collection, The National Archives.
31. Fletcher, *loc. cit.;* statements by Mr. Arthur J. Sweetman and Commander J. P. Norfleet, USN (Ret.), to the author.
32. "Casualties since Landing U.S. Naval Forces Vera Cruz, Mexico." U.S. Atlantic Fleet, Flagship *Arkansas,* Veracruz, Mexico, April 24, 1914. Naval Records Collection, The National Archives.
33. Vice Admiral Paul F. Foster, USNR (Ret.), to the author.
34. Fletcher, *loc. cit.*
35. "Heroism at Vera Cruz," *loc. cit.*
36. *Ibid.; Mexican Herald,* April 25, 1914; Howze, *loc. cit.*
37. Vice Admiral Paul F. Foster, USNR (Ret.), to the author.
38. Canada, *loc. cit.;* Howze, *loc. cit.*
39. Captain H. B. Grow, USN (Ret.), to the author.
40. Fletcher, *loc. cit.*
41. *Ibid.*
42. Lieutenant Commander J. F. Peck, USN (Ret.), to the author.
43. Howze, *loc. cit.;* "Heroism at Vera Cruz," *loc. cit.*
44. Howze, *loc. cit.*

45. Rear Admiral George M. Lowry, USNR (Ret.), to the author.
46. Log of the *Prairie,* April 22, 1914, *loc. cit.*
47. Mr. Arthur J. Sweetman to the author.
48. Log of the *Chester,* April 22, 1914, *loc. cit.*
49. Logs of the *Chester* and *Prairie,* April 22, 1914, *loc. cit.*
50. Howze, *loc. cit.*
51. *Ibid.;* Canada, *loc. cit.*
52. Howze, *loc. cit.*
53. Thomas, *op. cit.,* p. 178.
54. Howze, *loc. cit.*
55. "Heroism at Vera Cruz," *loc. cit.*
56. Howze, *loc. cit.*
57. *Washington Post,* April 24, 1914.
58. Vice Admiral Carleton H. Wright, USN (Ret.), to the author.
59. Mr. Arthur J. Sweetman to the author.
60. Howze, *loc. cit.*
61. "Heroism at Vera Cruz," *loc. cit.*
62. Captain J. A. Saunders, USN (Ret.), to the author.
63. Ellyson, "Letter," *loc. cit.*
64. Captain R. B. Hammes, USN (Ret.), to the author.
65. Howze, *loc. cit.; Washington Post,* May 10, 1914.
66. *Washington Post,* May 4, 1914.
67. Badger to Daniels, Naval Records Collection, The National Archives.
68. Veracruz *La Opinión,* April 23, 1914.
69. Captain Roy Dudley, USN (Ret.), to the author.
70. "Report of Duty Performed by the *Minnesota* Battalion." Headquarters, 3rd Seaman Regiment, Veracruz, April 25, 1914. Naval Records Collection, The National Archives.
71. Fletcher, *loc. cit.*

Chapter Eleven

1. Naval Records Collection, The National Archives.
2. Canada, *loc. cit.*
3. Howze, *loc. cit.*
4. Arthur S. Ruhl, "Vera Cruz: The Unfinished Drama." *Collier's Magazine,* Vol. LII (May 30, 1914).
5. O'Shaughnessy, *op. cit.,* p. 314.
6. *Ibid.,* p. 316.
7. *Ibid.,* p. 323.
8. *Ibid.*
9. London, "With Funston's Men," *loc. cit.*
10. Rear Admiral George M. Lowry, USNR (Ret.), to the author.
11. Mr. Arthur J. Sweetman to the author.
12. *Washington Post,* April 24, 1914.
13. Letter, subject: "Mexican Casualties" from Division Surgeon to Commanding Officer, U.S. Naval Forces on Shore, Division Headquarters, Veracruz, April 24, 1914. Naval Records Collection, The National Archives; Howze, *loc. cit.;* Rear Admiral George M. Lowry, USNR (Ret.), to the author.

14. "Casualties since Landing U.S. Naval Forces, Vera Cruz, Mexico," *loc. cit.*
15. Fletcher, *loc. cit.*
16. *Ibid.*
17. Howze, *loc. cit.*
18. Vice Admiral Paul F. Foster, USNR (Ret.), to the author.
19. *Ibid.*
20. *Ibid.*
21. *Ibid.*
22. Fletcher, *loc. cit.*
23. Rear Admiral George M. Lowry, USNR (Ret.), to the author.
24. *Washington Post,* April 23. 1914.
25. Rear Admiral George M. Lowry, USNR (Ret.), to the author.
26. Lieutenant Commander J. W. Greenslade, "Information concerning landing in Force." *Michigan* Battalion Headquarters, Veracruz, April 30, 1914. Naval Records Collection, The National Archives.
27. *Ibid.*
28. Fletcher, *loc. cit.*
29. O'Shaughnessy, *op. cit.,* p. 304.
30. *Ibid.,* p. 285.
31. *Ibid.,* pp. 247, 276.
32. *Ibid.,* p. 287.
33. *Ibid.,* pp. 286–89.
34. *Ibid.,* p. 305.
35. *Mexican Herald,* April 25, 1914.
36. *Ibid.*
37. Quirk, *op. cit.,* p. 108.
38. Mexico City *El Imparcial;* quoted in the *New York Herald,* April 29, 1914.
39. *Washington Post,* April 30, 1914.
40. O'Shaughnessy, *op. cit.,* p. 392.
41. Quirk, *op. cit.,* pp. 110–13; *The New York Times,* April 29, 1914.
42. The evacuation had an ugly aftermath. The American refugees boarded Mayo's ships under the impression that they would be permitted to return to Tampico as soon as the rioting subsided. Most of them had carried nothing more than the clothing they wore on their backs and many had left homes and businesses unattended. The State Department had no intention of letting them back into the picture, however, and Mayo was ordered to ship them to Galveston. The refugees' surprise was as unbounded as unpleasant. Free quarters and paid passage to their Stateside homes failed to dispel their resentment, and in the weeks that followed their angry protests received wide publicity. Wishing to deflect this latest barb from a policy already under attack, Daniels announced that the decision to withdraw from the Pánuco on April 21 had been made by Admiral Mayo. A poor choice for a scapegoat, Mayo replied with a sharp rebuttal endorsed by Admiral Badger. Daniels was in no position to pursue the matter; the messages were a matter of record, but the threat of further embarrassment was averted when the press allowed the story to die. Quirk, *op. cit.,* p. 113.

Notes

43. O'Shaughnessy, *op. cit.*, p. 295.
44. *Ibid.*
45. *Ibid.*, p. 296.
46. *Ibid.*, p. 297.
47. *Ibid.*, pp. 306–09.

Chapter Twelve

1. Reprinted in *Our Navy,* Vol. VIII, No. 3 (July, 1914).
2. *The New York Times,* April 22, 1914.
3. *Washington Post,* April 23, 1914.
4. *The New York Times,* April 22, 1914.
5. *Washington Post,* April 23, 1914.
6. *The New York Times,* April 22, 1914.
7. Quoted in Foreign Office File 414/239, Public Records Office, London.
8. *Chicago Tribune,* April 22, 1914.
9. *Ibid.*
10. *Literary Digest,* Vol. XLVIII, No. 18 (May 2, 1914).
11. Quoted in the *Washington Post,* April 24, 1914.
12. *New York Herald,* April 22, 1914.
13. *The New York Times,* April 22, 1914.
14. The vote was 72 to 13.
15. *Washington Post,* April 23, 1914.
16. *New York Herald,* April 23, 1914.
17. Karl Schriftgeisser, *The Gentleman from Massachusetts,* p. 265.
18. *The New York Times,* April 23, 1914.
19. *New York Herald,* April 24, 1914.
20. Quirk, *op. cit.*, p. 118.
21. Fletcher, *loc. cit.*
22. Brigade Order No. 5, Veracruz, April 24, 1914. Naval Records Collection, The National Archives.
23. O'Shaughnessy, *op. cit.*, p. 315.
24. London, "With Funston's Men," *loc. cit.*
25. O'Shaughnessy, *op. cit.*, p. 313.
26. Brigade Orders, Naval Records Collection, The National Archives.
27. Greenslade, *loc. cit.*
28. Rear Admiral George M. Lowry, USNR (Ret.), to the author.
29. Howze, *loc. cit.*
30. *Ibid.*
31. Fletcher, *loc. cit.*
32. *Washington Post,* May 3, 1914.
33. Fletcher, *loc. cit.*
34. Vice Admiral Paul F. Foster, USNR (Ret.), to the author.
35. Fletcher, *loc. cit.*
36. *Ibid.*
37. *Ibid.*
38. *Ibid.*
39. *Ibid.*
40. *Ibid.*; Subcommittee of Veterans' Affairs, *op. cit.*, p. 143.

41. London, "With Funston's Men," *loc. cit.*
42. *New York Herald,* April 29, 1914; *Washington Post,* April 30, 1914; O'Shaughnessy, *op. cit.,* p. 326.
43. Mr. Arthur J. Sweetman to the author.
44. Ruhl, *loc. cit.*
45. Howze, *loc. cit.*
46. *Washington Post,* June 24, 1914.
47. Vice Admiral Paul F. Foster, USNR (Ret.), to the author.
48. *Washington Post,* June 24, 1914.
49. Brigade Order No. 1, Veracruz, April 11, 1914. Naval Records Collection, The National Archives.
50. Vice Admiral Paul F. Foster, USNR (Ret.), to the author.
51. *Washington Post,* June 24, 1914.
52. Kenneth W. Munden (compiler), *Records of the Military Government of Veracruz.*
53. Vice Admiral Paul F. Foster, USNR (Ret.), to the author.
54. Fletcher, *loc. cit.*
55. *New York Herald,* April 29, 1914.
56. Fletcher, *loc. cit.*
57. Canada, *loc. cit.*

Chapter Thirteen

1. London, "With Funston's Men," *loc. cit.*
2. *The New York Times,* April 29, 1914.
3. Fletcher, *loc. cit.*
4. Quirk, *op. cit.,* pp. 106–07.
5. *Washington Post,* April 30, 1914.
6. *New York Herald,* April 29, 1914.
7. *Washington Post,* May 2, 1914.
8. Vice Admiral Carleton H. Wright, USN (Ret.), to the author.
9. Captain Roy Dudley, USN (Ret.), to the author.
10. In *The International Socialist Review* for October, 1913.
11. *Washington Post,* May 1, 1914.
12. Langford, *op. cit.,* p. 287.
13. Quirk, *op. cit.,* p. 128.
14. Joan London, *Jack London and His Times,* pp. 348–49; Irving S. Stone, *Sailor on Horseback,* pp. 312–13.
15. Langford, *op. cit.,* p. 288.
16. *Ibid.,* pp. 288–89.
17. Quirk, *op. cit.,* pp. 150–52.
18. *Washington Post,* May 1, 1914.
19. Quirk, *op. cit.,* pp. 105–06.
20. Lieutenant Colonel Aristides Moreno, USA, "Notes on the Occupation of Vera Cruz, Mexico, April 21-November 23, 1914." Naval Records Collection, The National Archives.
21. Jack London, "Lawgivers," *Collier's Magazine,* Vol. LIII (June 20, 1914).
22. Major Paul A. Wolf, "History of the Department of Public Works,"

Notes

Adjutant General's Office File, The National Archives.

23. Jenkinson, *loc. cit.*
24. Quirk, *op. cit.,* pp. 130–34.
25. Jenkinson, *loc. cit.*
26. Hamilton Peltz in the *New York Herald,* April 29, 1914.
27. O'Shaughnessy, *op. cit.,* pp. 326–28.
28. General Douglas MacArthur, *Memoirs,* pp. 40–43.
29. Quirk, *op. cit.,* pp. 118–19.
30. Link, *op. cit.,* pp. 415–16.
31. Quirk, *op. cit.,* pp. 158–66.

Chapter Fourteen

1. "Tribute to Those Who Died at Vera Cruz," *Outlook,* Vol. 107 (May 23, 1914).
2. Subcommittee of Veterans' Affairs, *op. cit.,* pp. 758–66.
3. Thomas, *op. cit.,* p. 180.
4. The fascinating story of this ill-fated message is told in Barbara W. Tuchman, *The Zimmermann Telegram.*

Epilogue

1. Palomares, *op. cit.,* pp. 203; 217–18.
2. Captain William L. Sayre, USNR (Ret.), to the author.

BIBLIOGRAPHY

Published Works

Books

Annual of the USS Arkansas. NP: 1913.

Baker, Ray Stannard. *Woodrow Wilson, Life and Letters*. 8 vols. New York: Doubleday, 1927–37.

Bryan, William Jennings and Mary Baird Bryan. *The Memoirs of William Jennings Bryan*. 2 vols. Chicago: Winston, 1925.

Daniels, Josephus. *The Life of Woodrow Wilson*. Chicago: Winston, 1924.

Gruening, Ernest H. *Mexico and Its Heritage*. New York: Century Company, 1928.

Jane, Fred T. (ed.) . *Fighting Ships*. London: Sampson, Low, Marston & Co., Ltd., 1914.

Langford, Gerald. *The Richard Harding Davis Years*. New York: Holt, Rinehart, and Winston, 1961.

Link, Arthur S. *Woodrow Wilson: The New Freedom*. Princeton: Princeton University Press, 1956.

London, Joan. *Jack London and His Times*. Garden City: Book League of America, 1939.

MacArthur, Douglas A. *Memoirs*. New York: McGraw Hill, 1964.

O'Shaughnessy, Edith. *A Diplomat's Wife in Mexico*. New York: Harper, 1916.

Palomares, Justino M. *La Invasión Yanqui en 1914*. Mexico City: (Published by the author) , 1940. Very useful, though colored by the author's anti-Americanism.

Parkes, Henry B. *A History of Mexico*. Cambridge: Houghton Mifflin, 1938.

Quirk, Robert E. *An Affair of Honor: Woodrow Wilson and the Occupation of Veracruz*. Lexington: University of Kentucky Press, Mississippi Valley Historical Association, 1962.

Schriftgeisser, Karl. *The Gentleman from Massachusetts: Henry Cabot Lodge*. Boston: Little, Brown, 1944.

Schuon, Karl. *U.S. Navy Biographical Dictionary*. New York: Franklin Watts, Inc., 1964.

Stone, Irving S. *Sailor on Horseback: The Biography of Jack London*. Cambridge: Houghton Mifflin, 1938.

Terry, T. Philip. *Terry's Guide to Mexico*. Boston: Houghton Mifflin, 1909.

Thomas, Lowell. *Old Gimlet Eye: The Adventures of Smedley Darlington Butler*. New York: Farrar and Rinehart, 1933.

Thompson, Charles W. *Presidents I've Known and Two Near Presidents*. New York: Bobbs-Merrill, 1929.

Tuchman, Barbara W. *The Zimmermann Telegram*. New York: Viking Press, 1958.

Tumulty, Joseph P. *Woodrow Wilson As I Know Him*. Garden City: Doubleday, Page, 1921.

Walsworth, Arthur S. *Woodrow Wilson: American Prophet.* 2 vols. New York: Langman's Green, 1958.

Periodicals

"Beating Swords into Shovels at Vera Cruz," *Survey,* Vol. 30 (October 3, 1914).

"Heroism at Vera Cruz," *Our Navy,* Vol. VIII, No. 3 (July, 1914).

Hinckley, Ted C. "Wilson, Huerta, and the Twenty-One Gun Salute," *The Historian: A Journal of History,* Vol. XXII, No. 2 (February, 1960).

Jenkinson, Charles. "Vera Cruz: What American Occupation Has Meant to a Mexican Community," *Survey,* Vol. XXX (November 7, 1914).

London, Jack. "With Funston's Men," *Collier's Magazine,* Vol. LII (May 23, 1914).

————. "Lawgivers," *ibid.,* Vol. LIII (June 20, 1914).

————. "Our Adventurers at Tampico," *ibid.,* Vol. LIII (June 27, 1914).

McCormick, Medill. "Army in Vera Cruz," *Outlook,* Vol. 107 (May 30, 1914).

McNeely, R. W. (translator). "The Tragic Days of Vera Cruz," *U.S. Naval Institute Proceedings,* Vol. 40, No. 3 (May–June, 1914). (A translation of the Veracruz newspaper *La Opinión* for April 22–23, 1914.)

"News from Vera Cruz," *Fleet Review* (March, 1913).

"Problems in Vera Cruz," *Outlook,* Vol. 108 (November 25, 1914).

Ruhl, Arthur S. "Vera Cruz: The Unfinished Drama," *Collier's Magazine,* Vol. LII (May 30, 1914).

"Tribute to Those Who Died at Vera Cruz," *Outlook,* Vol. 107 (May 23, 1914).

"Under Fire," *Outlook,* Vol. 107 (June 20, 1914).

"USS *Florida* at Veracruz," (A Page from the Old Navy), *U.S. Naval Institute Proceedings,* Vol. 87, No. 8 (August, 1961).

————. (Notes, Comment and Discussion), *U.S. Naval Institute Proceedings,* Vol. 87, No. 11 (November, 1961).

"Vera Cruz: A Crusade for Decency," *Outlook,* Vol. 107 (July 4, 1914).

"With Mayo at Tampico," *Literary Digest,* Vol. XLVIII, No. 18, (May 2, 1914).

Public Documents

Munden, Kenneth W. (compiler). *Records of the Military Government of Veracruz.* Preliminary Inventory No. 138, The National Archives. Washington: 1962.

Register of Alumni 1845–1964. Annapolis: U.S. Naval Academy Alumni Association, Inc., 1964.

U.S. Department of State. *Papers Relating to the Foreign Relations of the United States, 1913.* Washington: 1920.

————. *Papers Relating to the Foreign Relations of the United States, 1914.* Washington: 1924.

U.S. Senate. Subcommittee of Veterans' Affairs of the Committee on Labor and Public Welfare. *Medal of Honor Recipients 1863–1963.* Washington: 1964.

Bibliography

Newspapers

Brooklyn Daily Eagle
Chicago Tribune
Mexican Herald
New York Herald
The New York Times

New York Tribune
Springfield Republican
Washington Herald
Washington Post

Unpublished Sources

The National Archives, Washington, D.C.

Records of the Bureau of Naval Personnel. Record Group 24, Ships' Logs, April 21–22, 1914, for the following vessels: USS *Arkansas, Chester, Florida, Louisiana, New Hampshire, Prairie, Utah, Vermont.*
Naval Records Collection (Office of Naval Records and Library).
Record Group 45, Subject File "WE-5."
Box 661
    a. Dispatches sent by Admiral Fletcher to the Navy Department, March 5—April 30, 1914.
    b. Telegrams sent from the *Prairie* by Admiral Fletcher, April 21–28, 1914.
    c. Correspondence of Admiral Fletcher, April 22–28, 1914.
Box 662
    a. "Seizure and Occupation of Vera Cruz, 21–30 April, 1914." Report of Rear Admiral F. J. Fletcher, USN, Commanding United States Naval Forces on Shore to the Commander-in-Chief, United States Atlantic Fleet, 13 May 1914.
    b. Miscellaneous reports pertaining to the occupation of Veracruz. Includes the after-action reports of the *Michigan, Minnesota,* and *San Francisco* battalions, the only three which appear to have survived.
Box 663
    a. "Journal of the Commander of the Naval Brigade Operating Ashore at Vera Cruz, Mexico, April 13–30, 1914." Submitted by Lieutenant Gerald Howze.
    b. "Notes on the Occupation of Vera Cruz, Mexico, April 21—November 23, 1914." Lieutenant Colonel Aristides Moreno, USA, 1926.
Naval Records Collection (Office of Naval Records and Library). Record Group 45, Area File, Caribbean: Telegrams and letters sent to the Navy Department, April 20–26, 1914.
Naval Records Collection (Office of Naval Records and Library). Not indexed: "Organization of the U.S. Naval Forces on Shore at Vera Cruz, Mexico, April 21–30, 1914." Compiled by Ensign Mark L. Hersey, Jr., USN. Press of the USS *New Jersey.*

Public Records Office, London

Admiralty File 1/8374. "Second Attack by Rebels in Tampico 26th March to 14 April and their subsequent retirement. Incident of Demand by United States Rear Admiral Mayo for salute to the United States flag." Report of Rear Admiral Sir Christopher G. F. M. Cradock, RN, Com-

mander, Fourth Cruiser Squadron and Senior Naval Officer, West Atlantic.
Admiralty File 53/41085. Log of HMS *Essex,* April 21–24, 1914.

Naval Historical Foundation, Washington, D.C.

Ellyson, Lieutenant (jg) T. Gordon. Letter to Mrs. Ellyson, May 4, 1914.

Interviews and Correspondence

Information enclosed within parentheses indicates the rank and organization of the individual at the time of the landing.

Arnett, Roscoe, Lieutenant Colonel, USMC, Retired. (First Sergeant, USMC.)
Brownell, John, Commander, USN, Retired. (Ensign, USS *Florida.*)
Comstock, Lewis D., Captain, USN, Retired. (Ensign, USS *Vermont.*)
Cregan, George, Commander, USN, Retired. (Boatswain's Mate 2nd Class, USS *Florida.*)
Crosby, Ralph M. (Mail Clerk, USS *Arkansas.*)
Cumming, J. W. W., Rear Admiral, USN, Retired. (Lieutenant [jg], USS *Arkansas.*)
Dale, George S., Lieutenant Commander, USN, Retired. (Ensign, USS *South Carolina.*)
Dudley, Roy M., Captain, USN, Retired. (Ensign, USS *Florida.*)
Foster, Paul F., Vice Admiral, USNR, Retired. (Ensign, USS *Utah.*)
Gillespie, George U., Captain, USN, Retired. (Ensign, USS *Arkansas.*)
Grow, Harold B., Captain, USNR, Retired. (Ensign, USS *Utah.*)
Hammes, Roman B., Captain, USN, Retired. (Ensign, USS *South Carolina.*)
Hunter, L. L., Rear Admiral, USN, Retired. (Ensign, USS *South Carolina.*)
Johnson, John Robert, Chief Radio Engineer, USN, Retired. (Electrician 2nd Class, USS *Florida.*)
Lapham, E. B., Captain, USN, Retired. (Ensign, USS *Utah.*)
Lowry, George M., Rear Admiral, USNR, Retired. (Ensign, USS *Florida.*)
Mills, Schuyler S., Captain, USN, Retired. (Ensign, USS *New Jersey.*)
Nickerson, Henry N. (Boatswain's Mate 2nd Class, USS *Utah.*)
Norfleet, James P., Commander, USN, Retired. (Ensign, USS *New Hampshire.*)
Peck, Joseph, Lieutenant Commander, USN, Retired. (Seaman, USS *Arkansas.*)
Saunders, John A., Captain, USN, Retired. (Ensign, USS *New Hampshire.*)
Sayre, William L., Captain, USNR, Retired. (Electrician, USS *Texas.*)
Sweetman, Arthur J. (Quartermaster 3rd Class, USS *New Hampshire.*)
Wright, Carleton H., Vice Admiral, USN, Retired. (Ensign, USS *New Hampshire.*)

INDEX

Index

ualties, 123; confers with Admiral Fletcher, 123; and continued sniping, 139; mentioned, 121, 144

San Francisco, USS: Fletcher requests, 45; reaches Veracruz, 95; shells selected targets, 107; mentioned, 43, 99, 122

San Francisco battalion: 95, 101, 103

Sanitary Wharf, Veracruz: *Esperanza* moors at, 57, 90; *San Francisco* anchors off, 95; *Chester* anchors off, 96; mentioned, 73, 127, 153

San Juan de Ulúa. *See* de Ulúa, San Juan

San Sebastian Hospital, Veracruz: 100

Schnepel, Ordinary Seaman Fred J., USN: 79

Schumaker, Coxswain J. F., USN: 71, 72

Second Advanced Base Regiment, USMC: 44

Second Aero Section, USN: 147

Second Company, *Florida* battalion: 67, 68. *See also Florida* battalion

Second Division, USA: 125

Second Seaman Regiment: organization of, 97; objectives assigned to, 98; landing of, 100; advance of, 103; repulse of 107, 166; reforms and resumes advance, 109–10, 115–16; fired on from harbor, 114; occupies Military Barracks, 117; entrenches lines, 121; mentioned, 127. *See also New Hampshire* battalion; *New Jersey* battalion; *South Carolina* battalion; *Vermont* battalion

Secretary of War: 160

Sellers, Commander David F., USN: 144

Semple, Chief Gunner Robert, USN: 81–82

Senate, United States: 40, 45, 136

Seventh Infantry Regiment, USA: 125

Seymour, Lieutenant (junior grade) Philip, USN: 80–81, 85

Shively, Senator: 135

Siefert, Coxswain G. H., USN: 32, 35

Simpson, Captain Roy, USN: 137

Sims, Captain W. S., USN: 42

Sinnett, Seaman Lawrence C., USN: 71

Smith, Seaman George J., USN: 110–11

Smith, Boatswain's Mate Second Class Harry, USN: 117

Society of Defenders of the Port of Veracruz: 60

Solace, USS: reaches Veracruz, 101; mentioned, 43, 54, 75, 83

Soledad, Mexico: 143

Somer, Chief Turret Captain Abraham de. *See* de Somer, Chief Turret Captain Abraham

Sonora: 83, 114

South Carolina, USS: 97

South Carolina battalion: 100, 105–06, 117

Standard Oil Corporation: 9, 31, 156

State Department, U.S.: leaks news of Lind mission, 18; informs Wilson of Tampico Incident, 36; and *Ypiranga,* 44, 91; Consul Miller protests to, 47; mentioned, 6, 13, 24, 39, 128, 160

Staton, Lieutenant Adolphus C., USN: 118

Stewart, Charles H.: 151

Stickney, Commander Herman O., USN: 51, 57, 151, 155

Stirling, Lieutenant Archibald, USN: 80

Stone, Lieutenant H. W., USMC: 96, 97

Stout, Gunnery Sergeant, USMC: 3–4, 5

Strawbensie, Lieutenant, RN: 128

"Stripers." *See rayados*

Index

Sulzberger, Cyrus L.: 134
Sumner, USS: 151
Svenson, Gunner's Mate First Class Johan, USN: 113
Sweetman, Quartermaster Third Class Arthur J., USN: 86, 117, 143

Taft, William Howard: 11, 12
Tamaulipas State Guard: 33
Tampico, Mexico: naval life at, 29; description of, 30–31; US naval forces at, 43; affairs eclipsed at, 47; Mayo ordered to withdraw from, 46; Fletcher's estimate of situation at, 54; ships reach Veracruz from, 95, 96, 101; rioting at, 130; *Ypiranga* at, 155; mentioned, 39, 44, 45, 53, 137
Tampico Bar: 30, 43, 45, 47
Tampico Incident: 36, 39, 91, 130, 136, 165
Tejar, Mexico: 137
Tejería, Mexico: 60, 100
Templadora, Mexico: 132, 133
Terminal Hotel. *See* Hotel Terminal
Terminal Plaza, Veracruz: 67, 83, 93, 111
Terminal Station, Veracruz: rolling stock withdrawn from, 62; occupied, 64, 65; mentioned, 92, 115, 123
Terminal Wharf. *See* Pier Four
Terminal Yard, Veracruz: 67
Texas City, Tex.: 125
Texas Oil Company: 31
Third Company, *Florida* battalion: 67. *See also Florida* battalion
Third Seaman Regiment: 97, 137
Thompson, Charles W.: 16, 17
Topeka, Kan.: 134
Torreón, Mexico: 22, 24
Towers, Lieutenant J. H., USN: 148
Townsend, Ensign Laurence, USN: 111
"Tragic Ten Days": 11, 16
Tryon, Max: 30, 31, 32, 33

Tumulty, Joseph P.: Presidential secretary, 17; on decision to seize Customs House, Veracruz, 47–49; mentioned, 36, 91
Turnbull, Lieutenant A. D., USN: 114
Tweedie, Commander Hugh J., RN: 143
Twenty-eighth Infantry Regiment, USA: 125, 153
Tyderic, Ordinary Seaman Emil, USN: 106
Tyrell, Sir William: 24

United States: résumé of relations with Mexico, 7–8; and the Mexican revolution, 11–12; Mexican opinion of seizure of Veracruz, 167; mentioned, *passim*
United States Steel Corporation: 9
Uribe, Cadet Virgilio: 77
Utah, USS: ordered to intercept *Ypiranga*, 46; armament, 52; recalled from search, 52, 57; Marines disembark, 58; lands battalion, 73; sights *Ypiranga*, 76; sights *Arkansas*, 97; gun landed, 99; mentioned, 44, 77, 92, 99, 111, 125, 145, 149
Utah battalion: lands, 79; consolidates positions, 85, 93; second day's objectives, 97; action on second day, 101, 110–11; artillery, 117; mentioned, 53, 95. *See also* Fourth Company, *Utah* battalion

Veracruz, Mexican gunboat: 32
Veracruz, Mexico: Lind at, 3–5, 22; naval life at, 29; incident at, 39; US naval forces at, 44; forces available for defence of, 52, 53; landing forces available at, 54; situation morning 21 April, 61, 68; appearance and geography, 62–63; sanitation at, 63; outbreak of firing in, 70;

219

courses of action, 53; reaches Veracruz, 76; Fletcher reports arrival, 90; discharges arms, 155; mentioned, 57, 73, 91, 164

Zapata, Constitutionalist leader: 160

Zaragoza, General Ignacio Morelos: Mayo's opinion of, 32; Mayo's ultimatum to, 35, 37; and rioting at Tampico, 130; mentioned, 33, 45

Zaragoza, Mexican gunboat: 32, 130

Zayas, Major Diego E.: 62

Zimmermann, Alfred: 165

zopilotes: 63, 167

Zuiderveld, Hospital Apprentice First Class William, USN: 72

Jack Sweetman received a Bachelor of Arts degree in history and a reserve commission as a second lieutenant in the United States Army when he was graduated from Stetson University, Deland, Florida, in 1961. His college ROTC led to two years' active duty with the Army in the Medical Service Corps. After the basic officers' course at Fort Sam Houston, Texas, he was assigned to the 582nd Medical Company (Ambulance) at Stuttgart, Germany, eventually serving as its commanding officer.

Mr. Sweetman has the Army to thank for his wife, Gisela Auguste, whom he met during his duty in Germany. She was a nurse in the hospital where he was stationed. They have one daughter, and presently reside in Orlando, Florida, where Mr. Sweetman was born in 1940.

Since his return to Orlando, Mr. Sweetman has been engaged in the construction operations of Sweetman-Herb Construction and Realty, Incorporated, a firm headed by his father. He is a captain in the Army Reserve.

The study of military history and the collection of military medals and decorations are his hobbies.

The text of this book is set in ten-point Baskerville, with two points of leading.
The chapter numbers and titles are set in eleven-point Times Bold, capitals.

The book is printed offset on Hopper's bulk opaque paper, natural.
The cover is of Milbank linen and Elephant Hide paper.

Editorial production by Louise Gerretson.
Book and jacket design by Nick Kirilloff.

The book was composed, printed, and bound by Kingsport Press, Incorporated,
Kingsport, Tennessee.

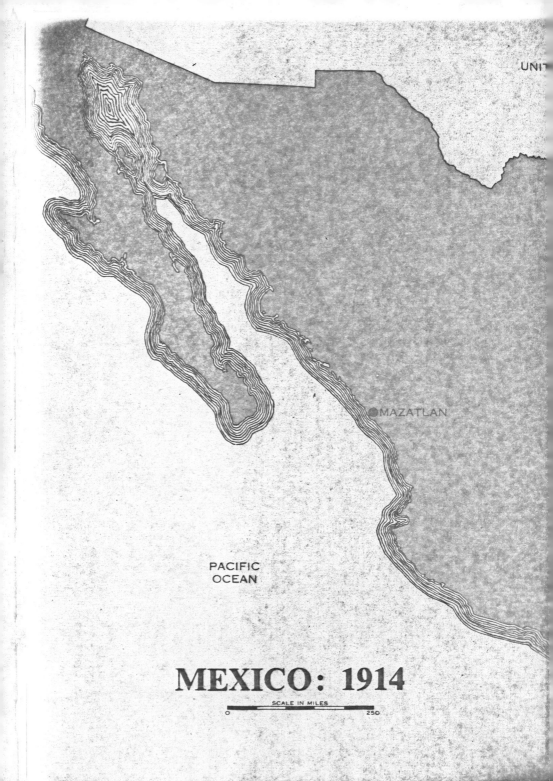

UNIT

PACIFIC
OCEAN

●MAZATLAN

MEXICO: 1914

SCALE IN MILES

O   250